1974

The German Stage
in the
Nineteenth Century

by

MARVIN CARLSON

The Scarecrow Press, Inc.
Metuchen, N.J.   1972

Library of Congress Cataloging in Publication Data

Carlson, Marvin A   1935-
   The German stage in the nineteenth century.

   Bibliography: p.
   1. Theater--Germany--History. 2. Theater--Vienna--
History. I. Title.
PN2653.C35   792'.0943   72-6636
ISBN 0-8108-0542-1

To My Parents

iii

CONTENTS

INTRODUCTION

The Thirty Years' War at the beginning of the seventeenth century brought Germany to the brink of destruction
politically, economically, and culturally, and was the major
reason for this country's relatively late development of a significant theatrical tradition. Hanseatic cities, principalities,
electorates, and kingdoms were ravaged by this fratricidal
conflict which devastated the countryside and crushed the
people. Many areas suffered greater loss during these years
than during the worst plague years of the middle ages; in
parts of Germany only a quarter of the population survived.
For the rest of the century Germany recovered slowly from
this brutal period.

However, with the return of some stability the cities
were rebuilt, learning revived, and the arts began to develop. The theatre was stimulated by the return of traveling
companies from France, Italy, and particularly from England. These provided a model for native German companies
which brought simple comedies and pantomimes to German
audiences during the seventeenth and eighteenth centuries.
The only established theatres during this period were at the
courts, and their dominant genres opera, ballet, and spectacles, strongly influenced by court offerings in France and
Italy. Germany at this time, and on into the nineteenth
century, was a hodge-podge of governmental units, kingdoms,
small principalities, and individual cities, still as self-suf-
ficient as in feudal times. While this pattern was not encouraging to the country's political development, it had certain advantages for the theatre. Each court established its
own theatre, and though these had a tendency, like the courts
that sheltered them, to be small and impecunious imitations
of Versailles, they at least dotted Germany with established
theatres where none had existed before. Decentralization of
the theatre, a much-sought-after and still unachieved goal of
the French, English, and American traditions, was a feature
of the German stage from the outset.

During the eighteenth century the German stage developed its first significant theatre artists--actors, play-

1

wrights, and critics--and the foundations of a major theatrical tradition. Gottsched and Neuber in Leipzig between
1727 and 1739 made the first serious attempt to create a
theatre of real literary and artistic distinction. The goals
and the inspiration of this experiment were carried on
through an intervening generation and led in 1765 to the
founding of the first German National Theatre in Hamburg.
The major lasting contribution of this venture was the collection of criticisms, the Hamburg Dramaturgy, written for
it by Lessing, but it served as a model for later organizations. It was the first German theatre with a real con-
tinuity of purpose and a repertoire of artistic respectability.

By the end of the century, most of the major cities
of Germany and many minor ones had some sort of mod-
erately well-established repertory theatre. Even the best
established were still oriented toward touring, however,
using one or two cities as a base. Many of these were
called national or state theatres, terms originally devised to
distinguish established theatres offering German plays from
regular touring companies or from the court theatres which
offered foreign plays and operas. It was a rather arbitrary
distinction, and somewhat misleading, since there was as
yet no German nation and the state theatres were not ordinarily maintained by the state. Some were outright private
enterprises and all were to some extent dependent upon the
box office. Moreover some court theatres in fact differed
from state theatre only in the source of their patronage and
not at all in repertoire or general organization. Some which
catered to both the aristocracy and to the new bourgeoisie
called themselves court and state theatres (Hof-und Stadts-
theater). This pattern of many small local theatres, each
related in a somewhat different way to its court or munici-
pality, remained the dominant one for most of the nineteenth
century, from Goethe at Weimar to Duke Georg at Meiningen.

Weimar, of course, dominated the German stage at the
opening of the century, and served as a kind of lost Eden
for the nostalgic epigones later in the century. Here, with
a largely undistinguished company and with inadequate facilities, Goethe and Schiller created the highest expression of
the classic movement on the German stage. In addition to
their inestimable literary contributions, Goethe and Schiller
created at Weimar a style of interpretation which added a
new sense of dignity, simplicity, and pictorial harmony to
German acting. The genius of these two men created here
a classic revival of a stature unequalled elsewhere in Europe

during this century. As a result, the arrival of romanticism differed greatly in Germany from its later and more spectacular arrival in France. Hugo led his revolt against a neo-classicism which was weak and derivative, but in Germany romanticism was launched during exactly the same years which saw Goethe and Schiller most keenly interested in classic themes, subjects, and treatment.

Whatever the classicists' eminence, it was hardly to be expected that German letters could ignore the wave of irrationalism and emancipation which swept Europe at the beginning of the nineteenth century. Most of the great battles of the Napoleonic wars were fought on German soil, and though Goethe could continue a production in Olympian aloofness while the gunfire from Jena echoed above his actors' voices, others may be excused for taking a less detached view. For them the sense of harmony, wholeness, placidity, and restraint of classicism seemed to have little relation to these apocalyptic times. German romanticism, however, contributed little to the theatre. Its willful disregard of all rules, its ecstatic fantasy appeared most effective in lyric poetry. In drama its most important contribution was the brilliant Shakespearian translations of Schlegel, since original works, such as the plays of Tieck or Grabbe, almost destroyed themselves in their contempt for order.

The movement toward a united Germany was begun, somewhat ironically, by Napoleon himself, both directly, by reducing the administrative states in Germany to less than forty, and indirectly, by encouraging the growth of a nationalistic outlook. France had fired all Europe with the ideals of liberalism and democracy, and German patriots fought the French themselves in pursuit of these ideals. Their exultation at the defeat of Napoleon gave way to bitter disillusionment after 1815 when repressive political regimes were installed throughout Germany. All German life was dominated by the conservative courts, and their bureaucracy and censorship created a heavy burden for Germany's theatres. Opera and ballet became once again the favored genres, and since most theatres presented these as well as spoken drama the latter naturally suffered. Vienna was the first city to separate spoken drama from opera, in 1821, and first Schreyvogel, and later in the century Laube and Dingelstedt, demonstrated the advantages of this division by building here an outstanding producing ensemble despite the constant interference of court and censor.

The range of production expected of an average German theatre in the 1820's was staggering: old German
musical plays and the new romantic operas of Weber, Italian
and French operas, the German and French classics, the
melodramatic fate tragedies which appeared during the romantic period, the sentimental middle-class comedies and
dramas of writers like Iffland and Kotzebue, contemporary
French comedies and vaudevilles, and local farces and skits.
Critics from Goethe and Schiller to Laube fifty years later
protested these conditions, but aside from the separation of
opera and drama, few theatres achieved much specialization.
These difficult demands, with the problems of working under
a rigorous censorship and a court-appointed supervisor who
was normally both unfeeling and uninformed about the theatre, discouraged dedicated theatre leaders. By 1830 most
of the strong creative drive which had been apparent in theatres all over Germany since the beginning of the century
had disappeared. The Napoleonic era had seen Goethe at
Weimar and Liebich at Prague, and the fifteen years following were those of Tieck's influence in Dresden, Brühl's
in Berlin, Klingemann's in Braunschweig, Schmidt's in
Hamburg, and Schreyvogel's in Vienna--all important con-
tributors to the German stage. When this generation retired, few new leaders of any stature appeared to replace
it. The new theatre directors were for the most part
bureaucrats rather than artists, concerned primarily with
running a successful commercial enterprise or with pleasing
their sponsoring sovereign.

The early nineteenth century was a period of great
acting, producing some of the German theatre's most distinguished names--Esslair, Schröder, Devrient, Seydelmann--
but the particular circumstances of the period turned this
blessing into a curse before the century was half completed.
The decentralized theatres, headed by courtier-managers
with little interest in the art, renounced the building of
stable ensembles in favor of the quick attraction of a touring
star. The guest engagement became Germany's dominant
theatre offering, and audiences came not to see a play, but
a Devrient, an Esslair. The play became a vehicle, the
resident company a nondescript background for the star.
During Goethe's time there were two major schools of
acting in Germany; his own "classic" style and the "realistic" style of Hamburg and Berlin. The worst faults of
each became apparent as actors developed the conspicuous
and striking mannerisms which were expected of the new
virtuoso. Unchecked by forceful directors, the demands of

the script, or any feeling for the whole, the realists sought
brilliant but erratic emotional effects while the classicists
turned to artificial, operatic mannerisms. Even the great
actors already mentioned did not escape this degeneration in
their later years, and lesser talents emulated them all over
Germany.

This virtuoso period, which may be roughly dated
from 1830 to 1870, therefore seems a dark and depressing
valley between the great peaks reached by the German stage
at either end of the century. It is understandable that many
German critics looking back on this period from the late
nineteenth or early twentieth century viewed it almost as a
new dark age for the theatre. Nevertheless, the ideals of
Goethe and others were continued in some theatres, such
as that of Immermann in Düsseldorf during the 1830's, and
more importantly, the groundwork was laid during the virtuoso period both in playwriting and in production for the great
creative period at the end of the century.

The late romantics had in general passively accepted
Metternich's conservatism, turning to remote or fanciful
worlds as a form of escape. But after 1830 a new movement, Young Germany, challenged the status quo with works
of strong political realism. As in the previous period, the
major dramatists were outside the predominant literary
movement, but Ludwig, Büchner, the Austrian Anzengruber,
and Hebbel, whose powerful studies of man and society prepared the way for Ibsen, all showed the influence of Young
Germany's concern with contemporary reality. The only
dramatists of any importance associated directly with Young
Germany were Gutzkow and Laube, and Laube's contribution
as a theatre director was far more significant than his
writings.

Between 1850 and 1870 Laube was one of Germany's
two most important theatre directors. The other was Dingelstedt, who directed in Munich and Weimar while Laube directed in Vienna, and who ultimately succeeded him at the
Burgtheater there. Though both opposed the bureaucracy,
dilettantism, and virtuoso playing of their day, their alternatives to these conditions were in many respects dia-
metrically opposed. Through much of the century there was
a conflict in Germany between two general tendencies in
production. On the one hand there was the elaborate scenic
tradition historically associated with the opera and with court
spectacles. During the nineteenth century this turned to

detailed visualization of locale with every aid that perspective
painting and modern machinery could provide. Partially in
reaction to this and partially in an attempt to recapture the
spirit of the Greek and Elizabethan stages there developed,
on the other hand, a weaker but still significant tradition of
simplified staging. The Berlin stage under Brühl championed
the elaborate style early in the century while Tieck and later
Immermann worked on simplified stages. Dingelstedt followed in the tradition of Brühl, Laube of Tieck and Immermann.

        There were other equally striking differences between
these contemporaries. Laube sought to develop a modern
repertoire, relying heavily on the French social drama of
the Second Empire; Dingelstedt emphasized the classics.
Laube worked for an actors' theatre, where the spoken word
was the central medium; Dingelstedt sought a theatre which
would fuse all arts--acting, poetry, painting, dancing,
music--into a single effect. Laube therefore worked as an
independent creator, while Dingelstedt was a brilliant co-
ordinator of the visions of others. Yet for all this it must
be remembered that they shared an ideal of an artistically
effective theatre which was otherwise rarely encountered in
Germany at this time. Viennese critics in the 1870s were
fond of saying that if a director could be found who combined
the abilities of Laube and Dingelstedt he could revolutionize
the German stage.

        Georg II, Duke of Saxe-Meiningen, seemed almost
an exact fulfillment of that rather wistful hope. The contributions not only of Laube and Dingelstedt, but of Tieck,
Immermann, Goethe, Brühl, and many lesser figures all
helped to prepare the way for the enormously influential
Meininger productions. First Berlin, then most of Europe
marveled at the concern for color and composition, the
richly detailed scenery and costumes, the manipulation of
crowds and the total production control which the tours of
the Meininger demonstrated. Two great innovative ventures
of the 1870s--the Meininger and Wagner's festival at Bay-
reuth--effectively ended the virtuoso period. Both championed an ensemble, not only of an entire company (as the
scattered opponents of the virtuosi had always done) but of
every element of production. Moreover, they together
brought to its culmination the concept which had been implied
in much of the work of their predecessors--the idea of a
single controlling artistic consciousness which would attempt
to insure this desired unity. The modern idea of a director

was thus born at Bayreuth and Meiningen.

These great theatrical experiments came at a time
when a whole new German society was emerging.   Prussia's
defeat of Austria in 1866 and of France in 1870-71 opened
the way to the establishment of the long-awaited German
state.   While this did not mean an end to the geographically
diversified German theatre, since Munich and other major
cities continued to make important contributions, Berlin now
became the theatrical center of Germany as it became the
political and cultural hub of the new state.   Vienna, ex-
cluded from the new Germany, naturally continued its own
distinct development, with the Burgtheater under Wilbrandt
maintaining its reputation as one of Europe's great ensembles.

Berlin more than any other German city felt the
effect of the new European literary movement of this period
--naturalism.   The writings of Marx and Engels, of Zola,
Tolstoy, Dostoevski, and Ibsen combined in Germany with
the heritage of Hebbel and Young Germany to create a rough
and bitter militant drama of social protest--protest against
the bourgeoisie, the status quo, and many of the conventions
of the traditional theatre.   Conservatism, commercialism,
and censorship not surprisingly denied this new movement
any place in the established theatre, so Brahm's Freie
Bühne, modeled on the Théâtre-Libre of Paris, became the
home of naturalist drama.   Hauptmann, discovered by this
theatre, was one of the movement's greatest authors, but
like most of his colleagues he soon forsook naturalism for
experiments in other directions, becoming one of Germany's
first symbolist dramatists as well.   The Freie Bühne's
career was brief, but Brahm went on to direct the new
Deutsches Theater, which he made into the new nation's
outstanding theatre.   From his company came Max Reinhardt, a far more eclectic director than Brahm, who carried into the new century the Wagner and Meininger ideal of
an all-powerful director creating a rich ensemble of the
arts.   Berlin made another important contribution to the
theatre of the new century by developing a theatre for the
proletariat--the Volksbühne, begun in 1890 and developed
despite official indifference and outright hostility, to become
the greatest populist theatre in Europe.   Thus at the beginning of the twentieth century more Germans were attending the theatre, and there was available to them a higher
quality of theatre than ever before.   Moreover the German
stage, through the contributions of such innovators as Wag-

ner, Georg of Meiningen, Hebbel, Wedekind, and the whole tradition of simplified staging, contributed more than any other single European country to determining the direction taken by the twentieth century theatre.

I. THE ROMANTIC PERIOD
1800-1830

The Napoleonic wars and the Metternich reaction seem an unlikely political background for the development of a significant theatre, but the opening years of the nineteenth century were nonetheless full of notable achievements. More of these were to be found in acting and directing than in playwriting, but there were important literary contributions as well. The masterpieces of Schiller opened the century, and Kleist, Tieck, Grabbe, Grillparzer, and Raimund made important lesser contributions, some almost unrecognized until our own century. The political upheaval and the variety of theatre organizations makes a coherent view of this fluid period difficult to obtain, but it may be useful to remember that most theatres with any distinct style could be generally described by the position they took on the basic theatrical polarities of the time: classicism versus romanticism in playwriting, elaboration versus simplicity in production, naturalness versus elevation in acting. All of these terms are admittedly somewhat arbitrary, but they do allow us to sort out tendencies in different theatres.

Weimar, the bastion of classic theory and interpretation, is the obvious point of departure for a consideration of the nineteenth century German stage. Goethe and Schiller, the two dominant literary figures of the period, worked together for seven years, from 1798 until 1805, in this hitherto obscure ducal theatre, and made it the reference point for most German theatre throughout the century. Yet despite their great influence, Goethe, Schiller, and the Weimar company were distinctly isolated from much German literary activity of their time. The same years that saw the great historical dramas of Schiller in Weimar saw the full tide of romanticism affect poets and critics elsewhere, resulting in such extravagant experiments as the folk and fairy plays of Tieck.

The sprawling and chaotic romantic movement developed no distinct theatrical center in Germany to correspond with classic Weimar, but the Dresden theatre under Tieck was clearly the most distinguished of the many the-

atres which showed the effects of romanticism. Tieck was
the major dramatist of the early romantics, though the works
of his contemporaries Kleist and even Grabbe have proven
more enduring. The wild fancies of Grabbe were too extreme even for Tieck, but he alone of the prominent writers
of his day recognized the genius of Kleist and initiated the
serious study of his works. He also pursued a life-long
interest in Shakespeare and a lesser interest in Calderon
which contributed greatly to establishing these two dramatists
as the major foreign classic dramatists presented on the
nineteenth century German stage. Tieck's interest in the
theatre was predominantly literary, but like Goethe and
Schiller he developed, as a director, a keen and often in-
sightful interest in the techniques of production. It is
therefore not surprising that his study of Shakespeare led
him to make the first significant steps toward the simplified
staging which eventually replaced the alternate heavy and
elaborate productions of these works which we now think
of as typical of the nineteenth century.

        The theatre which was in these early years most
associated with this elaborate style of production was Berlin.
Tieck had little interest in spectacle, Goethe was interested
but could not afford it, but Berlin, especially after 1815,
when Brühl became director, offered pageantry, rich historical costuming, and lavish settings unequalled anywhere
in Germany. Here Schinkel, like his French contemporary
Ciceri, brought romantic scene design to its fullest expression. During these same years Berlin also possessed the
most famous of the German romantic actors, Devrient,
though his greatest years were those of his earlier engagement in Breslau.

        Doubtless a modern appraisal of Devrient's acting
would find it exaggerated, even bombastic, similar in style
to the great English romantic actor, Kean. Yet to German
critics of the time, the Berlin theatre, even with such ex-
tremists as Devrient, was the major center of realistic
acting, the inheritor of the realistic tradition of Hamburg.
In part this was because Berlin was also the home of the
great popular bourgeois dramatists of the period--Kotzebue,
Iffland, and later Raupach--whose dramas frequently tried
to capture the emotional rhythms of contemporary life, but
Berlin's reputation for realistic interpretation included even
remote romantic and historical dramas. The distinction
was apparently based on the greater emphasis on emotion,
movement, and color in Berlin, since the outstanding

example of the opposing style of interpretation was Weimar, where clarity and formal beauty were sought through an approach which stressed solemnity, dignity, and elevation.

A number of other German theatres achieved real stature during this productive period--most notably those of Munich, Prague, Braunschweig, and Leipzig--but the only theatre center comparable to Weimar, Dresden, and Berlin in influence was Vienna. Though the Austrian theatre, with its strong folk tradition, maintained a distinctive approach to drama throughout the century, it nevertheless reflected each major movement in the north. Schreyvogel at the Burgtheater carried on many of Goethe's ideals, and his major dramatist, Grillparzer, began his career with a romantic fate-tragedy, and then turned to works which, like Schreyvogel's productions, achieved a striking balance between German classicism and Austrian realism. In the folk theatre, on the other hand, it was romanticism which during this period created the most successful synthesis with tradition, particularly in the works of Raimund, one of the greatest authors in the rich folk tradition.

Another glory of the Vienna theatre early in the century was its opera, unquestionably the best in Germany. The opera, like the folk theatre, was strikingly changed by the advent of romanticism. Exotic and mysterious subjects, a passion for freedom and a new national spirit, all common romantic themes, could be clearly seen in the development of a native Germanic operatic tradition, culminating in the works of Weber. Though his triumph was not complete, Weber established a powerful alternative to the Italian tradition, particularly as represented by Rossini, his major rival. Then, with the passing of these two masters, Parisian artists emerged as the leaders of the romantic opera and ballet, indeed, of most of the contemporary theatre. Scattered stages attempted after 1830 to continue the tradition of Weimar, Berlin, Dresden, and Vienna, but clearly a period of decline had begun.

1. Goethe and Weimar

In the decentralized German theatre of the early nineteenth century the fortunes of any individual venture might vary widely according to the interest of the community or court and to their success in attracting important theatre artists. Probably nothing illustrates the arbitrariness of this

system better than the dominant position in German cultural
life enjoyed by the little Weimar court stage at the opening
of the century.   Twenty years before, this theatre had been
little more than a toy for the amusement of the Weimar court,
one among many minor courts which then covered Germany.
The theatre followed, on a small scale, the pattern of most
such theatres since the Renaissance.   The Duke and his court
were the actors; the playwrights, composers, and designer
were all members of the Duke's staff.   Then the young Duke
Karl August brought the young Goethe to Weimar and placed
the theatre under his supervision.   Goethe in turn brought
Schiller and drew the attention of all literary Germany to
Karl August's hitherto insignificant theatre.

The great years of Weimar were those between 1798
and 1805 when Goethe and Schiller worked there together.
Though Goethe had been chief director of the theatre since
1791, his interests in these early years ran to other things,
particularly to science and the theory of color.   Though he
fulfilled his directorial duties competently and thoroughly, the
company he led achieved nothing to distinguish it from any
other minor German house.   The conditions in Weimar were
in any case hardly calculated to inspire a development of
theatrical art.   The theatre was poor and small, though certainly large enough for Weimar, which had only about 6000
inhabitants.   A few wings and back-cloths had to do for the
scenery for all productions.   When Iffland came on tour in
1796 he was unable even to obtain a chair to collapse into at
an emotional moment in his Dienstpflicht, and had to sink to
one knee instead.   A few basic costumes did multiple duty.
Though after 1791 the theatre relied upon professional actors
rather than amateurs from the court, the salaries given them
were so small that the quality of interpretation scarcely improved.   The company, about twenty in number, had little
familiarity with drama of any quality and none at all with
verse.   "Even the most experienced members of the company
found it impossible to memorize a role written in poetic
lines," reports Genast.   "It had to be written out in prose
with a thick line drawn after each verse" [1 end of Part I].
Though Goethe introduced Schröder's technique of beginning
with "reading rehearsals" dedicated solely to proper interpretation of lines, the actors still preferred to rely on their
ability at improvisation or on the prompter rather than to
memorize their parts.

Little wonder that during these early years of his administration Goethe attended rehearsals infrequently, leaving

much of the responsibility for the company with his stagemanager Franz Joseph Fischer or with his business manager
and later assistant director Franz Kirms. Fischer in turn
discharged his duties with more resignation than pleasure.
His relations with the company worsened steadily, and by
1793 he was glad to return to his native Prague. The only
promising talent in this early Weimar company was the young
Christine Neumann (1778-1797), who alone engaged Goethe's
attention. Her simplicity and natural charm soon made her
a general favorite and during her unhappily short career she
achieved success as Emilia Galotti, Minna von Barnhelm,
Amalie in Die Räuber and Luise in Kabale und Liebe. After
her death, Goethe and his public shifted their support to
another young actress, Amelie Malcomi (1780-1851), who
under Goethe's tutelage became the theatre's leading tragedienne, playing such roles as Iphigenie, Antigone, and Ophelia.

Goethe's interest in the theatre was strongly stimulated
in 1796 by the guest appearance in Weimar of August Wilhelm
Iffland (1759-1814), the first major actor to visit the little
theatre. To prepare his company for this event, Goethe for
the first time carefully and personally supervised their rehearsals. His play Egmont, written in 1788 but never yet
presented at Weimar, was prepared for presentation. Goethe
informed his actors that the great Iffland should serve as an
example to them, but that he wished them in turn to demonstrate how well they could work together in supporting him.
His double emphasis was significant. Clearly Goethe was
impressed by Iffland's versatility if not by his depth; he
played fourteen widely varied roles during his brief visit.
At the same time he recognized that none of his own company
possessed even a latent ability for such achievement, and
wisely emphasized with them the development of an ensemble
which placed less demand on any individual actor. It should
be noted, however, that this was not an idea that came to
Goethe after working with his actors; he promised some such
emphasis even in the prologue which opened the theatre in
1791:

>   Allein bedenken wir, dass Harmonie
>   Des ganzen Spiels allein verdienen kann
>   Von euch gelobt zu werden, dass ein jeder
>   Mit jedem stimmen, alle mit einander
>   Ein schönes Ganzes vor euch stellen sollen
>   So reget sich die Furcht in unsurer Brust. [2]

In the late 1790s, however, Goethe became more

clearly interested in the practical achievement of this goal,
most notably in his production of Schiller's <u>Wallensteins</u>
<u>Lager</u> in 1798.   Goethe had during the previous year inspected
theatres in Frankfurt, Ludwigsburg, and Stuttgart, and commissioned the Stuttgart court architect Friedrich Thouret and
the Stuttgart theatre designer Karl Heideloff to rebuild the
Weimar theatre, which opened with Schiller's new play on
October 12.   The new theatre was still modest, but much
more elaborate than its predecessor.   Its parterre was surrounded by pillars painted to resemble granite, with Goethe's
own box at the rear.   The pillars supported a gallery with
the Duke's box at the rear above Goethe's, and above this
gallery was a balcony, supported by classic columns of sim-
ulated yellow marble with bronze capitals topped by Greek
masks in low relief.   Each social class had its own designated place--the court in the balcony, the working class in
the gallery, students and the bourgeoisie in the pit.   The old
tallow candles were replaced by oil lamps, and the chandelier
over the auditorium could be raised into a recess in the
ceiling to dim the house during performances.   The stage
was slightly more than seven meters deep with a proscenium
opening of somewhat more than nine meters.   Scenery and
machinery were very simple, with five sliding wings on each
side and a back cloth which had to be rolled up to be changed,
as there was no loft-space above the stage.   "The design is
tasteful, " reported Goethe in his description of the new theatre in the <u>Allgemeine Zeitung</u>, "serious without being heavy,
pompous, or pretentious. "   Schiller's Prologue called the
theatre a cheerful temple, full of harmony and dignity.

     The process of creating an authentic, yet harmonious
and beautiful stage picture now fascinated Goethe, and his
experiments in this direction, beginning with <u>Wallensteins</u>
<u>Lager</u>, are surely his major contribution to the non-literary
side of the theatre.   He collected wood-cuts and other pictorial material of the Thirty Years' War, even carrying off
an old stoveplate with a seventeenth-century camp scene em-
bossed on it from the public house in Jena.   With the aid of
Georg Melchior Kraus (1762-1827) as costume designer and
Heinrich Meyer (1760-1832) as scene painter, Goethe created
a lively and picturesque composition with a richness of detail
unlike anything yet seen on the German stage.   He described
the opening scene in a letter of October 15, 1798:

          Soldiers of all types and colors were gathered
          around a canteen tent.   Here were empty dishes
          that seemed to promise still more guests, there

> were heaps of rubbish and trash. To one side lay
> Croats and sharpshooters around a fire with a
> kettle hanging over it, and not far from them other
> soldiers playing dice on a drum. The canteen pro-
> prietress and her assistants wandered here and
> there, serving the humblest and the most important
> with equal care, while the rough song of the sol-
> diers resounded continuously from the tents. [3]

The soldiers' song was one of many elements Schiller added
to the play at Goethe's request, and it did much to establish
the mood. One verse of it was sung before the curtain
opened, and some subsequent verses were sung by the actors
on stage, others from the wings to create the impression of
a much larger camp than that shown. Goethe gave particular
attention to stage groupings and carefully rehearsed even the
most insignificant actors to achieve the most effective total
impact. In all such concerns we can see the beginning of
the staging ideas which would reach their full fruition later
in the century with the Meininger.

    In 1799 Schiller moved from nearby Jena to Weimar
and joined Goethe in daily work with the theatre. He was
given a private box in the new house, just next to the Duke,
and under the double tutelage of Goethe and Schiller, the
company began to develop an ability in the physical and vocal
delivery of poetic drama which soon became a model for
others. This growing ability was already apparent in the
production of Piccolomini (1799), the second play of Schiller's
Wallenstein trilogy. Heinrich Vohs, who had given the Prologue to open the new theatre and was generally acknowledged
as the troupe's leading male actor, played Max, while Wallenstein was portrayed by Johann Jakob Graff (1768-1848),
whose dark, mysterious manner and clear reading of lines
endeared him to Schiller. The settings were designed by
Heideloff with the help of Conrad Horny, a painter from
Mainz.

    The success of these two productions made the open-
ing of Wallensteins Tod (1799), which completed the trilogy,
a major event, and the audience included the Prussian royal
couple and hundreds of students from the university at Jena.
Vohs and Graff again played the leading roles, supported by
Karoline Jagemann (1777-1848), who had accompanied Iffland
on his first tour to Weimar and later returned to stay. She
had already achieved great success in Mozart's operas, but
it was the Wallenstein trilogy which established her fame as

a dramatic actress.

Later in this same year there appeared in the journal
Propylaën an article by Wilhelm von Humboldt on the contemporary style of tragic acting in France.   Humboldt praised
Talma's ability in harmonizing words and actions, and noted
with approval the musical quality of French spoken verse and
the beauty of the stage groupings.   The lengthy article concluded by suggesting that German actors, in striving for a
natural quality, had neglected an aesthetic appeal to the eyes
and ears of their audiences.   Clearly these observations were
closely in line with Goethe's concerns, and the article made
a great impression on him.   "No friend of the German theatre, " he observed, could read Humboldt's report "without
wishing that, without prejudice to the road we have taken, we
might be able to assume the good qualities of the French
theatre. "[4]   Thus in seventy years the German stage had come
full circle.   In the 1730s Gottsched had translated French
tragedies as models of beauty and harmony for the German
stage.   In the 1760s Lessing condemned this as the darkest
sort of betrayal of national culture.   Now the new century
opened with Goethe translating Voltaire's Mahomet and Tan-
crède and Schiller Racine's Phèdre, departing from Gottsched
only in using blank verse instead of alexandrines.

The first translation finished was Mahomet, presented
in 1800 with Vohs and Karoline Jagemann in the leading roles,
but the public found Voltaire too alien, and the production
failed.   This was shortly followed by Schiller's translation,
or rather adaptation of Macbeth, a considerably more successful offering.   Aside from its popularity, Macbeth was
significant for two reasons.   It was apparently the first play
in which Schiller himself worked with his actors, and it, even
more than Mahomet, demonstrated the growing interest in a
"classic" approach at Weimar.   The hero played by Vohs was
depicted as consistently noble, the guiltless victim of Fate,
personified in the three witches which were played by men in
Greek robes.   Unity of mood was stressed, which involved
such changes as the replacing of the porter scene by a pious
song.

The great event of 1800 was unquestionably the presentation of Schiller's Maria Stuart.   Anton Genast (1765-
1831), now stagemanager, reports that by this time the actors
had become so accustomed to Schiller's blank verse that they
would often improvise with it in private life.   They were enthusiastically received by an audience of nearly 800 persons

packed into the 500-seat house. Vohs played Mortimer and his wife Friderike Maria, but Karoline Jagemann as Elisabeth dominated her more beautiful rival by the power of her interpretation.

Goethe's Tancred (1801) was condemned by many critics for its sentimentality, but Karoline Jagemann made Amenaide one of her most popular roles, and the play was frequently revived not only in Weimar, but in Berlin, Vienna, and elsewhere. Classic experimentation went much further in Einsiedel's translation of Terence's The Brothers, for which the actors wore half-masks in modified antique style. This experiment was well received, but when masks were used again for Schlegel's adaptation of Euripides' Ion in 1802, the audience's laughter drove Goethe to rise from his chair and demand silence. One more quite different experiment with masks was Schiller's adaptation of Gozzi's Turandot, produced in a modified commedia dell'arte style soon after Ion. The play seems an odd selection for classic Weimar, but it was apparently the mask tradition itself which attracted Goethe's interest, while Gozzi's sentiment and poetic possibilities appealed to Schiller. The play, possibly as a relief from the severity of Ion, was warmly received in Weimar, but gained little approval elsewhere.

Goethe's Iphigenie auf Tauris (1802) clearly suffered from diverging visions in its author and in Schiller, its director. Goethe saw the work as a rather ethereal drama of the soul while Schiller sought to introduce more life and passion through theatrical, even melodramatic means. Goethe prevailed over Schiller's attempt to personify the Furies and bring them on stage, but the actors Frau Vohs, Friedrich Cordemann and Friedrich Haide were torn between the opposing views and their interpretations were naturally vague and confused. In 1807, after Schiller's death, the play was produced to far greater success by Goethe with Pius Alexander Wolff, then the company's leading actor, Wolff's wife Amalia, and Carl Ludwig Oels.

In their manner of dealing with their actors, Goethe and Schiller could hardly have been more unlike. Goethe was brusk, formal, Olympian, while Schiller was always amiable, enthusiastic, and easy-going. The one was universally loved, the other respected but feared. August von Kotzebue (1761-1819), the popular and prolific dramatist, spent 1801 and 1802 in Weimar and was encouraged by these differences to attempt to drive a wedge between the leaders of the theatre.

Goethe frequently mounted Kotzebue's plays as a concession
to popular taste (600 of the 4136 performances under Goethe's
direction were works of Kotzebue, while Schiller received
361 performances and Goethe himself only 238), but he personally considered Kotzebue a shallow moralizer and refused
any dealings with him outside of purely commercial ones.
Kotzebue, irritated by this rebuff and by the veneration
Goethe enjoyed among the romantics, sought occasions to promote Schiller at Goethe's expense. These culminated in
plans to present a special ceremony in Schiller's honor in the
theatre in 1802. Goethe raised mild protests, but it was the
burgomaster who cancelled the ceremony, fearing that the
potentially huge crowd might damage the theatre. Soon after,
Kotzebue departed for Berlin, while the friendship between
Goethe and Schiller continued unaffected.

1803 was probably the Weimar theatre's most outstanding year. Schiller's Die Braut von Messina, directed by
Goethe, was one of the most successful of the Weimar classic
experiments, amply rewarding the unusually long period of
preparation--six reading rehearsals spread over four weeks
followed by eight rehearsals on stage. Goethe gave special
attention to the chorus, dividing the speeches among them
and balancing high and low voices to give a musical effect.
Goethe's own Natürliche Tochter featured Karoline Jagemann
in a classic drama which dealt with themes taken from the
French Revolution, but despite the talent of the actress and
the timeliness of the subject, Goethe's cold and abstract
treatment stimulated little interest in the public. The play
was to have been the first part of a trilogy, but the sequels
never appeared. Indeed, after this Goethe wrote only one
more theatre work in addition to Faust, Des Epimenides
Erwachen, an occasional piece to celebrate the peace of 1815.

Schiller's Die Jungfrau von Orleans was premiered
this year not in Weimar, but in Leipzig, where the theatre
possessed the larger company and more elaborate scenery
and costumes demanded by this play. The Leipzig actors,
however, had no experience with Schiller and were unsuccessful in their attempt to capture the spirit of this unusual combination of heroic drama and lyric romance. Later in
Weimar, on the contrary, it was presented to great acclama-
tion, even though parts had to be doubled and trebled and
settings ingeniously fashioned from cardboard and tinfoil.
Both Goethe and Schiller protested the use of a blue silk
curtain for the coronation robe and were finally allowed to
purchase one of imitation velvet. Genast noted that this was

the only item of value in the theatre's wardrobe and that it
became the standard royal costume thereafter. The work of
translation continued too, the most distinguished contributions
that year being Friedrich von Einsiedel's Die Fremde aus
Andros from Terence and Porträt from Cervantes, Schlegel's
Julius Caesar and two works by Schiller drawn from plays of
his popular French contemporary Picard--Der Neffe als Onkel
and Der Parasit.

The presentation of Schiller's Wilhelm Tell (1804)
strained the resources of the little company again, but the
generally high level of interpretation, with Haide as Tell and
Graff as Attinghausen, and the topicality of a plea for freedom at a time when Germany was suffering under the Napoleonic invasions stimulated enormous enthusiasm. This
success encouraged Goethe to revive his own youthful freedom
drama, Götz von Berlichingen, though his ideas on theatre
had so changed in the intervening years that he called in
Schiller to help him rework the play for production. Their
major task was cutting the sprawling drama, but even after
revision the play ran six hours, and exhausted the most politically sympathetic houses. In 1809 and again in 1819
Goethe promised new revisions, but his later classic version
achieved at last only a dilution of the play's youthful fire.

The now-ailing Schiller completed only two more
works before his early death in 1805. One was a small occasional piece, Die Huldigung der Künste, for the arrival of
Maria Paulovna, daughter of the Czar, as the bride of Prince
Karl Friedrich, the other his adaptation of Phèdre, completed at the request of the actress Christiane Becker. After
Schiller's death, the theatre closed for a period of mourning,
and a memorial program, with an Epilogue written by Goethe,
was presented in the neighboring theatre of Lauchstädt.

After the death of Schiller, Goethe's interest in the
theatre once more began to wane, and his influence was not
particularly positive. Deprived of the balance Schiller had
provided, Goethe became more and more the autocrat, demanding lifeless, mechanical interpretations from his actors.
A sort of spoken opera seems to have been his goal; Wolff
reported "He was constantly appealing to the analogy of music
in his instruction. The cast members were trained to speak
their lines the same way an opera is rehearsed: he determined the speed, the fortes and pianos, the crescendos and
diminuendos, and carefully watched them."[5]

His Rules for Actors, dictated in 1803 to the young
Wolff and to Franz Grüner, set forth 91 commands for the
actors' physical and vocal control. Exact arm, hand, and
head positions were described, as well as specific methods
of delivering lines. All punctuation marks were scrupulously
observed and given relative weights--one beat pause for a
comma, two for a semicolon, four for a colon, six for an
exclamation point, eight for a question mark, ten for a
period. Movements were controlled with similar care on a
stage marked out in squares for absolute precision. Wolff
insists that the acting remained natural and convincing, but
not surprisingly, his opinion was not shared by most observers. In any case, Goethe was not interested in natural
or convincing acting. Harmony, grace, and dignity were his
chief concerns; his principle was "Beauty first, then truth"
(Erst schön, dann wahr).

The irony of this situation was that the company that
Goethe was attempting to convert to puppets was, in the years
just after Schiller's death, the best that Weimar had ever
possessed. Pius Alexander Wolff (1782-1828) and his wife
Amalia (1780-1851), Carl Ludwig Oels (1780-1833), Heinrich
Becker (1764-1822) and his wife Christiane were all among
the best German actors of the period. Whatever effect
Goethe may have had on their creativity, he apparently did
nothing to diminish their dedication or spirit of ensemble.
The company continued to perform in 1806 even on the night
the guns of the battle of Jena could be heard in Weimar. In
1807, without the aid or even the encouragement of Goethe,
they produced a much-praised Torquato Tasso. The fame of
Weimar was now such that patrons of the theatre from many
parts of Germany and elsewhere in Europe began to make
pilgrimages here whenever the tides of war allowed. In the
summer of 1807 the company was invited to make guest appearances in Leipzig, where their ensemble work created a
great sensation.

The major new works of the following years were
primarily drawn from the now-dominant romantic school.
The most popular theatrical manifestation of this movement
was the fate-tragedy (Schicksalstragödie), conceived by the
romantics as a modern equivalent of the classic tales of
doomed houses. Zacharias Werner (1768-1823), the most
noted writer in this genre, brought his historical tragedy
Wanda, Königin der Sarmaten to Weimar in 1807. Goethe
himself directed it, and the success was such that Werner
was widely regarded as the most likely successor to Schiller.

Goethe encouraged Werner to create a modern tragedy with a classic interest in fate, and the result was the archetypical Der vierundzwanzigste Februar (1810). This dark and grotesque tragedy in one act tells of a family haunted by a dying grandfather's curse, delivered on a fatal 24th of February. One by one the family members have met violent and melodramatic deaths on this date and the play shows the final such catastrophe. The father, reduced to poverty, kills a stranger for his money, only to discover that it is his long-lost son, come home to save him.

The great success of this work inspired a whole series with similar subjects. In 1812 Werner's play was produced by an amateur company in Weissenfels. The father was played by Gottfried Müllner (1774-1829) who then set to work to create a crude but popular imitation, Der neunundzwanzigste Februar (1812) with a similar family catastrophe, here heightened by incest. Müllner followed this with his most noted play, Die Schuld (1813). In it, a Scandinavian woman visiting in Spain is frightened by a gypsy prophecy into adopting a Spanish child and taking him home to rear as her own. The child, unaware of his origins, returns to Spain, falls in love with a woman there, and kills her husband, only to find that it was his own brother. Similar situations were developed by the other major writer in this genre, Ernst von Houwald (1778-1845), whose Die Heimkehr (1818), Das Bild (1820) and Der Leuchtturm (1820) were all widely produced. Unlike Werner and Müllner, Houwald insisted on a certain measure of justice in his catastrophes, and replaced blind fate with a benevolent if unyielding providence. However cruel the sufferings in his plays, all are merited and most result in purgation and elevation of the soul. The great years of such works were 1810 to 1820, by which time their exaggerations were becoming increasingly the source of humor rather than agreeable thrills. As early as 1818 Castelli and Jeitelles published their parody Der Schicksalstrumpf, though the finishing blow to the genre is generally considered to have been given by Count Platen's Die verhängnisvolle Gabel (1826).

To turn to the more respectable offerings at Weimar, Heinrich von Kleist's Der zerbrochene Krug was given in 1808, but its lusty peasant humor proved totally beyond the reach of Goethe's company, and it was not repeated. Only one of Schlegel's Shakespearian translations was attempted, Romeo und Julia in 1812, so heavily classicized as to be almost a travesty. The interest the romantics had aroused in

the Spanish was reflected in translations of three works by
Calderón: <u>The Constant Prince</u> in 1811, in which Wolff
achieved a great personal triumph, <u>Life is a Dream</u> in 1812,
and <u>Zenobia</u> in 1815.

Taken as a whole, the repertoire in Weimar was not
greatly different from that of most other better German theatres of the period--some German classics and occasional
translations of classic works of other nations, but the great
majority of offerings contemporary sentimental comedies,
bourgeois dramas, fate-tragedies and melodramas, ballets
and operettas. Goethe attempted to balance his program and
at least during the first decade of the century maintained a
fairly regular sequence of opera or operetta on Tuesday,
classics and experimental works on Thursday and light fare
on Saturday. After 1810 he put up less resistance to the
continuing pressure to emphasize the non-literary side of the
program. The major representative of this pressure was
Karoline Jagemann, who had become official mistress of the
Duke. In 1809 she was elevated to the nobility and her
power in the theatre grew until by 1814 her authority there
was officially recognized in a position rivalling Goethe's own.
Still it was another three years before Goethe could bring
himself to break completely with a theatre which had occupied so much of his life. The final insult was a performance
of <u>Der Hund des Aubry de Mont-Didier</u>, a translation of a
popular French melodrama by Pixérécourt in which a leading
role is played by a trained dog. A man called Kaspar was
at this time touring the theatre capitals of Germany with a
poodle whose interpretation of the role was considered outstanding. Duke Karl August, a dog-lover, expressed interest
in the play and Goethe's horrified reaction led Karoline to
demonstrate her power by encouraging the Duke. Goethe
threatened to resign if this travesty appeared on his classic
boards, and carried through his threat when the Duke and his
mistress persevered. He travelled to Jena expressly to be
out of Weimar when the sacrilege occurred, and submitted
his resignation shortly after.

In later years, Goethe relented to the extent of occasionally attending the theatre, but his dealings with it were
few. When the house burned in 1825, the Duke himself
arranged for the rebuilding. The new theatre opened with a
celebration of the fiftieth anniversary of his rule featuring a
production of Goethe's <u>Iphigenie</u> and a prologue praising the
"world-famous director." Another festival in Goethe's honor
was held for his 78th birthday in 1827. <u>Tasso</u> was presented

and Karoline Jagemann showed her willingness to be reconciled with Goethe by crowning a bust of him in the first scene
instead of one of Virgil. Goethe was indeed sufficiently mol-
lified to return to the theatre to coach the actors for the
first Weimar presentation of Faust I, given for his 80th
birthday in 1829.

    This Weimar production was actually the third offering
of at least part of Goethe's masterpiece. In 1819 a brief
excerpt was presented at the private theatre of Prince Radzi-
will. Count Brühl from Berlin was the director, Pius Wolff
played Faust and Duke Karl of Mecklenburg was Mephisto.
A few months before the Weimar production of 1829 a more
extended version was presented for the first time in a public
theatre in Braunschweig. This rather stylized interpretation
featured Eduard Schütz (1799-1868) as Faust, Heinrich Marr
(1797-1871) as Mephisto, and Wilhelmine Berger (1805-1837)
as Gretchen. The director, August Klingemann, subsequently
toured this popular production to Dresden, Leipzig, and
Frankfurt. Goethe's own production suffered, as usual, from
an over-spiritualized interpretation. Karl von La Roche
(1794-1872), who played Mephisto, boasted in later years that
he remembered every word, every step, every gesture that
Goethe had given him. The result, suggested one observer
"was no flesh and blood devil who ran about like a bellow-
ing lion to spy out what mischief he could engage in. He
was a symbolic apparition, standing on the peak of the
poem. "6

    Goethe's death in 1832 was marked, as Schiller's had
been, by a period of closure followed by a commemorative
program. An enormous crowd supplemented the faithful of
Weimar for a presentation of Tasso followed by an epilogue
which concluded "only his appearance has departed; his works
remain forever!"

2. Tieck and the Romantics

    Thanks to the power of Goethe and Schiller, the
classicism which the German romantics opposed was no half-
moribund tradition, as it was in France, but a living and
thriving force, and in the theatre as least as powerful as
they. There was no real need in early nineteenth century
Germany for a vital new movement to revivify the tradition.
Weimar classicism had done that in a way that the sterile

neoclassic revival of Napoleonic Paris was far from emulat-
ing. This surely helps to explain why the roots of German
romanticism lie more in philosophical, political, and social
movements of the time than in the artistic ones. No German artist or literary figure stimulated romanticism so much
as Fichte, with his interest in the universe as reflected in
the self, Schelling, whose concern with nature provided much
of the movement's subject-matter, or Schubert, who encouraged blendings of dream and reality. The Napoleonic
wars clearly were another powerful influence, both in their
encouragement of the ideals of patriotism and liberty and in
the emotional and spiritual turbulence they brought to the
country which saw most of their major engagements. Against
this turbulent background, so little related to the calm harmony of Goethe's ideal world, grew up a literature of moods,
of caprices, of willful disregard of all order, to the extent
that a work could turn upon and refute its own rules. Under
these conditions lyric poetry managed well enough, but though
romanticism dominated the German literary world for the
first thirty years of the century, it did not produce a single
major theatrical work.

The German theatre nevertheless owes a great debt to
the romantics if only for the translations of Shakespeare
undertaken by August Wilhelm Schlegel (1767-1845) and completed by Count Baudissin and Ludwig Tieck's daughter Dorothea. This collection is generally considered the best rendering of Shakespeare into any other language and served as
the basis for the subsequent strong German interest in the
English dramatist. Wilhelm Schlegel was the leader of the
group which has come to be known as the early romantics--
the Frühromantiker--a group of young writers who gathered
at Jena at the end of the eighteenth century. The critical
spokesman of the school was Wilhelm's brother Friedrich
(1772-1829) in the literary periodical Athenäum, founded in
1799. Aside from Wilhelm's translations, the brothers each
produced only a single play: Friedrich Alarcos (1802), based
on a Spanish romance, and Wilhelm Ion (1803), taken from
classic themes. Both, despite their authors' literary stance,
were classic in form, both were produced by Goethe in
Weimar, and both were resounding failures.

The only member of the Frühromantiker primarily
associated with the theatre, therefore, was Ludwig Tieck
(1773-1853), whose work forms a sort of compendium of
reasons why this movement produced no major dramatist.
Tieck met Friedrich Schlegel in 1797, the two writers drawn

together by a mutual admiration of Goethe's early poetry, an
aversion to rationalism, and an interest in such foreign
authors as Shakespeare, Cervantes, and Dante. Wilhelm met
Tieck the following year, and the Schlegel brothers and Tieck
strongly influenced each other thereafter in the authors they
supported and in the kind of drama they favored. Tieck encouraged Wilhelm in his translations of Shakespeare, sixteen
of which were completed by 1803, and together they discovered Calderon, five of whose plays Schlegel translated
along with one more Shakespeare (his last translation) between 1803 and 1809. Tieck's Buch über Shakespeare, which
occupied him throughout his life, had already gone through
its first draft before he met the Schlegels, but under their
influence later versions became more theoretical, even
ethereal. Such influence can already be seen in the first
parts of his Briefe über Shakespeare which appeared in the
single volume of the periodical Das poetische Journal in 1801,
but theoretical concerns never led Tieck totally away from an
interest in how the plays were actually staged, and he made
significant contributions to such study. The Briefe über
Shakespeare first expresses his central idea that the Shakespearian theatre had an upper stage, supported by pillars,
with a stairway leading to it on either side, and a third tier
above for musicians. Both the main stage and the upper
stage, he thought, were hung with curtains.

The Schlegels apparently also encouraged Tieck in the
sprawling, disconnected plays he was writing, an unfortunate
side-effect of romantic expression, since Wilhelm at least in
theory preached unity and coherence and Tieck's plays are
manifestly the worse for their arbitrariness. The best-known
of these strange works were based on old fairy and folk tales,
which Tieck apparently considered a possible basis for a new
sort of Aristophanic comedy. His first such work was Ritter
Blaubart, which appeared in the collection Volksmärchen
(1782-86), an excellent example of Tieck's "Romantic irony."
This was a term frequently and variously used by first-gen-
eration romantics. For Schlegel it apparently meant a kind
of god's-eye view in literature, the appraisal of the relative
and conditional in the light of cosmic absoluteness. For
Tieck it meant above all the arbitrary destruction of his own
poetic illusion as a kind of ultimate rejection of form.
Everything is mixed together in Ritter Blaubart--the real and
the imaginary, the remote and the contemporary, farce,
horror, pathos, and spectacle. Characters are willfully con-
tradictory and erratic, and the play ridicules them, ridicules
itself, ridicules its own author and raises total confusion on

all levels.   Immermann put it successfully on the stage in
1835, but with that single exception, producers and audiences
have found the work too diffuse and arbitrary to maintain
interest.

       Similar characteristics are found in all Tieck's plays,
the best-known of which was his next, Der gestiefelte Kater
(1797), based on Puss in Boots as Ritter Blaubart was based
on Bluebeard.   After a prologue ridiculing contemporary plays
(particularly the popular sentimental dramas of Kotzebue and
Iffland) and their audiences, the play, or actually the play
within a play, tries to tell its story, discuss itself, and experiment with a variety of genres all at once.   Zerbino and
Die verkehrte Welt (both 1799) are even more extreme sequels.   Zerbino is a fantastic parable about the son and heir
of Puss in Boots who takes a pilgrimage in search of Good
Taste, encountering literary figures, past and present, and
a series of inanimate but vocal objects.   At one point Zerbino tries to destroy his own play, forcing it to run backward until editors, readers, and critics appear to set things
to rights.   Die verkehrte Welt reverses its prologue and
epilogue and introduces the author who in a sort of Aristophanic parabasis advocates confusion.   The plot is also
vaguely Aristophanic, concerning the clown Skaramuz who
usurps Parnassus to turn it into a tourist attraction.   Eventually Apollo defeats the upstart, though Skaramuz is supported by "spectators" from the audience.

       Leben und Tod der heiligen Genoveva (1800) and
Kaiser Octavius (1802) are more typical romantic expressions, less distorted by Tieck's idiosyncratic mixing of elements.   These two epic works are set in the imaginary
Middle Ages so popular with romantic authors and in their
lyric passages, emphasis on emotion and exaggerated situations both suggest opera more than drama.   Kaiser Octavius
was hailed by the romantics as a masterpiece and its opening lines have ever since been cited as one of the most com-
pact expressions of the romantic school:

           Mondbeglänzte Zaubernacht,
           Die den Sinn gefangen hält,
           Wundervolle Märchenwelt,
           Steig auf in der alten Pracht. [7]

Goethe, however, deplored the complexity and diffuseness of
the work, and Schiller called Genoveva "uncultured prattle."
Later critics have generally cast their votes with Goethe and

Schiller, but Schiller at least showed himself susceptible to Tieck's influence, particularly in Die Jungfrau von Orleans.

By 1800 most of Tieck's original playwriting was completed, though he returned to the Aristophanic fairy-tale a final time in Leben und Tod des kleinen Thomas (1811) to ridicule, among other things, the then-popular fate-tragedies. During these years Tieck's interest was steadily growing in the early drama of Spain, Germany, and particularly England. His work with Schlegel on Calderon influenced the composition of Genoveva and Octavius and in 1818, at the suggestion of K. W. F. Solger, Tieck turned to Lope de Vega. He somehow developed and never renounced the idea that almost all pre-Shakespearian work of doubtful authorship--some sixty-two plays--was by Shakespeare, and this odd notion stimulated him to supplement Schlegel's translations with important other examples of early English drama. His Alt-Englisches Theater (1811) contained King John, The Pinner of Wakefield, Pericles, Locrine, The Merry Devil of Wakefield, and the old King Lear. In 1817 he published Deutsches Theater, a two-volume collection of drama from Sachs to Opitz, Gryphius, and Lohenstein with influential critical prefaces. The same year he visited England to collect more early English material, and at the British Museum copied fourteen plays and parts of eleven others which were published in Shakespeares Vorschule (1823, 1829, and posthumously) and Vier Schauspiele von Shakespeare (1836). He also regularly attended the English theatre, seeing Kean, Booth, Young, Macready, and the farewell performances of Kemble. Understandably, he deplored the general substitution of Cibber for Shakespeare, and he had little praise for English acting style. Naturalness had been destroyed there by French influence, he felt, and Kemble in particular he scorned as more a declaimer than an actor.

The later romantics, who came to prominence during the Napoleonic era, were far more disparate geographically and theoretically than Tieck and his circle had been. Most of the major figures in this younger generation--Achim von Arnim (1781-1831), Joseph von Eichendorff (1788-1837), Clemens Brentano (1778-1842) and others--dabbled in the drama, but with no more success than their predecessors. Brentano attempted French-style vaudeville in Die lustigen Musikanten (1803), with music by E. T. A. Hoffmann, but most of his plays reflected the influence of Tieck. Gustav Vasa (1800) copied the devices of Der gestiefelte Kater and Tieck's interest in historical drama and in the Spanish cape and sword

plays could be seen echoed in <u>Ponce de Leon</u> (1804) and <u>Die</u>
<u>Gründung Prags</u> (1815).   The patriotic fervor which charac-
terized much romantic writing during and just after the wars
of liberation had little opportunity to develop in the theatre,
which almost immediately suffered from the censorship imposed by the conservative reaction.   A kind of muted nationalism, however, appeared in the historical dramas of the
Swabian Ludwig Uhland (1787-1862), <u>Ernest von Schwaben</u> and
<u>Ludwig von Bayern.</u>

The most powerful German dramatist of the period
after Schiller went almost without recognition during his lifetime.   This was the tormented and solitary Heinrich von
Kleist (1777-1811).   Though Kleist had little association with
the romantics, he did share with them a revolt against reason
and standardized attitudes, confirmed by a study of Kant, and
a search for new bases of human action which would be
meaningful and yet cognizant of the subjective and emotional
side of existence.   To some authors of the time, this search
was invigorating and elevating.   For Kleist it was a journey
through horror.   He became obsessed with the illusory nature
of the world of appearance, which seemed almost malevolently
determined to thwart the expectations of human reason.   Even
the lightest of Kleist's works are darkened somewhat by this
insoluble problem, and the tragedies express it directly.
Every step of the disaster which overtakes all in his first
play, <u>Die Familie Schroffenstein</u> (1803), is the result of a
perfectly rational mistake in judgment.   Two branches of a
princely house destroy each other in mutual suspicion arising
from a law which decrees that if either line lacks a direct
male heir, its possessions will go to the other.   The play
owes something to <u>Romeo and Juliet,</u> and even more to the
"Sturm und Drang" tradition, but its development is pure
Kleist.   Some critics have called it an argument against reason, since the reasonable assumption in every case proves
both wrong and catastrophic, but Kleist's pessimism seems
to go much deeper.   There seems to exist in the world of
the Schroffensteins a power of active malevolence which
arranges traps for the destruction of those mortals foolish
enough to attempt to understand and react meaningfully to
their situation.

Kleist began another tragedy at about this same time,
<u>Robert Guiskard,</u> but in 1803, during one of his frequent
bouts with despair, he burned the manuscript.   All that remains of it are several scenes which he recreated from
memory in 1808 to publish in the magazine <u>Phöbus.</u>   This

fragment remains one of his darkest and most powerful works,
its hero pitted against a merciless universe graphically represented by the plague. In scope and poetic power the play
suggests a Greek tragedy, complete with a chorus (from
which, however, individuals speak for the group). For several years after the destruction of Robert Guiskard, Kleist
shunned writing, but in 1806 he resumed his career and in
the next four years completed six of the most significant
German plays of the period. First came Der zerbrochene
Krug (1806), which Goethe produced without success in Weimar, but which has since come to be generally acknowledged
as one of the greatest German comedies. Again illusion and
error form the basis of the plot. Adam, the judge in a
small Dutch village, has attempted to seduce Eve, a village
girl, but was interrupted at the crucial moment by her fiancé
Ruprecht. Ruprecht dealt his rival some heavy blows in the
dark but failed to recognize him. Eve could identify her
would-be seducer, but to her fiancé's dismay she keeps si-
lent, knowing that Adam would avenge a scandal by sending
Ruprecht to the army. The potential melodrama in such a
situation is avoided by the rough humor of the characters,
particularly of Adam, holding court over his own crime and
developing the most preposterous lies to explain how he has
lost his wig and scarred his face.

Kleist's reworking of Amphitryon (1807) considers a
similar triangle with distinctly more serious implications.
The inscrutable universe that worked against all human plans
was abstract and remote in the early tragedies; here, in this
strange comedy, it becomes personified as Jupiter. What
Adam attempted Jupiter achieves, and with such success that
even when she is aware of the deception the tormented
Alkmene cannot determine her real husband. For Molière,
the focus of the play was on the confusion of the deceived
husband, for Kleist it was on the psychological and moral
ambiguity experienced by the confused wife.

Alkmene served as a sort of preliminary study for
Kleist's two deepest and richest female studies, Penthesilea
(1808) and Käthchen von Heilbronn (1808). Kleist conceived
of these as companion pieces, but his plan must have been
for them to illuminate each other by opposition, for two more
different works within the general romantic tradition would be
difficult to imagine. Penthesilea is a sprawling, chaotic
dramatic poem, a depiction of cruelty, passion, and irra-
tionality perhaps unmatched in dramatic literature since
Seneca. This is the most internal of Kleist's works; no

conflicts with an inscrutable universe destroy his barbaric
Amazon Queen, but the emotional storms within herself that
arise from her love-hate relationship with Achilles. Kleist's
savage and blood-crazed Queen has often been cited as a
purely romantic creation in contrast to Goethe's classic intellectual, almost ethereal Iphigenia. One is clearly Diony-
sian, the other Apollonian. Käthchen on the other hand fol-
lows conventional dramatic form, shuns the luxuriant but idiosyncratic verse of most of Kleist's other works and notably
of Penthesilea, and faithfully includes all the cliches of standard German romantic chivalric drama, such as a duel, a
nocturnal tempest, and a besieged castle. Good and evil are
clearly defined and suitably rewarded, and the heroine Käthchen is all that Penthesilea is not--a medieval figure of self-
sacrifice and devotion. Never did Kleist make so many concessions to popular taste as in this work, and it is hardly
surprising that during the rest of the century it was the most
frequently adapted and performed of his works. It is surely
no less surprising that in our own century the more irrational
and psychologically richer Penthesilea has proven much more
attractive.

Like many writers of his generation, Kleist reacted to
the conquests of Napoleon by turning to Germanic themes.
When the Emperor attacked Austria in 1805, Kleist wrote to
his friend Rühle forecasting with bitterness but resignation
the downfall of the hopelessly divided and disorganized German states. The loss of Bavaria, Württemberg, and other
principalities, the defeats of Jena and Auerstädt and the hu-
miliating Peace of Tilset confirmed Kleist's gloomy prediction
and doubtless left their mark on his last plays, all of which,
from Kätchen on, concern the German spirit in adversity.
Die Hermannsschlacht (1808) showed a brilliant leader uniting
feuding German tribes to throw off the yoke of the Romans,
but Kleist was so concerned with drawing historical parallels
that this became the weakest of his mature works. The play
was not even allowed to capitalize on the feelings of the time,
for it was scheduled for production in Vienna when Napoleon
captured the city and Kleist was forced to leave for Prague.

Prinz Friedrich von Homburg (1810), concerning a
leader who conquers pride and fear to sacrifice himself to
his duty and to the German state, could have been another
study of narrowly contemporary interest, but in his consideration of the conflict between the individual and society,
Kleist created in his last play one of his most universal
statements. Once again his hero's fate is in the hands of an

external force, here the Elector, which seems determined to
thwart all his reasonable expectations, but the relation between the two is a very complex one. Most of Homburg's
illusions are self-imposed, and the play begins with the
clearly symbolic action of the Elector awakening him from a
deluding dream. The reversals of the drama temper Homburg, increase his stature and bring him a deeper knowledge
of himself. For all this the Elector is responsible, but there
is a certain almost demonic coldness in the process by which
he manipulates Homburg's fate. His final act is to pardon
Homburg after the condemned Prince has accepted the justice
of his execution. In his own life, Kleist was unable to
achieve this balance, and the year after writing the Prinz von
Homburg he committed suicide. Only two of his works had
been presented in his lifetime, and only one, Käthchen von
Heilbronn, had achieved any success.

Almost the only critic in the first half of the nineteenth century who recognized Kleist's genius was Tieck, who
began collecting the dramatist's work about 1816. In 1821 he
published Prinz von Homburg, Die Hermannsschlacht and all
that remained of Robert Guiskard, and was instrumental in
getting the first of these produced in Dresden. The city had
established a court theatre not long before Tieck settled there
in 1819, but its fare was the usual selection of French comedies and vaudevilles mixed with native farces and the dramas
of Iffland and Kotzebue. During Tieck's first two years in
Dresden a production of Macbeth in 1819 and of Hamlet in
1820 were the only offerings of any literary interest. Not
surprisingly, Tieck showed little interest in this venture and
devoted his time to his editing and to leading the town's literary circle. Hans von Könneritz, the intendant of the royal
theatre, seems to have had a vision of making Tieck into a
kind of Lessing for his organization, however, and he urged
Tieck to begin a series of dramatic criticisms for the
Dresden paper, the Abendzeitung.

The project had little appeal for Tieck, since the
paper was headed by Könneritz' secretary Winckler, whose
adaptations of French vaudevilles were making him wealthy
and who looked with great misgivings on any reforms Tieck
might propose. Könneritz however refused to consider a
production of so odd a play as Kleist's Prinz von Homburg
unless Tieck agreed to prepare the public in the Abendzeitung.
Tieck agreed, with several beneficial results. The production was an unequivocal success, Tieck became more interested in the workings of the Dresden theatre, neither Tieck

nor Winckler found the other as troublesome as both had
feared, and within another year Tieck indeed became a regular contributor to the paper. The high standards, dignified
tone and clear style of Tieck's articles do in fact suggest
Lessing, but Könneritz was not fortunate enough to inspire
another Hamburg Dramaturgy. Tieck rarely considered general questions of theatre art in these articles, but spent most
of his time in specific discussions of the plays, particularly
the minor ones, in hopes of improving the repertoire. He
scathingly condemned Anna Boleyn by Eduard Gehe, a friend
of Winckler, and the crude comedies of Clauren, Töpfer, and
Frau von Weissenthurn. He seized on the occasion of a production of Houwald's Der Leuchtturm to denounce the entire
genre of fate-tragedy. On the positive side, the theatre
under his urging produced The Merchant of Venice in 1821,
Romeo and Juliet in 1823, King Lear in 1824, and comedies
by Holberg, Goldoni, and various English writers in adaptations by Schröder. Kleist's Käthchen von Heilbronn followed
his Prinz von Homburg and in 1826 Tieck published the collected works of Kleist with an introductory essay which became the basis of Kleist criticism for most of the century.

In 1822 Tieck was contacted by a young dramatist
even more eccentric and original than Kleist, Christian Dietrich Grabbe (1801-1836), who sent a copy of his first play,
Herzog Theodor von Gothland. The work was a demonic
vision of life, going beyond the fate-tragedies and Sturm und
Drang plays which had in part inspired it to a grotesque
world suggestive of Shakespeare's Titus Andronicus. While
Tieck expressed shock at such despair and cynicism in an
author so young, he told Grabbe that his play showed great
promise and urged him to continue writing. In reply, Grabbe
sent his fantastic comedy Scherz, Satire, Ironie und tiefere
Bedeutung (1822). The extravagant imagination of this work,
its reveling in satire and burlesque, and its verbal exuberance
were surely developed in part with Tieck's own dramatic experiments in mind, but Tieck's romantic irony is conspicu-
ously absent. Except for a freewheeling discussion of heaven,
hell, and literature between the devil and the poet Ratbane in
the second act, and the sudden and totally unexpected appearance of Grabbe himself at the conclusion of the piece,
Grabbe's farcical elaborations take place within a reasonably
conventional and consistent framework. Tieck was less encouraging this time, but at Grabbe's insistence, offered him
an acting position in Dresden. Grabbe enjoyed little success
there, and after a disappointing series of similar attempts in
Leipzig, Braunschweig, and Hannover, Grabbe returned to his

home in Detmold and took up practice as a lawyer. During
these travels he completed a dark historical tragedy, Marius
und Sulla (1823), which he apparently considered the conclusion of his theatrical career.

Then in 1827 Grabbe's interest was revived by an offer
from George Ferdinand Kettembeil, a friend of his in Frankfurt, to publish his plays. A volume containing his three
early works with a rather weak Italian tragedy, Nannette und
Maria, was published that same year and met with considerable success in Germany and abroad. His confidence restored, Grabbe rapidly produced a series of ambitious and
staggeringly diverse dramas: two epic historical pageants,
Friedrich Barbarossa and Heinrich IV (1828), a fairy-tale
comedy Aschenbrödel (1829), a vast romantic tragedy Don
Juan und Faust (1828), and an odd, almost Brechtian, historical saga, Napoleon oder die hundert Tage (1831). During
these productive years Grabbe was the pride of his town and
in 1829 his Don Juan und Faust was presented in the Detmold
court theatre. Grabbe's odd and wayward genius did not
adapt well to the theatre, however, and this was the only
production of any of his works in his lifetime. A new period
of uncertainty and personal crisis followed. The prospect of
a productive relationship with the theatre in Düsseldorf in
1834 raised his spirits once more and encouraged his work
on a new series of experimental history plays. Of these only
an expressionistic Hannibal (1835) and Die Hermannsschlacht
(1836) were completed. Immermann in Düsseldorf proved no
more capable of assimilating Grabbe than Tieck in Dresden
had been, and the discouraged author returned home to Detmold, where he died in 1836.

For much of the nineteenth century, Grabbe fared far
worse than Kleist. Not one of his plays was performed from
the time of his death until 1875. Then at the end of the century, with the development of modern experimental movements, his strange techniques, his pessimism, and his violent
themes no longer seemed so grotesque. During our own century, the expressionists, the theorists of "epic" theatre, and
the absurdists have each in turn recognized him as a precursor of certain of their own approaches.

Shortly after the brief and unfortunate sojourn of
Grabbe in Dresden, the intendant Könneritz retired, and his
successor Adolf von Lüttichau invited Tieck to become the
theatre's dramaturg, a position which involved giving literary
advice on the selection of the repertoire and coaching the

younger actors.   Tieck and Lüttichau began their new administration in 1824 by traveling about to observe theatres in
such major cities as Prague, Munich, Vienna, Stuttgart,
Frankfurt, and Braunschweig.   This was a disappointing trip
for Tieck, who found the plays mediocre and the acting
worse.   He returned to Dresden hopeful that he could make
it a model for other theatres, but the indifference of Lüttichau
and the public and the mutual antagonisms of Winckler and
the three actors who served in turn as stage managers--
August Werdy (1770-1847), Ludwig Pauli (1793-1841), and
Friedrich Julius (1776-1860)--negated most of his efforts.
His greatest influence predictably was on the repertoire, and
Dresden during the 1820's produced more Shakespeare than
any previous German stage had attempted.   Other significant
offerings included Lope de Vega's Star of Seville, Calderón's
Phantom Lady, Goethe's Tasso, Kleist's Der zerbrochene
Krug, and Grillparzer's Ein treuer Diener seines Herrn.   In
honor of Goethe's 80th birthday in 1829 the theatre gave
Faust I, though with extensive cuts to remove anything possibly offensive to religion or morality or offering too great
a challenge in staging.

These years also saw a series of important new theatrical articles from Tieck.   The essays Costüm and Dekorationen (1825) each began by attacking the stylized and arbitrary traditional designs--the standard eighteenth century
heroic costume, worn whatever the period of the play, the
settings composed of bare rooms with wings for walls or
landscapes in symmetrical perspective in the Italian style.
One would expect such a beginning to lead to a plea for historic accuracy or at least for local color, but on the contrary, Tieck condemned strongly the Berlin experiments in
that direction.   He argued instead for a stage based on simplified medieval and renaissance elements (as he understood
them) and a poetic and colorful costume essentially theatrical
rather than realistic.   In the rest of the nineteenth century,
as historicity triumphed, this attitude was generally condemned as reactionary or even self-contradictory, but when
Tieck argued for example for modern dress in preference to
scrupulously authentic historical costuming of Shakespeare,
his arguments clearly anticipated those of many twentieth century producers. [8]

His Über des Tempo (1825) was a useful corrective to
Goethe, urging actors to respect the poetic rhythm of their
speeches but to avoid such obvious conventions as a pause
following each line.   He was an astute observer and appraiser

of actors, as we may see in his lengthy critiques of the almost thirty members of the company which appeared in 1827
in Das Dresdener Hoftheater.   In 1826 he collected his
articles since 1821 for the Abendzeitung and other writings
on the theatre which were published as Dramaturgische Blätter.   Two major articles the next year, Über die neueren
französischen Stücke and Das deutsche Theater continued his
unsuccessful campaign to wean his audience from French
comedy and vaudeville and mediocre native farce and melodrama.

Tieck's most important work of these years, however,
was unquestionably his continuing editorship of the early
English plays.   The two volumes of Shakespeares Vorschule
appeared in 1823 and 1829 with long and important prefaces
tracing English drama from 1580 to 1620.   In 1829 Tieck
completed his translations of Edward III, The Life and Death
of Thomas Lord Cromwell, and Sir John Oldcastle, which
were published in 1836 with Count Baudissin's translation of
The London Prodigal as Vier Schauspiele von Shakespeare.
In 1831 Tieck encouraged his disciple Eduard von Bülow to
collect the plays and adaptations Schröder had prepared for
the stage, including many foreign works with acting versions
of Elizabethan and Restoration authors.   Tieck's influential
introduction to this four-volume work discussed the development of the European theatre up to 1800, and called for a
German national drama and the development of a native bür-
gerliches Drama.   Most significantly, he supervised translations by Count Baudissin and his daughter Dorothea of nineteen more Shakespearian plays which with Schlegel's seventeen earlier translations were published in a nine-volume
edition between 1825 and 1833 to become the basis of Shakespearian study and production in Germany.

Tieck remained dramaturg until his departure from
Dresden for Berlin in 1842, but indifference and opposition
to his reforms had destroyed most of his interest in the post
by 1830.   During the following decade, he achieved much
more recognition for his twice weekly dramatic readings,
which became a major attraction in the city.   Grillparzer
reported in his diary that the readings had the effect of an
excellent performance and they indeed came in time to rival
the attractiveness of the national theatre itself.   Here, freed
from the necessity of arguing his goals with stubborn collab-
orators, Tieck continued to promote his favorite authors--
Shakespeare, Jonson, Calderon, Lope de Vega, Gozzi, and
Goldoni.

The Prussian monarch Friedrich Wilhelm IV invited
Tieck to his court theatre at Potsdam near Berlin in 1841 to
stage the Greek tragedy Antigone. The production, with
choruses by Mendelssohn, was presented in an attempted reconstruction of a Greek stage, with permanent settings and
no curtain. The actors entered from the orchestra and played
far downstage in a kind of bas-relief. The following year
Tieck accepted an invitation from the king to settle in Berlin
permanently. He supervised a production of Medea, with
music by W. G. K. Taubert, at Potsdam in 1843 and later that
same year presented his most important production, A Midsummer Night's Dream. This was a culmination of Tieck's
investigations into the Shakespearian stage, which had continued throughout his years in Dresden. He designed an
architectural stage (Raumbühne) with minimal scenery for the
Romeo and Juliet production of 1823 and a sketch in the
Goethe papers, probably from 1828, shows a variation of his
three-level stage for A Midsummer Night's Dream. For the
Dresden Macbeth of 1836 he created a permanent setting with
a staircase that served both as a mountain ascent for the
witches and a way from the castle yard to the upper living
quarters, and the same year he, Baudissin and the architect
Gottfried Semper worked out a reconstruction of the Fortune
theatre.

Gerst, the scene painter for the royal theatre, designed the settings for the 1843 Midsummer Night's Dream
according to Tieck's directions, and the result was the most
complete embodiment of Shakespearian staging which Tieck
achieved. The stage, built in the Neues Palais, had two
levels with a musicians' gallery, each level divided into three
usable sections. The side sections on the lower level were
staircases, on the upper, smaller acting areas. There was
no moveable scenery, no curtain, and a drop for the single
interior. The cast numbered over a hundred, and Tieck required more than thirty rehearsals. The production was so
great a success that it was taken from Potsdam to Berlin
and repeated more than 150 times during the next forty years.

Tieck's failing health made this the last of his major
undertakings. His Der gestiefelte Kater and Blaubart were
presented in Berlin in 1844 and 1845 against his wishes and
both were failures. The Frogs (1843), Oedipus at Colonus
(1845), Racine's Athalie (1845) and Euripides' Hippolytus
(1851) were given on the pseudo-antique stage at Potsdam,
but none equalled the success of Antigone. Tieck blamed
these failures and others on the decline of German acting,

now so poor, he maintained, that Shakespeare had been destroyed and Goethe and Schiller were living on their reputations alone. He still encouraged promising young playwrights, most notably Gustav Freytag and Eduard von Bauernfeld, but he was bitterly opposed to the Young Germany movement which included most of the better writers of the 1830s and 1840s and he refused to recognize the importance of either Hebbel or Grillparzer. He thus became more and more isolated from the theatre of his time. He died in Berlin in 1853.

3. Iffland and Brühl in Berlin

Though as the capital city of the powerful state of Prussia Berlin became in the early nineteenth century one of the major theatre centers of Germany, the theatre traditions of the city was rather undistinguished. During the eighteenth century, Berlin was host to a number of companies, German, French, and Italian, competing with each other in a series of unsuccessful attempts to establish a permanent theatre in the city. It was the popular author and actor August Wilhelm Iffland (1759-1814) who at last brought stability and fame to the Berlin theatre at the end of the century. In the 1780s and early 1790s the two most influential theatres in Germany were Ackermann's theatre in Hamburg, managed now by Schröder, and the Hof- und National-theater in Mannheim which Baron von Dalberg had founded in 1779. Iffland was associated with the latter venture and when it closed in 1796 he accepted the offer of Friedrich Wilhelm III to establish himself in Berlin.

His repertoire in Berlin was essentially the same as that of Mannheim and indeed differed little from that of most German theatres of the period. The authors most popular and most frequently performed were Iffland and his somewhat younger contemporary August von Kotzebue (1761-1819). Even in Weimar Goethe produced 31 of Iffland's plays and 87 by Kotzebue as against nineteen of his own, eighteen by Schiller, and eight by Shakespeare. Iffland's works were meticulous if sentimental depictions of middle-class home life called Familienstücke. In politically turbulent times, these offered relief by their careful exclusion of any possibly disturbing references to politics, social problems, or history. Instead they demonstrated the inevitable triumph of persecuted virtue over vice and of deserving poverty rewarded with honor and

prosperity.   The most popular works of Iffland, such as Die
Jäger (1781), Die Hagestolzen (1791), Der Spieler (1796), and
Dienstpflicht, were all frequently revived until late in the
nineteenth century.

Kotzebue's range was broader, his humor lower, his
catering to his audiences' prejudices and conceit more blatant,
and his success proportionately greater than Iffland's.   His
first and greatest success was Menschenhass und Reue (1787),
a tearful melodrama which gained him a European reputation
rivalling that of Goethe.   Kotzebue came to join Iffland in
Berlin in 1802 after being briefly associated with each of the
other major German theatres at the turn of the century, the
Burgtheater in Vienna and Goethe's theatre in Weimar.   He
was already the author of more than fifty plays, but he would
almost double that number before leaving Berlin in 1806, and
add another hundred before his death.   Two new works by
Kotzebue inaugurated the new Berlin theatre in 1802, an historical drama, Die Kreuzfahrer, and a spectacular fairy
opera, Des Teufels Lustschloss.   He was lionized by the
public and even made a member of the Berlin Academy of
Science, but he was not without influential enemies, particularly among the romantics, the followers of Goethe and
Schiller, and other literary critics who deplored his appeal
to the lowest tastes of his audiences.   The magazine Zeitung
für die elegante Welt regularly attacked him, but Kotzebue
responded by founding a rival journal, Der Freimüthige, in
1803, to attack such figures as Goethe and Schiller.   The
same year he founded the Almanach dramatischer Spiele
which until his death regularly published his new comedies
and parodies.   He also continued to produce a wide variety
of other works: comedies of manners such as Die deutschen
Kleinstaedter (1803), an amusing consideration of status-seek-
ing in a small German town; comedies of character, such as
Blinde Liebe (1806), whose Baron Qualm is a rather vulgar
blend of Don Juan and Tartuffe; farces like Pagenstreiche
(1804), which deals with the love-intrigues of a witty page
derived from Mozart's Cherubino; adaptations from Molière
and Holberg; mythological parodies and travesties such as
Das Urtheil des Paris (1804); chivalric dramas and historical
plays such as Hugo Grotius (1803); patriotic plays like Die
Hussiten vor Naumburg im Jahr 1432 (1803); bourgeois dramas such as Die Sticknadeln oder Der Weg zum Herzen
(1805); and children's plays such as Die Uhr und die Mandel-
torte (1804).

Napoleon's victory at Jena caused Kotzebue to retire

first to Königsberg, then to Russia, where he continued his
work as a playwright and produced several important volumes
on German history.   In 1816 he was commissioned by Czar
Alexander to return to Weimar to study the political climate
of France and Germany.   Though he shared with the young
liberals of the period a hatred of Napoleon, he disagreed
openly with them on the more volatile matter of the Metternichian conservatism which had followed, and expressed a
solidly conservative viewpoint in his periodical Pudende oder
Archiv der Thorheiten unserer Zeit, founded in 1817.   As a
result, his Geschichte des deutschen Reiches was burned
along with the Napoleonic Code in student demonstrations that
year.   Kotzebue replied with a widely-read article in Das
literarische Wochenblatt attacking the universities as centers
of anarchy where academic freedom was invoked to excuse
simple license.   He was in turn accused of serving as an es-
pionage agent for the Czar.   The bitterness between the popular author and his liberal enemies increased until Kotzebue
was assassinated in 1819 by a patriot student, Charles Fred-
erick Sand.   This assassination and an attempt on the life of
the regent of Nassau unleashed a veritable terror in German
intellectual society.   Professors were expelled and arrested,
schools closed, periodicals suppressed, constitutional liberties
rescinded.   Many German intellectuals held Kotzebue responsible for this, and the contempt previously held for his
work was reinforced by a hatred for his political position.
German literary critics therefore continued to heap abuse on
his works long after the other popular and equally insubstantial authors of the period such as Iffland and Raupach were
mercifully forgotten.

    The plays which Iffland personally favored were those
in the spirit of the eighteenth century enlightenment, which
brought him into close harmony with the opinions of Friedrich
Schulz, Berlin's first systematic theatre critic.   Schulz'
Berlinischer Dramaturgie (1799) scorned romantic experiment
and looked to Lessing as the highest authority in all theatrical
matters.   As a theatre director, however, Iffland was distinctly more eclectic than he was as a dramatist or an actor.
He offered eighty plays of Kotzebue and twenty-six of his
own, revivals of Lessing, and parodies of the early romantics and particularly of Tieck such as Heinrich Beck's Das
Chamäleon (1800).   On the other hand, he brought several of
the Schlegel translations to Berlin: Hamlet in 1799, Julius
Caesar in 1804, The Merchant of Venice in 1810, and Romeo
and Juliet in 1812.   Kleist and Tieck were never offered,
but Werner's Söhne des Tales (1805) was presented after its

success in Hamburg, and Iffland encouraged the creation of Werner's Luther play, Die Weihe der Kraft (1806). This role, indeed, became one of Iffland's favorites and was the last in which he appeared. Eichendorff, who saw the play in Berlin in 1810, noted in his Tagebuch (28 February) that Iffland even utilized a certain romanticism in production:

> Luther (Iffland)'s prayer while a flute played. A truly romantic scene. Luther with Melancthon and his father, Katharina at their feet, Therese and Theobald (Mlle Schick) sitting before them on the ground. Behind them a duet singing (heavenly!), an accompanist with a horn, Wildeneck standing in the middle. A great procession, full of pomp, with rich, authentic costumes. All the electors on horses, etc. The noble figure of the ruler (Bethmann) on horseback under a canopy. [9]

After 1800, a romantic note even crept into certain of Kotzebue's plays--in such historical tragedies as Johann von Montfaucon (1800), Gustaf Vasa (1801) and Hussiten vor Naumburg (1803) and in such comedies of local color as Beiden Klingsberg (1801), Deutschen Kleinstädter (1803) and Pagenstreiche (1804). Iffland did draw the line at such extreme romantic manifestations as the fate-tragedies, however, which had to wait for the next administration to be produced in Berlin.

Between 1799 and 1806 Iffland also drew heavily on the Weimar repertoire, giving Schlegel's Ion in 1802, and most of Goethe's works--Egmont and Tancred (1801), Iphigenie (1802), Näturliche Tochter (1803), and Götz von Berlichingen (1805). The Schiller productions of these years were Iffland's major achievements as a director. For Piccolomini and Wallensteins Tod in 1799 and Maria Stuart in 1801 the leading roles were taken by an outstanding group of actors: Iffland himself, Friedericke Bethmann-Unzelmann (1760-1815), Johann Ferdinand Fleck (1757-1801) and Franz Mattausch (1767-1833). Despite their success in working together, these actors represented two distinctly divergent styles of interpretation, for Iffland made no more attempt in the acting of his company than in its repertoire to encourage a single, distinctive approach. Iffland approached his roles in a clearly objective way, carefully building them up from small but significant details--the correct gesture, the right sort of walk, the proper trimming on a costume were matters of great importance to him; though it must be noted that unlike the romantics he was concerned primarily with theatri-

cally effective detail rather than with detail which was necessarily authentic or even colorful. The charming and youthful
Frau Unzelmann had a style close to Iffland's and was his
most common leading lady, and Mattausch, though he lacked
Iffland's power and imagination, built characters in essentially
the same way. Fleck, on the other hand, employed an intui-
tive emotional approach which clearly looked forward to that
of the great romantic actors such as Devrient.

Though in his early pronouncements at least Iffland
preached a unified style, he made no attempt to adjust his
own acting to Fleck's or vice versa. He achieved instead at
least a superficial unity in his theatricalized surroundings,
which somewhat muted the occasional clashes in style by placing them in a consistent environment. All Iffland productions
used elaborate costumes and scenery, pageantry and lively
movement, quite unlike the stately, restrained, and deliberate
productions of Weimar. Again it was theatrical effectiveness
Iffland sought, rather than romantic historicity or local color,
but his productions clearly prefigured the more purely romantic offerings of his successor Count Brühl. After Fleck's
death in 1801 Iffland assumed most of his roles, with lesser
parts shared between Jonas Beschort (1767-1846) and Josef
Böheim (1752-1811), and the Iffland style for a time dominated
Berlin productions. Schiller in a letter to Körner remarked
on its difference from the Weimar style:

> Madame Unzelmann plays Maria Stuart with great
> charm and great understanding; her delivery is
> beautiful and full of meaning; yet one might wish
> her a bit more tragic style and elevation. The in-
> fluence of natural playing still dominates her so
> that her delivery approaches conversation and every
> phrase becomes realistic in her mouth. This is
> Iffland's school and it gives a general tone to Ber-
> lin productions. When nature is graceful and noble,
> as with Madame Unzelmann, one can't help enjoying
> it, but generally the natural is unbearable, as we
> saw in the presentation of Die Jungfrau in Leipzig.[10]

The roles that Iffland inherited from Fleck were modified in
a similar way; Fleck's Wallenstein, for example, had been a
demonic, haunted, romantic figure, while Iffland's was a pro-
saic, even bourgeois man of affairs.

Iffland's Schiller productions were also physically his
most ambitious. Goethe's friend Karl Zelter reported that if

Schiller really wished to see his <u>Jungfrau von Orleans,</u> he
must come to Berlin:

> The pomp for our production of this play is more
> than regal; the fourth act alone, which includes
> more than eight hundred people complete with music
> and other effects creates so brilliant an impression
> that the audience is raised to ecstasy. The setting
> is a long arcade through which the procession
> passes, backed by a cathedral, elaborately decorated
> in the Gothic style. [11]

Little wonder that Iffland and his designer Bartolomeo Verona
felt it necessary to have a new theatre with more elaborate
scenic possibilities by 1802. Here Iffland was able to produce
<u>Wilhelm Tell</u> in 1804 with huge Alpine settings and an even
more formidable <u>Jungfrau von Orleans</u> to commemorate Schiller's death in 1805. Not surprisingly, Shakespeare was given
similar treatment. For his 1804 production of <u>Julius Caesar,</u>
Iffland demanded that Schlegel reduce the number of scenes so
that, like Irving later in the century, he could make the remaining ones more impressive scenically. The same care for
detail which characterized his acting and the realistic interiors
of his own plays still lay behind these exaggerated spectacles.
Obviously Iffland preferred dramatists with a feeling for a
dramatic situation that could be heightened by scenery and
costume to those who placed their emphasis on language.
Schiller was far more popular in Berlin than Goethe.

Between 1806 and 1809 the theatre was under French
occupation and the repertoire was composed largely of opera
and ballet. The political reorganization which followed gave
Iffland the opportunity to organize the theatre under a Ministry
of Culture, which would have had a dignity similar to the
Academy of Science, but Iffland preferred to be subordinate
to the police and the Bureau of Trade, apparently feeling this
might intimidate critics of the theatre and avoid the establishment of more of the notorious Prussian bureaucracy. Whatever his motives in this decision, it became increasingly
apparent in Iffland's later years that he was much less concerned with making his theatre artistically distinguished than
with making it popular. Between 1809 and 1814 the repertoire
was dominated by successful but minor figures such as Kotzebue and Schiller's disciples Collin and Theodore Körner.

On one of his final tours in 1814 Iffland performed
Kotzebue's <u>Menschenhass und Reue</u> in Breslau. He played the

old Bitterman and opposite him, playing his son, was an actor who had never done the role before, but who was nevertheless so powerful that Iffland saw in him a successor to the great Fleck. He therefore invited Ludwig Devrient (1784-1832) to Berlin, and some of his last arrangements before his death were for the hiring of this new leading actor. His successor, Count Karl Brühl (1772-1837) welcomed Devrient to the capital in 1815. The actor's dissolute life and empassioned manner of performing had already taken their toll; he came to Berlin already past the peak of his power; still he remained until his death one of the most dominant actors of the time.

Devrient more than any other actor embodied the spirit of romanticism on the German stage, as Kean, his contemporary, did in England. The eldest son of a respectable merchant in Berlin, he showed little promise in his early years of his future calling, unless an inability to make a success of either studies or business might be so interpreted. He attended the Berlin theatre, where he saw Iffland and Fleck, but he seems to have developed no particular interest in theatre until 1803 when, visiting Leipzig, he saw the performances of Ferdinand Ochsenheimer (1767-1822). Ochsenheimer was a leading player in one of the many lesser but respectable companies of the time which were not sufficiently prosperous to settle permanently in one city and so regularly divided the season among three or four. Ochsenheimer's company had temporary homes in Leipzig, Dresden, and Prague, and its leading actor, a lean figure with grotesque but extremely flexible features, was a popular interpreter of villains; Franz Moor in Die Räuber and Wurm in Kabale und Liebe were particular favorites.

Inspired by this demonic figure, Devrient applied for employment in the minor Lange company, making his debut at Gera in 1804 as Princess Isabella's messenger in Schiller's Braut von Messina. In this, and in a series of young lovers' roles which followed, he was so insecure and gauche that but for the encouragement of the leading actor Julius Weidner he would doubtless have renounced acting forever. Then he achieved a sudden and astonishing success as the last-minute substitution for a part in K. F. Hensler's folk play Das Donauweibchen. The part was a traditional comic rogue in the Hanswurst tradition, here called Kaspar Larifari. Devrient, who had just been reading Shakespeare's Henry IV and was fascinated with Falstaff, attempted to inject some of that character into his role. His fellow actors and audience discovered to their astonishment that though Devrient was

hopelessly bad in the simple parts that most mediocre actors
could do with ease, he had a kind of genius for the odd and
grotesque. He was changed at once from young lovers to
character roles and on his way to fame.

After a year with the Lange company Devrient joined
the more prosperous Bossan troupe permanently established in
Dessau. Here he shook off his tendency to imitate Ochsenheimer and created his first striking original characterizations, beginning with Kanzler Fessel in Iffland's Die Mündel.
On the darker side, here he also began to exhibit that pro-
fligacy and weakness for drink which like his brilliant but
erratic style he shared with Kean, his English counterpart.
By 1809 he had reached his full artistic maturity, and was
accepted by the national theatre of Breslau, the second most
important city of Prussia. The theatre, founded in 1797, had
been raised to a position of significance by a series of excellent directors from Professor Rhode to the present Streit.
When Devrient arrived the leading actors were Friedrich
Julius, an ex-soldier who specialized in "dignified" parts and
who later worked with Tieck in Dresden, Thürnagel, who
went on to perform for the Duke of Baden and write a work
on the theory of dramatic art, Becker, who had worked under
Goethe in Weimar, and an excellent comedian, Schmelka
(1780-1837). Just before Devrient left the Breslau theatre in
1814 the company gained Heinrich Anschütz (1785-1865), who
went on to become another of Germany's great actors and a
pillar of the Vienna Burgtheater.

Devrient's first role in Breslau was Franz Moor in
Die Räuber. The part was traditionally associated with Iffland's interpretation, which made Moor a grotesque embodiment of evil with a hump and a thatch of red hair. Devrient
merely darkened the lines around his mouth and eyes and concentrated on exposing an internal corruption, which audiences
generally found more horrible than anything suggested by Iffland's monstrous appearance. Klingemann described his interpretation as

> ... more than truth--more than artistic perfection
> .... His facial play was in itself thrillingly great;
> the eyes now flaring up in frenzy, now dying down
> in hippocratic ashiness with the exhaustion of utter
> despair; and with this the wild Gorgon-like hair with
> its loose locks twining about his forehead and neck
> like the snakes of the Furies--all this in terrifying
> combination formed a picture ... immeasureably far

removed from what is ordinarily called acting, so
that everything else in comparison seemed but artifice and make-believe, and even Iffland's performance dwindled to a shadow in our recollections. [12]

Devrient continued to win praise as Wurm and Fessel
and in 1810 began performing Lear in the new Schlegel translation.   The enormous physical demands of his interpretation
put a great strain on him.   Karl von Holtei recalled as a
youth in Dresden seeing Devrient collapse in a sort of epi-
leptic fit at the conclusion of the second act, and the play had
to be abruptly concluded at this point not once, but many
times.   Nine years later, F. L. Schmidt described a similar
attack which occurred in Hamburg.   In his later years, Devrient had to give up the part of Lear altogether.   His Shylock,
on the other hand, was one of his richest and yet best controlled creations.   Unlike Kean, who saw Shylock as powerful
and middle-aged, Devrient portrayed an old man, quite broken
by the end of the play.   He gave Shylock a distinctly oriental
cast, reinforced by the costume, which Devrient believed to
be an exact reproduction of the dress of a Renaissance Vene-
tian Jew.

When Devrient arrived in Berlin in 1815, Count Brühl
had already begun to develop an approach somewhat different
from Iffland's.   Staatsminister von Hardenberg had given him
an impressive commission: "Make the best theatre in Germany, and then tell me what it cost. "[13]   Brühl took von
Hardenberg at his word.   When Iffland died, the theatre was
13, 244 Taler in debt.   The new director more than doubled
that deficit during the first year of his administration and by
February, half way through the following year, there was already a new debt of 46, 660 Taler.   Large new productions
often required more than 1000 Taler apiece above receipts,
and Brühl often had more than thirty such premieres a year.

Von Hardenberg and the court were apparently satisfied with the productions, which were certainly the most
sumptuous in Germany, though Brühl's administration never in
fact achieved the renown of Goethe's at Weimar or Schreyvogel's in Vienna.   It was a complex administration, almost
a failure in some areas, such as organization and repertoire,
a qualified success at best in acting and the development of
an ensemble, yet extremely important and influential in other
areas, most notably in costume, scenery, and operatic presentation.   To begin with the most negative aspects, Brühl
imposed on the theatre almost at once just the sort of elabo-

rate bureaucracy which Iffland had carefully avoided, contributing not a little to its inefficiency and expense. He apparently began with an idea of building an impressive repertoire, but was unwilling to risk untried authors. He returned, as Iffland had done, to the Weimar dramatists, but to their less significant works. His first production, Goethe's Epimenides Erwachen (1815), was an occasional piece on the Congress of Vienna and therefore an understandable choice, and Terence's Brothers, with the same masks used at Weimar, had the virtue of experimental novelty at least for Berlin, but the same year saw Schiller's undistinguished Glocke, Werner's Vierundzwanzigste Februar, which Iffland had refused as too melodramatic, and the next year Brühl even offered the notorious Hund des Aubry, which had driven Goethe from the theatre.

In foreign works Brühl did somewhat better. Calderon was surprisingly well represented. The Constant Prince was a great success in 1816, apparently due in part to a wave of religious mysticism which swept Berlin after the liberation. The popularity of this offering encouraged Brühl to offer Life Is a Dream in 1818, The Surgeon of his Dishonor in 1820 and The Open Secret in 1821. When these proved less attractive, no more Calderon was attempted. The great popularity of Devrient as Falstaff in Henry IV Part I (1817) led to productions of Henry IV Part II in 1820 and The Merry Wives of Windsor in 1826, but the only other Shakespearian offerings were undistinguished new translations of Twelfth Night in 1820, Macbeth in 1825 and Richard III just at the end of Brühl's regime in 1828. The vast majority of foreign works were French, and these, except for Chateaubriand's Germanicus in 1817 and Molière's Tartuffe in 1823, were all minor contemporary comedies, vaudevilles, and melodramas. Few such works had been presented during the war years 1810 to 1816, but with peace they came like a flood to the Berlin stage in the translations of Karl Blum, Castelli, Lebrun, and Hell. In 1824, for example, seventeen out of twenty-eight new plays were from the French.

To a great extent these French imports filled the void left by the deaths of Iffland in 1814 and Kotzebue in 1819, but gradually a new German rival appeared for them in Ernst Raupach (1784-1852). Like Kotzebue he wrote prolifically and with little literary distinction in all genres. His first great success in Berlin was Erdennacht (1821) and in the next twenty years another 76 of his plays were presented here (he wrote 117 in all). He made his home in Berlin in 1825 after the enormous success of his Russian tragedy Isadore und Olga, and according to the actress Karoline Bauer, tyrannized king, court, theatre intendant, actors, and audiences alike for the next fifteen years. Among his many popular offerings during the Brühl regime were the tragedy Raphaele (1826), the drama Vater und Tochter (1828) and the comedy Ritterwort (1828).

Brühl's repertoire, as we have already seen in the cases of Shakespeare and Calderon, was a pragmatic one, and any important success encouraged him to present similar works. The popularity of Werner's Vierundzwanzigste Februar therefore made Berlin one of the centers for the production of the gloomy fate tragedies of Müllner and Houwald and led in 1818 to the production of Grillparzer's Die Ahnfrau. On the more positive side, the success of Die Ahnfrau led in turn to the production of the more significant Grillparzer plays Sappho in 1818 and Medea in 1826. After the failure of Der zerbrochene Krug in 1822 and the only moderate interest shown by the public in Die Familie Schroffenstein in 1824, Brühl attempted no more "pure" Kleist, but turned to Holbein's "improved" version of Käthchen von Heilbronn in 1824 and Ludwig Robert's bowdlerization of Der Prinz von Homburg in 1828. Not a single new German dramatist of any significance appeared in Berlin during the thirteen years of his administration.

Brühl's early interest in the Weimar theatre led him to bring Pius Alexander Wolff and his wife Amelia from there to become, with Devrient, the leaders of his company. As a result, he insured a conflict of styles as serious as any under Iffland's directorship. The Wolffs were representatives of the elevated, deliberate style of Weimar, a style more concerned with suggesting inner nobility than natural emotion. Devrient's style, on the contrary, somewhat recalled Fleck's, but was even more chilling and demonic. August Lewald called it a "Rembrandt" style: "through the dazzling points of light that he places before us he leads us to guess what lies hidden in the deepest shadows." While the Wolffs strove for beauty of form, Devrient sought "with a sort of demonic drive the most extreme manifestations of humanity."[14] It seems strikingly appropriate that Devrient's closest friend in Berlin was the haunted romantic author E. T. A. Hoffmann, whose stories inspired feelings similar to those associated with Devrient's acting.

Brühl's solution to this wide divergence between his major actors was simple, if somewhat ruthless. The first year of his engagement, Devrient was allowed to present his

full range of roles, beginning with Franz Moor, then going on
to Gessler in Wilhelm Tell, Falstaff, Harpagon, Richard III,
Mephisto, Sheva in Cumberland's The Jew. The next year,
however, Brühl turned all major tragic roles over to Wolff
and to a minor disciple of Iffland, Friedrich Wilhelm Lemm
(1782-1837) and allowed Devrient only comic parts. Fortunately, even with this restriction Devrient's range was great,
from Harpagon to Falstaff, to the cook Syrus in The Brothers,
and to the burlesque and farce roles demanded by the Possen
mit Gesang (the German equivalent of French vaudevilles)--
such roles as Rochus Pumpernickel in Matthäus Stegmeyer's
play of that name or the tailor Kakadu in Wenzel Müller's
Zwei Schwestern von Prague (1794). The Danish author Oehlenschläger, visiting Berlin at this time, admired Devrient
greatly, but did not even realize that he could play anything
but comedy.

        Only outside of Berlin could Devrient exhibit his true
range, and during the 1820's he filled his vacations with ex-
hausting tours that further undermined his weakened constitution. After the death of Hoffmann in 1822 he declined rapidly,
but as late as 1828 he gave a final magnificent series of all
his greatest roles in Vienna, beginning with Shylock and ending with Franz Moor. It was his last great triumph, but he
returned to Berlin where he continued to perform with his
strength almost gone and his memory failing, until his death
in 1832.

        Among the other actors in Brühl's company, the most
popular was Auguste Stich-Crelinger (1795-1865), who assumed most of the roles of Iffland's partner, Frau Unzelmann.
Like her predecessor, Frau Crelinger was much more effective in broad sentiment than in tragic passion, and she gained
her reputation primarily as an interpreter of Raupach, playing
opposite the actors Wilhelm Krüger (1791-1857) and Jonas
Beschort. During Brühl's early years, the company presented both spoken drama and opera. Thus Beschort sang
Don Giovanni and Orestes, while Frau Crelinger sang Dona
Anna and the Countess in The Barber of Seville. On the other
hand, performers hired primarily for their singing ability
were expected to contribute to the spoken drama as well. The
tenor Friedrich Eunike (1764-1844) regularly portrayed princes, and Margarete Schick (1773-1809), whose singing of
Gluck's Armide was one of the theatre's greatest attractions,
also played the Marquise Mondekar in Don Carlos. In Brühl's
later years the opera became more and more dominant and
this sort of doubling diminished. Attention shifted to virtuosi,

often guests, devoted solely to opera or dance--Henriette
Sontag, Wilhelmine Schröder-Devrient, and Fanny Elssler.

Brühl's administration is probably most remembered
for his interest in costume and scenic reform, particularly
after the destruction of the theatre by fire in 1817 gave him
the obligation and the opportunity to replace the entire stock.
Iffland had been quite interested in costume, as may be seen
in the twenty-two volume Kostüme auf dem kgl. National-
theater zu Berlin which appeared between 1802 and 1812, but
he was far less concerned with costumes suitable to the period or the social situation than with costumes that would be
theatrically effective. It was the romantics who introduced
the idea of historically and geographically correct costuming
in such works as Adolf Müllner's Ideen zu einem Theaterlexikon and Schlegel's Verlesungen über dramatische Kunst
(1809-1811). Brühl applied these ideas first on the stage,
attempting not only to recreate historical dress, but to make
it from the correct materials and even decorate it with the
proper trimmings. He insisted on authentic hair styles and
with historic characters even attempted to make up actors to
portrait likenesses. This involved new costumes for at least
the major characters in every production, and a clear move
away from the standardized dress of the previous century and
toward the scrupulous accuracy of the Meininger. In practice, however, Brühl was not so close to the Meininger as
he was in theory. Lessing and Schröder from the previous
century and the more modern works of Schiller, Iffland, and
Kotzebue were played not in the dress of their time, but in
contemporary Empire style. Only the purely historical works
of these authors were costumed in period, and even these
costumes were simplified in line and color-keyed to Empire
harmonies. The goal was therefore not in fact authenticity,
but as the Vossische Zeitung commented on the costumes for
the Jungfrau von Orleans, was rather the combination of historical accuracy with tasteful elegance.

Brühl encouraged the development of stage design in
Berlin by replacing the mediocre Bartolomeo Verona with
Carl Friedrich Schinkel (1781-1841), who became the outstanding romantic designer of the German stage. The introduction
to Schinkel's Dekorationen auf den beiden kgl. Theater unter
der Generalintendantur des Herrn Grafen Brühl in 1819 suc-
cinctly summarized his goals:

> This directorship was taken as its basic principle
> that the most characteristic design is always to be

sought, that each costume must be integrated with
the setting and not distracting.... The ideal designer will have certain indispensable assets: a
basic knowledge of the general and specific stage
history of all times and peoples, the utmost skill
and accuracy in perspective, a knowledge even of
archeology, a thorough acquaintance with all the
schools of painting, particularly landscape painting,
and the actual colors of things, yes even with
botany and other studies which describe the various
forms of trees, plants, rocks, and hills in every
country. [15]

Schinkel, like his French contemporary Ciceri, was
less an innovator in design than a sensitive and intelligent
artist who drew together the scattered experiments from the
first decade of the century into a coherent whole. In 1800
the architect Johannes Breysig (1766-1831), who had been a
theatre designer in Magdeburg, Danzig, and Königsberg, and
the landscape painter Katz opened a panorama theatre in
Berlin, the Kosmostheater, for the presentation of "all the
phenomena of nature and art." Here one of the earliest
cycloramic backdrops was employed, but Breysig was most
interested in replacing the usual two-dimensional "painter's
stage" with an architectural environment. In this he was
supported by a number of other designers and critics, several of whom showed themselves important prophets. Louis
Catel in his Vorschläge zur Verbesserung der Schauspiel-
häuser (1802) advocated scene changes in darkness rather
than behind a closed curtain, arguing that this suggested a
closing of the eyes and was therefore more natural. L.
Pujoulx in his Neueste Gemälde von Paris (1801) was the
first theorist, apparently, to argue for an enclosed set instead of the traditional Italianate wings and drop.

None of these suggestions received much support at
the time. Goethe specifically condemned Pujoulx' enclosed
stage as a French corruption arising from Diderot's mis-
placed enthusiasm for reality. Ironically, the first notable
enclosed set in Germany was used in the first staging of
Goethe's own Faust, presented in an abbreviated version at
Monbijou Castle in 1819. This set was for Gretchen's room,
which Schinkel designed as a simple German interior with
real details--flowers, mirror, pictures, a crucifix, and so
on--instead of the usual painted ones. The audience praised
the innovation warmly, but Schinkel judged rightly that his
Berlin public would view it less favorably. No enclosed set

appeared on the Berlin stage until 1826 in Wolff's comedy
Die Steckenpferde and this was a total failure. It was difficult to light and both actors and audience complained that it
deadened all voices on the stage. Not until Laube's productions of French salon-plays in Vienna after 1850 was the enclosed set commonly used in German theatres.

       Schinkel was the culmination of this group of turn-of-
the-century stage reformers. Before his theatre appointment
he was even, like Breysig, involved in the operation of a
diorama theatre. He entered Brühl's service at the height
of his power and imagination, and probably no Schinkel design is better known than his first, for Mozart's Zauberflöte
in 1816. The design for the Queen of the Night scene has
been often cited as the essential Schinkel design, a distinctly
poetic, even symbolic vision of nature rather than an attempt
to suggest nature as it is observed--a simple, powerful and
stylized design with clear influence from neoclassicism which
yet suggests romanticism in its evocativeness and charm.
The designs for the entire production struck a similar classic-romantic balance. Romantic crags and stylized starry
heavens were juxtaposed in the opening scene with classic
architecture. Later Imperial halls with sphinxes and other
Egyptian motifs were shown filled with exotic birds and the
most fanciful decoration.

       After another opera, Hoffmann's Undine in 1816,
Schinkel created the following year his first design for the
spoken theatre, Die Jungfrau von Orleans. Here he demonstrated the same ability in Gothic motifs which he had earlier
shown in classic ones. He returned to the classic for
Gluck's Alceste, but showed a romantic concern in his painstaking archeological research and his attempt to create a
plastic setting. For the same production, Brühl attempted
for the first time to use authentic Greek costumes. Spontini's Ferdinand Cortez gave Schinkel the opportunity to experiment with stylized Aztec designs, and for Armide's en-
chanted garden he created an exotic landscape in the style of
Claude Lorrain. Despite their disparate inspiration, all
these designs shared an emotionality, a stylized exaggeration,
a plasticity, an interplay of light and shadow by which
Schinkel sought to create what he called visual music.

       It was naturally Schinkel who was entrusted by Brühl
with the task of designing the new royal theatre, which was
to be an "aesthetic church, " a "museum of theatre art, " the
greatest such establishment in Germany. The influence of

Palladio and of classic theatre design on the new building was
very strong, not only in exterior decoration but in the entire
shape of the structure. Schinkel renounced the baroque
horseshoe shape standard in German theatres until then to
create a huge 1600 seat half-circle. The stage itself was
not so revolutionary as the house, nor as Schinkel first
planned. He considered a major enlargement of the hitherto
insignificant proscenium arch to create a deep recess framed
by Corinthian columns in the French fashion between scenery
and audience. Though this design was modified in the final
theatre, the actors still tended to play in front of, rather
than within Schinkel's settings. Despite their plasticity, these
remained essentially backgrounds.

The cornerstone of the new theatre was laid in the
Gendarmenmarkt in January, 1818 by Prince Wilhelm, the
future first Kaiser of Germany. It contained an iron cross,
a commemorative medal, and a portrait of Iffland. The new
house, a model for German theatres for some time after,
opened in 1820. It was a huge structure containing in addition to the theatre a concert and ballroom, rehearsal rooms,
painters' shops, and a large storehouse. Its opening year
saw also one of the theatre's most important offerings,
Weber's Die Freischütz, the triumph of German romantic
opera. Though the new house allowed Schinkel more scope
for his designs, none of his later works achieved the renown
of the Zauberflöte or Jungfrau von Orleans. Brühl's increasing interest in light comedy and bourgeois drama gave him
less opportunity to employ either fantasy or historical research in his designs. Only twice in these later years did
he create new settings as imaginative and powerful as his
early work, for Kleist's Käthchen von Heilbronn in 1824 and
Der Prinz von Homburg in 1828.

4. Schreyvogel and the Viennese Theatre

While Berlin possessed only one permanent dramatic
theatre until the last years of Brühl's administration, Vienna
began the century with four. The oldest of these was the
National Theatre, founded in 1776 by Kaiser Josef II. Until
his death in 1790, he supervised hirings, selected the repertoire, served as censor, and provided a substantial annual
subsidy for the troupe. The company had no other real director, though Friedrich Schröder dominated it when he was
guest from 1781 until 1785. During these years the ground-

work was laid for that spirit of ensemble which has ever since been a major component of the Vienna theatre's heritage. After Schröder's departure, Franz Brockmann (1745-1812) carried on the struggle to impose order and artistic harmony on an extremely talented but wilful company.

The major difference between the theatrical fare of Vienna and that of northern German cities at the beginning of the century was the great popularity and power here of the old folk comedy. The broad burlesques of Hanswurst in his infinite forms gave rise here to a whole set of standard Viennese types, reinforced by the influence of the Italian commedia dell'arte (Vienna's ties to Italy were strong; Italian rivalled French as a standard language for the aristocracy). A folk comedy troupe headed by Matthias Memminger and featuring the popular comic rogue Johann La Roche (1745-1806) performed fairly regularly in Vienna after 1769 and settled there permanently under the direction of Karl Marinelli (1744-1803) in the new Leopoldstädter Theater in 1781. After Marinelli's death the theatre was directed by one of his authors, Karl Friedrich Hensler (1759-1825), who continued to present simple plays with standard characters, local settings, and topical jokes. Since the National Theatre supported by the court favored foreign plays, the folk theatre, despite its insubstantial fare, remained an important stimulus for native playwrights.

A second folk theatre opened in 1786 in the suburb of Wieden, and achieved its greatest success with Mozart's Zauberflöte. The profits from this noted production allowed Emanuel Schikaneder (1751-1812), who served the theatre as director, librettist, and leading actor and singer, to build a new, more central house in 1801. This was one of the largest and handsomest theatres in Vienna, equipped to handle the most ambitious operas or spectacle plays. For some productions, as many as 500 persons and fifty horses appeared here. Schikaneder's own statue in the character of Papageno fittingly stood over the door of the home Mozart's opera had built, called the Theater an der Wien. Finally, in 1788, the actor Karl Meyer (1750-1830) and his company settled in a third Viennese folk theatre, the Josefstädter Theater. He and his successor, Josef Huber, provided an important training ground for many of the great Austrian actors. As the new century began, the repertoire was dominated by the works of the popular and prolific Joseph Alois Gleich (1772-1841).

The early death of Josef II in 1790 marked the end of the first great period of prosperity for the National Theatre. Leopold II, his successor, died only two years later. His son, Franz II, fought four wars against Napoleon, and saw his capital conquered by French troops. During these turbulent years the Viennese theatres remained in operation, but the National stage could obviously depend on little government support or attention. In 1794 it was turned over to a private entrepreneur, the banker Baron Peter von Braun, who managed it until 1806. Braun appointed the author Johann von Alxinger his artistic secretary, a position which involved mostly struggling with the notorious censor Hägelin. The extremes of Metternich's censorship still lay ahead, but the theatre's problems were perhaps more serious now than they would be later since there was now almost no hope of appeal to royal protection. Alxinger's efforts were therefore largely wasted; almost every reference to customs, morals, religion or politics which might conceivably give offense to anyone was ruthlessly banned from the Viennese stage. Such dramatists as Goethe and Schiller disappeared almost entirely, in favor of the innocuous sentimental dramas of Iffland and Kotzebue. Their dominance was already so well established by 1798 when Alxinger died that Kotzebue was von Braun's first choice to replace him.

Though Kotzebue's position officially required little more than overseeing the theatre's correspondence and adjusting its repertoire to satisfy the censor, the new secretary, with von Braun's encouragement, was soon involved far more deeply in the development of the company. He edited a journal for the court discussing the plays and their interpretation, he supervised casting, began insisting upon rehearsals with rigorous discipline, and saw to it that a new play was prepared at least every three weeks. Most significantly, he actively sought new actors for the theatre, especially those whose talents seemed suited for the sort of natural presentation his own works and those of Iffland required. Two actors who arrived the same year as Kotzebue and remained popular members of the National Theatre until their deaths were Siegfried Koch-Eckhardt (1754-1831), whose preference was for classic works, and Friedrich Roose (1767-1818), who established himself as a major interpreter of Kotzebue's works in Die beiden Klingsberg (1799), the author's most successful Viennese work. Roose married Koch-Eckhardt's daughter Betty (1770-1808), who became the theatre's major tragic heroine. Her first great role was in Kotzebue's most significant production, Goethe's Iphigenie, presented here in 1800, two years before its production in Weimar.

Johanna von Weissenthurn (1773-1845) proved not a
popular interpreter of Iffland and Kotzebue, but after Kotzebue's departure, a very successful authoress of dramas in
the same manner. The most important of the young artists
encouraged by Kotzebue was Sophie Schröder (1781-1868),
whose major contribution to the theatre, however, came long
after his departure. Kotzebue discovered her in Reval, already at the age of sixteen a mother and a popular actress
in a minor provincial company. Though she became Germany's greatest female interpreter of romantic tragedy, her
talent had not yet matured in these early years in Vienna,
and for Kotzebue she played only soubrette roles. In 1800,
when he left, Sophie left also. She joined the theatre in
Hamburg, where she divorced her first husband, Stollmers,
to marry Friedrich Schröder, an actor and operatic singer
in Hamburg.

Though Kotzebue officially left the National Theatre
for reasons of health, a consideration of at least equal importance was the animosity he had created by his efforts to
drive the rather independent company to greater and more
impressive efforts. The spirit instilled by Schröder fifteen
years before seemed irretrievable. Ironically, von Braun
sought as Kotzebue's successor a young and enthusiastic
Viennese literary critic, Josef Schreyvogel (1768-1832), who
had very different ideas from Kotzebue about the repertoire,
but much the same concern with artistic discipline. Predictably, he received no more cooperation from his company
than Kotzebue had, and without strong backing from the public
or the administration, he had little authority to enforce his
demands. Having studied at Jena for two years, Schreyvogel
was deeply interested in the Weimar experiment and hopeful
of bringing its influence to Vienna. He was able to present
a heavily rewritten and bowdlerized Jungfrau von Orleans
under the name Joanna d'Arc in 1802 and Goethe's Tancred
the following year, but this pace was too slow for the new
secretary. The combined pressures of von Braun, the censor, and the public kept the repertoire virtually unchanged.
In 1803 Marianne von Eybenberg complained in a letter to
Goethe: "The National Theatre becomes more miserable
daily; we see nothing but Iffland, or what is worse, Kotzebue." The theatre's more serious offerings were the neoclassic tragedies of Heinrich von Collin and F. J. Holbein's
extremely popular if simple-minded dramatizations of Schiller's ballads. The discouraged Schreyvogel resigned in 1804.

He was followed by a minor author, Sonnleithner, who held
the post until Schreyvogel's return, under more favorable
conditions, in 1814.

It was under von Braun's administration that scenery
and costume for the first time became important concerns at
the National Theatre. Scenic reform had begun in the ballet
in 1792 with the designs of Joseph Platzer (1752-1806), who
worked in the baroque tradition of the Italian Galliaris. Then
in 1794 the dancer Salvatore Vigano brought Lorenzo Sacchetti (1759-1828) from Venice to Vienna to work with
Platzer. Lorenzo, his brother Vincenzino, and his son Antonio were the major Viennese designers of the Napoleonic
era. Their basic style was late baroque, but they used
classic, romantic, even contemporary middle-class elements,
applied to ballet, opera, and spoken theatre. Like their
contemporaries Verona in Berlin, Innocente Colomba (1717-
1793) in Stuttgart, Georgio Fuentes in Frankfurt, the Quaglios
in Munich, and de Loutherbourg (1740-1812) in London, the
Sacchettis, and Lorenzo in particular, formed a transition
between the Italian baroque and romantic settings. Lorenzo
used the diagonal perspectives of the Galli-Bibienas but without the baroque emphasis on high or deep rooms. A concern
with mass replaced concern with depth, though Lorenzo often
increased the plasticity of his sets with a double perspective,
an arcade or broken wall in the foreground and a background
with a different vanishing point behind it. Like Fuentes,
Lorenzo liked to increase the impressiveness of his setting
by painting extra actors on it. Exotic ruins, crags, gothic
halls, all the Sir Walter Scott trappings of romanticism appear among the more than sixty settings Lorenzo created,
along with neoclassic sphinxes and Biedermeyer interiors.
By the beginning of the nineteenth century the Burgtheater,
as it was then called, had the most extensive collection of
settings in Germany. A new theatre at Linz in 1803 considered itself unusually well equipped with eighteen settings,
among them two rooms, one gothic and one Roman hall, one
temple, one dungeon, and one large collonaded square, but
the Burgtheater possessed thirty-three room settings alone.

The costume collection was even more impressive; the
Weimar Journal des Luxus und der Moden of 1796 reported
that it was then known and admired throughout Europe. The
theatre hired its first costume designer, Vinzenz Chiesa, in
1791, and within ten years he had built a huge stock, though
not, it must be admitted, with any particular concern for
historical accuracy. One writer complained in 1804 that

"English hats are worn with German armor, modern shoes
with ancient trousers, French hair styles with old Spanish
servants' costumes. "[16] Still, the Burgtheater did normally
provide all the costumes for its actors, while it was common
for other German stages to require women to supply their
own historical dresses and for both women and men to supply
any modern clothing.

In 1807 von Braun retired and the court again became
involved in the administration of the theatre. A directorial
board was formed of a group of aristocrats called the Kavaliere: three princes (Schwarzenberg, Lobkowitz, and Esterházy), and five counts (Palffy, Lodron, Zicky, Nikolaus, and
Franz Esterházy). The same group also took over the administration of the opera and of the Theater an der Wien, so
that all three theatres now became in effect court theatres.
Count Palffy was given particular responsibility for the Theater an der Wien, which since 1802 had placed its major
emphasis on opera and concerts--the works of Cherubini,
Mozart, Haydn, and Méhul and the early symphonies of Beethoven under that composer's personal direction. Now this
house became a sort of experimental annex to the Burgtheater, and though opera, ballet, and Beethoven's later symphonies were presented here, emphasis shifted to the spoken
drama. The Prince von Lobkowitz managed the opera and
responsibility for the Burgtheater was divided among various
members of its company. The three leading senior actors--
Brockmann, Koch-Eckhardt, and Joseph Lange (1751-1831)--
were placed in charge of the repertoire and of new engagements. The staging was supervised by Roose, by Karl
Krüger (1765-1814), a character-actor brought by Schreyvogel
in 1802, and by a newly appointed actor of young heroes,
Joseph Koberwein (1774-1857). This division of labor may
have spared the actors, but it obviously further eroded the
old ideal of unity in production and program. Schreyvogel
complained of the 1808 productions of Kabale und Liebe and
Macbeth that both suffered from a lack of any sense of the
whole, and the aristocratic producers agreed. They appealed
to Iffland in Berlin to make a guest appearance in Vienna
during 1808, hoping that he might be induced to remain as a
guiding artistic spirit. These hopes were not fulfilled, however, and the theatre had to struggle on without such a spirit
until Schreyvogel himself returned there six years later.

In the meantime, significant changes occurred in staging, repertoire and company under the Kavaliere. The new
regulations of 1807 stipulated that costumes should henceforth

suit the characters and not be concerned wholly with vanity
and ostentation. The regisseur was now given the power,
especially in modern family dramas, to regulate the costumes
worn to keep them in harmony. This gave much more power
to the new costumer Philip von Stubenrauch (1784-1848), who
began designing for the Opera in 1807 and worked at the
Burgtheater as well from 1810 until his death. His publications of costume designs in 1807 and from 1810 to 1813 contained 1100 designs. Despite the official regulations, von
Stubenrauch, unlike his contemporaries in Berlin, clearly
preferred theatricality to historical accuracy. The 1809 Don
Carlos and 1810 Egmont costumes were full of fantasy elements, and though von Stubenrauch gave more attention to
period under Schreyvogel's administration after 1814, he
shared the new director's greater concern for beauty and
harmony in preference to accuracy.

In the repertoire, the same sort of grotesque changes
which had been inflicted on Jungfrau von Orleans were
wrought upon Kabale und Liebe before the censor would approve it in 1808, and Schreyvogel wrote bitterly that no people
could have a great stage when its masterpieces were banned.
A year later, despite his complaints, Don Carlos suffered a
similar fate. Napoleon's victories over Austria in this same
year placed Vienna itself under French occupation, and even
bowdlerized Goethe or Schiller disappeared from the Burgtheater, to be replaced by contemporary French fare. Napoleon, in residence at Schönbrunn, even called upon the
Burgtheater actors to present Phédre there. Yet this experience, however bitter for national pride, had a most beneficial ultimate effect on the theatre. A resurgence of German
patriotism in 1810 provided fertile ground for the development of native authors, who as French influence faded enjoyed a new freedom of expression. Theodor Körner's Zirny,
a national drama in historic dress somewhat in the manner
of Collin, was given at the Burgtheater in 1810 without a
word of protest from the censor, and Körner followed this
work with other similar expressions until his death on the
battlefield in 1813. The classics also profited from the new
freedom. Goethe's Egmont and Die Braut von Messina were
given in their original form at the Burgtheater in 1810 also,
Kabale und Liebe was revived in 1811 with most of the 1808
changes removed, and a few months later came the major
expression of the new patriotic fervor, Wilhelm Tell. As a
means of encouraging the development of a German drama,
the Burgtheater was allowed for the first time in November
of 1810 to present spoken theatre exclusively, with all opera

and ballet transferred to the opera house, the Kärtnertor-
theater. Nowhere else in Germany was the spoken drama
given such encouragement.

The first important new actor employed during this
period was Ferdinand Ochsenheimer, the popular character
actor from Leipzig who a few years before had so inspired
the young Devrient there. Maximilian Korn (1782-1854), a
native Viennese actor, entered the theatre in 1802. He
studied with Roose and became as dashing a polished lover in
elegant comedies. Juliane Löwe (1786-1852) was added to the
theatre's interpreters of high comedy and Nikolaus Heurter
(1781-1844) came to share young heroic roles with Koberwein.
The author Körner encouraged his wife Toni Adamburger
(1790-1867) to join the theatre where her mother Anna Adam-
burger-Jaquet had already built a modest reputation as a
tragic heroine. Toni's Desdemona in Clemens Brentano's
version of Othello (1814) caused that author to call her one
of the most gifted artists of the theatre. She could become
great, he felt, under a good leader, but that was precisely
what the Burgtheater still lacked.

In 1814 Count Palffy, the aristocrat then in charge of
the theatre, provided this leader by calling Schreyvogel to the
position of dramaturg and secretary, promising to support
him in disputes with the censor or the company, and giving
him almost a free hand in the running of the theatre. Despite various changes in his administrative title, Schreyvogel
remained effectively in control of the theatre until shortly before his death in 1832, and during these years built it into
the greatest theatre in Germany. He was equally interested
in literature and theatrical art, and possessed the imagination, the determination, and the managerial skill to create
not only the best repertoire of plays among German theatres,
but also the best ensemble for their presentation.

Neither of these goals were achieved easily, but
Schreyvogel's diary gives an illuminating day-by-day account
of his tact and skill in building a repertoire under one of the
most conservative and rigorous censorships in Europe (for
the conservative reaction after Napoleon's defeat soon ended
the brief period of freedom begun in 1810) and in building an
ensemble from established and popular actors long used to
working according to their own inclinations. Circumstances
were more favorable for the development of a strong acting
ensemble. There was, of course, the tradition established
by Schröder which Kotzebue had attempted to revive, of dis-

ciplined ensemble work in the National Theatre, even though
many actors had resisted this. Second, Schreyvogel was
personally known to the company and generally liked by them,
even though as a critic and literary man he was suspected
of being somewhat naive about their craft. Just after his
appointment Schreyvogel reported happily in his diary (June
14, 1814): "most of the theatre personnel seem pleased with
me, especially the actors. Koberwein speaks very favorably
of me. This is necessary if I am to achieve anything."[17]
Finally, the new dramaturg set to work almost at once seeking new talents to supplement his already excellent company,
and these young actors were naturally chosen with an eye to
how they would contribute to the whole.

Brockmann had died in 1812; Roose died in 1818 and
Ochsenheimer in 1822. Baumann and Klingemann retired in
1821. Nevertheless, Schreyvogel kept through most of his
directorship the majority of the important actors he inherited
--the men Lange, Krüger, Koch, Heurter, Korn, Koberwein,
and the women Weissenthurn, Adamburger, and Korn. Indeed
one of his most notable accomplishments was keeping so
many important actors in Vienna when they could have enjoyed both better facilities and higher pay in the North. The
most important of the new actors Schreyvogel added to his
company was one of the first, Sophie Schröder, who came in
1815. We have already mentioned her brief earlier appearance in Vienna with Kotzebue, but since 1801 she had been
developing her talent in Hamburg, and though she left Vienna
a rather undistinguished soubrette, she returned a major
tragic actress. Doubtless the change was in large part due
to the influence, both direct and indirect, of Friedrich Ludwig Schröder (not to be confused with Sophie's husband, a
baritone in the Hamburg opera), who was still during his last
years the dominant figure in the theatre he had made the
best in Germany during the 1770's and 1780's. When Sophie
made her Hamburg debut the great Schröder was in retirement, but his ideals and devotion were carried on by his
successor as administrator, Jakob Herzfeld (1769-1812), and
his style of acting was passed on by his pupils. The most
important of these was Hamburg's great comic actor, Ludwig Costenoble (1769-1837), whose roles as character interpreter ranged from Truffaldino to Shylock. Under the tute-
lege of Costenoble, and later of Schröder himself, since he
returned from retirement in 1811, Sophie developed her rich
and resonant voice and a vehemence and intensity of playing
which allowed her to interpret the great tragic queens despite
her small size and rather plain features. Klingemann ob-

served: "her deep voice is one of the most masterful I have
ever heard, and is powerful as thunder without any of that
masculine quality which disturbs one in so many French
actresses."[18] Doubtless he was thinking of Mlle Raucourt
and her imitators, who in range of roles and even in tendency
toward a somewhat rhetorical delivery invited comparison
with Frau Schröder.

        Friedrich Schröder selected an unfortunate time to re-
turn to his theatre.   Hamburg, like Vienna, was soon conquered by the French.   Many of his best actors fled the city:
Stegmann and his wife, Gottfried Eule, Karl Leo, and others.
Since Steiger, who played many of the key leading roles, had
recently died, Schröder's possible repertoire was extremely
small.   To add to this difficulty, the French censor refused
to allow any plays which might encourage German nationalist
spirit--all of Goethe and Schiller, even most of Kotzebue.
Suspect words such as fatherland, freedom, tyrant, oppres-
sion, were of course purged from the few innocuous works
which passed the censor, and the very title of the theatre
was changed from Deutsches Theater to the more neutral
Theater am Gänsemarkt.   The spoken drama, weakened in
repertoire and in personnel, soon gave way in large part to
opera.   In the fall of 1812, Schröder was summoned before
the authorities and accused of attacking military conscription
by presenting Kotzebue's comic opera Das Dorf in Gebirge,
an occasional piece written in 1798 to honor the Viennese
volunteers in the first Italian campaign.   This attack convinced the old director that his position was impossible, and
he resigned from the theatre, this time permanently.   Herzfeld resumed the directorship, but the theatre continued to
decline, and Sophie Schröder gratefully accepted Schreyvogel's
offer to come to Vienna in 1815.   She was followed in 1817
by her old tutor Costenoble, who became one of the pillars
of the Viennese theatre.

        A major contribution to the interpretation of middle-
class comedy and drama was provided by Heinrich Anschütz
(1785-1865) and his wife Emilie (1795-1866).   Heinrich remained at the Burgtheater from 1821 until 1861, playing both
domestic drama and classic tragedy, and moving from young
heroes such as Theseus and Orestes to Wilhelm Tell and
Lear with no decline in popularity.   Among the younger
actors Schreyvogel brought, the most notable were Ludwig
Löwe (1795-1871) and Sophie Müller (1803-1830).   Löwe
specialized during Schreyvogel's regime in haunted, demonic
young heroes, making him an ideal interpreter for the youth-

ful roles of Schiller. During his career at the theatre, which
lasted more than forty years, he, like Anschütz, developed
a wide variety of roles, though it was some time before he
could command a sense of poetry and style to soften his
basically naturalistic delivery. Of his popular Don Cesar,
Costenoble complained: "He looked like a greasy peasant that
someone had dressed as a prince. "[19] Sophie Müller was an
attractive young heroine with a classic beauty that made her
a memorable Emilia Galotti, Desdemona, and Cordelia. She
therefore was an excellent partner for Löwe and an ideal
compliment to Sophie Schröder, whose specialty was such
dark and heavy tragic roles as Cleopatra, Lady Macbeth,
Brunhild (in Raupach's Nibelungen), and Medea. The theatre
was unfortunately soon deprived of the talent of Sophie Müller,
however. She died in 1830, and was replaced by Julie Gley
(1809-1866), who made an important contribution, but who
came to the theatre too late to be really integrated into
Schreyvogel's famous ensemble.

The other most important additions Schreyvogel made
to the company were Friedrich Wilhelmi (1788-1852), Karl
Fichter (1805-1873), and Karoline Müller (1806-1891). Wilhelmi, one of the best comics of the time and a specialist
in caricaturing the bourgeoisie, established his reputation in
Prague, and joined the Burgtheater in 1822. Fichter, who
came in 1824, specialized in young lovers in the Marivaux
style. Löwe generally took the more ardent, romantic roles
and Fichter the suave Viennese bonvivants. Karoline Müller
shared with Juliane Löwe the roles of society ladies in salon
comedies. It was, in all, a versatile and balanced company,
with an actor of considerable stature for almost any sort of
role.

Schreyvogel was quite aware, however, that building
an excellent company was effort largely wasted unless that
company could demonstrate its ability in a worthy repertoire.
The repertoire he inherited was based primarily on comedy
and middleclass drama--Schröder, Iffland, Kotzebue, French
comedies and vaudevilles, and local Viennese comedies.
Schreyvogel made no attempt to purge the repertoire of this
popular entertainment, but devoted much effort to supple-
menting it with more serious works, both native and foreign.
One of the first works he presented in 1814 was Maria Stuart
with Johanna Weissenthurn as Elisabeth and Sophie Koberwein
as Maria. All the influence Schreyvogel could muster at
court was brought to bear on the censor, and though a few
cuts were demanded, this was an important step forward, for

the play had previously been banned entirely. Later productions used Sophie Schröder and Juliane Löwe in what was
considered at the time to be the ideal casting. Toni Adam-
berger and Korn took the leading parts in Goethe's Iphigenie
in 1815 and Torquato Tasso in 1816, evolving under Schreyvogel's direction an inner style of playing distinctly different
from either the theatricalism of Berlin or the classic formality of Weimar.

In pursuing Goethe's ideal of a repertoire of significant native works and major foreign ones, Schreyvogel found
himself constantly at odds with Metternich's censor, Count
Sedlnitzky, but by appealing to the court either directly or
through his aristocratic superiors he was able to present
Schiller's Wallenstein (in a condensed but not bowdlerized
version), and faithful versions of Kabale und Liebe, Jungfrau
von Orleans, and Don Carlos. Shakespeare was represented
by Romeo and Juliet in 1816, Macbeth in 1821, King Lear in
1822, Othello in 1823, Hamlet in 1825, The Merchant of
Venice in 1827, and the two parts of Henry IV in 1828.
Oehlenschläger, Holberg, Voltaire, Molière, Racine, Sheri-
dan, Goldoni, and Wycherly were among the other foreign
dramatists represented, along with the inevitable translations
of such contemporary French authors as Picard and Duval.
Schreyvogel hoped to do for the Spanish what the romantics
had done for Shakespeare and translated a number of Spanish
classic plays under the pseudonym of West. Three of these
were presented at the Burgtheater with considerable success:
Moreto's Donna Diana in 1816, and Calderon's Surgeon of his
Dishonor in 1820 and Life is a Dream in 1822. Schreyvogel
showed no interest in the plays of such early romantics as
Tieck, but the Burgtheater gave Kleist his first major hear-
ing. Prinz von Homburg (under the title Die Schlacht von
Fehrbellin to evade the censor) was given with moderate success in 1820, and shortly followed by an extremely popular
adaptation of Käthchen von Heilbronn with Emilie Anschütz.
Die Familie Schroffenstein, adapted as Die Waffenbrüder,
came in 1823 and was such a success with Heinrich Anschütz, Sophie Schröder, Korn, and Müller in the leading
roles that it was a standard revival piece for the next fifty
years and gave Kleist a European reputation.

The only important new dramatist discovered by the
Burgtheater under Schreyvogel was Franz Grillparzer (1791-
1872). The young writer came to Schreyvogel's attention
through the publication of his partial translation of Calderon's
Life Is a Dream. Schreyvogel contacted Grillparzer and

encouraged him to attempt an original drama, and the result
was Die Ahnfrau (1817). Although Grillparzer complained of
critics classifying this play as a fate-tragedy, it is a classi-
fication the work clearly invites. Many of the trappings of
one of Müllner or Werner's exaggerated works are present:
a cursed family, all of whom are destroyed in the course of
the play, the ghostly figure of the title who seems to represent the figure of fate, a haunted and mysterious hero, a
setting of bandit-infested forest and haunted castle. It was
at Schreyvogel's suggestion that the family curse was added,
however; Grillparzer was more interested in the catastrophe
of the play's young lovers who discover they are in fact
brother and sister. Doubtless Schreyvogel, who knew his
audience, helped insure the play's success by this change,
but subsequent works showed how he had obscured Grillparzer's real concerns.

Since the author of the play was an unknown dramatist,
the premiere took place not at the Burgtheater but at the
more experimental Theater an der Wien, now also under
Schreyvogel's direction. For all its excesses, Die Ahnfrau
was so superior to the popular fate-tragedies it resembled
that it was a great success here, and was soon produced all
over Germany. Grillparzer's fame was assured, but it was
hardly the fame he desired, since he was viciously attacked
by literary critics as cheap and vulgar and by the clergy as
pagan and immoral. In Vienna, vulgarity was of no concern
to the censor, but immorality was, and the production was
saved only by the intervention at court of influential friends
of Sophie Schröder, who had chosen the first performance as
her benefit.

Grillparzer's next play, Sappho (1818), was clearly in
part an attempt to answer criticisms of Die Ahnfrau, even
though its major thrust was the expression of the problems
which haunted the young author. "I chose the simplest possible story," says he in his autobiography, "in order to prove
to the world and to myself that I could produce an effect by
sheer poetic power."[20] If Die Ahnfrau suggested the fate-
tragedies of Werner and the robber melodramas of Schiller,
Sappho's inspiration appeared to be the classic tragedies of
Goethe. In fact, the more perceptive critics soon realized
that these two apparently so dissimilar plays were dealing
with certain common themes. Grillparzer himself confirmed
the intellectual closeness of the two in a letter to Müllner
which explained that Die Ahnfrau "dealt with the unhappiness
of being, and Sappho with the indisputable unhappiness of be-

ing a poet. "[21] The dramatist's diary confirms that this was
a period of great isolation and agony for him, but this personal crisis was strikingly reflected in the macrocosm of
Restoration Germany. The utopian dreams of the Wars of
Liberation had been crushed by the Congress of Vienna, and
the peace and stability of the period which followed was
achieved at tremendous psychic cost. The Biedermeier
period has come to suggest a narrow and rather stuffy time
of concern with domestic comfort, but this turn to hearth and
home was based on widespread doubt as to the significance or
usefulness of idealism, particularly in public life. Schopen-
hauer's Die Welt als Wille und Vorstellung (1819), a central
statement of the decline in classic and romantic idealism,
was published the year after the production of Sappho.

Few dramatists of this period crystallized its restlessness and disillusionment more sharply than Grillparzer, and
the expression of his own misery stood for that of a lost
generation. The new age had left them rootless, and root-
lessness is a central image in Grillparzer's plays. His
major characters in all his early works are exiles, separated from the past and out of harmony with others and with
themselves. The outlaw Jaromir and the solitary poetess
Sappho both are drawn by love to attempt a reintegration
with humanity, but for both the idealism of this love is in-
separable from a degrading passion which leads each to outrage and at last to death. On the path to her disaster Sappho
attempts in vain another alternative, a return to a simple
pastoral life, but she finds retreat is as impossible as idealistic fulfillment.

With Sappho Grillparzer achieved one of his greatest
popular successes. He was now widely hailed as the most
important dramatist since Goethe and Schiller and his fame
spread well beyond the national frontiers. Byron called his
play "supurb and sublime." For the production Schreyvogel
had evolved a blending of German classicism and Austrian
realism which became the standard style of the Burgtheater
and an excellent medium for the interpretation of Grillparzer's
work. The role of the poetess was one of Sophie Schröder's
greatest creations, her rendering of its verse praised for its
evocation of the smallest nuances. The critic Solger complained in a letter to Tieck that this was not a purely artistic
triumph, that the play was given an extra piquancy by the
scandalous private life of the actress, which bore a striking
resemblance to that of Grillparzer's poetess. [22] In the
opinion of most of Vienna, however, the production was an

unqualified triumph for author, actors, and director.

Schreyvogel now had no difficulty getting Grillparzer
appointed the official dramatist of the Burgtheater, and in
this post he embarked on a far more ambitious creation, a
dramatic trilogy on the Medea legend called Das goldene
Vliess (1821). The first two parts, Der Gastfreund and Die
Argonauten, were quickly completed in 1818 (Grillparzer always created with amazing speed), but the suicide of the
dramatist's mother and quarrels with his bureaucratic superiors interrupted his work for two years before he could
complete his Medea. The unity of the trilogy did not suffer
from the delay, but the last play, more complex psychologically than the others, is the only one to have survived in
the active repertoire. Grillparzer's Medea and Jason basically resemble those of Euripides, the savage pagan thirsting
for revenge and the attractive but petty egoist who is both
her torturer and her victim. Grillparzer, however, frames
these with a far darker figure in Medea's evil nurse, Gora,
and a charming lighter figure in Creon's daughter Creusa.
Both Jason and Medea are softened, especially at the conclusion, where they part, not with curses, but with mutual
pity and even a measure of respect.

The golden fleece, constantly present, serves as a
kind of visual leitmotif suggesting the Schopenhauerian themes
of the futility of man's efforts, corrupted by passions and the
drive of life. Medea's horrifying and irreconcilable break
with her homeland made her another useful exile symbol for
Grillparzer, and Jason, though he returns to his home, suffers a similar tragic dislocation, since his liaison with the
alien Medea prevents his reintegration into his own society.
The idea that man's thought and will has cut him off from
the rest of the world obviously has much in common with
modern existentialism, but Grillparzer's heroes are denied
the existentialist solution of creating an independent life by
the drives of their passions which their reason cannot control. The only solution offered them is a recognition and
acceptance of this grim state of things, and Medea, in her
double role of woman and enchantress, is the first Grillparzer hero who seems to achieve this insight.

Schreyvogel, like Grillparzer, expected this trilogy to
be one of his greatest productions. His actors were now accustomed to effective delivery of Grillparzer's poetry; they
were working as an effective ensemble, headed by Schröder
and Korn. Moreover, Schreyvogel arranged for the produc-

tion scenic display such as the public was accustomed to
viewing only at the fairy plays of the folk theatres. The
costumes were, of course, designed by von Stubenrauch, and
the scene designer was Anton de Pian (1784-1851), inheritor
of the Sacchetti-Platzer tradition and the great classic designer of the Schreyvogel period. His settings used the same
arcades, colonnades, and staircases as those of his predecessors, but he placed even more emphasis on details--
gothic, oriental, or idyllic pastoral elements. The setting,
he felt, should heighten the mood of the play through its
shape, its specific elements, and particularly its chiaroscuro.
Like Stubenrauch's costumes, his settings were influenced
less by the Berlin emphasis on historicity than by Schreyvogel's concern with a unified effect, and much more attention was given to such matters as color harmonies between
setting and costume than to the action period or locale being
represented.

Despite the contributions of all these important creative artists, however, Das goldene Vliess proved too diffuse
and complicated to gain popularity. The intellectual harmony
of the trilogy was simply not supported by three equally
powerful plays, and later directors have agreed with Schreyvogel's analysis after the first reading rehearsal: "Medea is
a striking work. Der Gastfreund is adequate. Die Argonauten on the whole doesn't have much in it."23 The disappointed author, striving as usual to adjust to the public's
wishes, turned away from mythology to try his hand at Austrian history, a subject made widely popular at this time by
the writings of the "Austrian Plutarch," Joseph von Hormayr
(1782-1848). Hormayr's theatrical influence was first clearly
seen in the dramas of Matthäus von Collin (1779-1823), who
condemned Schiller for restructuring the past to fit the ideas
of the present and who attempted instead to depict objectively
the actual current of history, subjugating even his leading
characters to an inexorable march of events. None of his
dramas were produced, but their influence can be clearly
seen in the historical plays of Grillparzer, who found Collin's
fatalistic idea of the tide of history most congenial. Inspired
by Collin's preoccupation with facts, Grillparzer was the first
German historical dramatist to create a background as rich
as his foreground by including many authentic details not
actually required by the plot.

König Ottokars Glück und Ende (1825), unlike Collin's
plays, centered on a single hero, but destroyed him by setting his will against Collin's tide of history, which here

serves as an elemental force like that of passion in Grillparzer's earlier plays.   Opposed to the wilful Ottokar II is
the Emperor Rudolf, Grillparzer's first major character who
seems to have discovered a means of restoring harmony, by
subjugating his individual will to a concern for the welfare of
the whole.   Ill-fortune of every sort plagued this drama.   It
came into Schreyvogel's hands just as he was assigned a new
aristocratic supervisor, Count Czernin, who unlike his predecessors Palffy and Dietrichstein, was disinclined to support
Schreyvogel against the censor.   The director therefore had
to appeal personally for help to the Kaiser and Kaiserin to
get the play approved.   All this stir aroused public interest
of an unfortunate kind; though attendance was high, many in
the audience were sensation-seekers who found the play innocent and uninteresting.   Literary critics condemned Grillparzer for deserting classic themes after his triumph with
Sappho and at least the latter part of Das goldene Vliess to
curry popular support.   Finally, Czech nationalists, who considered Ottokar a national hero, besieged the unhappy dramatist with letters from Prague threatening his life for his
treatment of the King.   Not surprisingly, Grillparzer entirely
forsook playwriting for some time and left the scene of his
sufferings to travel in Germany.

Schreyvogel's difficulties increased steadily in the
final years of his administration.   Despite the major loss of
Sophie Müller, his company remained impressive and dedicated, but as Metternich's conservative regime felt itself
more and more threatened, censorship became an ever-
greater problem, and Count Czernin, far from protecting the
theatre given to his charge, resented Schreyvogel's independence and intrigued constantly to undermine his authority.
Under the circumstances, the 1827 production of Wilhelm Tell
was both bold and brilliant, with public acclaim drowning any
possible protest against this daring play.

Grillparzer's next work, Ein treuer Diener seines
Herrn (1828) was also enthusiastically received, but not so
fortunate politically.   The play was a new sort of experiment
for the versatile dramatist, a fable of loyalty in extreme
testing suggested by the works of Lope de Vega.   The specific source again was Hormayr, this time from Magyar history, and the tragic story qualifies, if it does not wholly undermine, even the tentative solution to the human dilemma
suggested in König Ottokar.   Again a corrupt and wilful
leader, Duke Otto, is opposed to a sympathetic figure, Bancbanus, who has been entrusted with the kingdom in the mon-

arch's absence and who, like Rudolf, elevates this charge
above all personal considerations.   No Schillerian affirmation
comes from his suffering in this trust, however.   Like the
medieval Griselda, Bancbanus with his humble total resignation engages our compassion, but his fate seems scarcely
preferable to that of the villainous Duke Otto.   The liberals
in Grillparzer's audience condemned this servility, but Austria's Emperor Francis was more concerned by the play's
representation of a debauched court, of nobles revolting
against their ruler, and of Hungary fighting Germany, and
after a single performance the play was suppressed.

Despite the political upheavals of 1830, Schreyvogel
mounted Goethe's Götz von Berlichingen, and in a version
near the original of 1773 instead of the much adapted one
given in Vienna in 1809.   He paid again for his boldness by
having the play banned after five performances, with enormous losses in settings and costumes.   The next year Grillparzer brought Schreyvogel two new plays, Des Meeres und
der Liebe Wellen and Der Traum ein Leben.   Perhaps to
answer complaints from his critics, perhaps to mollify the
censor, Grillparzer turned again away from history to classic
literature in the first and to a dramatic fairy story in the
second.   Perhaps because this genre suggested an offering
for the suburban theatres or perhaps because it challenged
comparison with Calderon, Schreyvogel expressed doubts over
the success of the second play and Grillparzer withdrew it.
Thus Des Meeres und der Liebe Wellen was the last Grillparzer work Schreyvogel produced.

Grillparzer's tale of Hero and Leander, called by
some later critics the German Romeo and Juliet, ends in
tragedy, but has a distinctly less pessimistic tone than Ein
treuer Diener seines Herrn.   Hero seeks to escape the un-
pleasantness of the world and to fulfill herself by becoming
a priestess of Aphrodite, which Grillparzer interprets as
equivalent to entering the strictest of nunneries.   Nature up-
sets this decision by arousing in her a sudden irrational love.
Since she has already joined the order, either obeying or
denying this love means destruction, but she accepts nature
and obeys it.   The love thus accepted has none of the destructive passion which it had in Grillparzer's first plays,
and the play thus suggests that Hero's choice is the right one
and in a more fortunate world she would be blessed for it.
It was perhaps the closest Grillparzer had yet come to a
harmony of the antagonisms of his dramatic world.

With the departure of Schreyvogel in 1831, the greatest years of the Burgtheater came to an end. Count Czernin
attempted to carry on his work with the aid of the writer
Ludwig Deinhardstein, but their efforts won little distinction.
The ensemble Schreyvogel had formed remained for some
years, however, and as an ideal, has never been forgotten.
Its style was perhaps never a national model, but it was a
distinct, rich, and unified one, an influential rival to Weimar
classicism and Berlin theatricalism. In staging and costuming Schreyvogel was not revolutionary, but here too his ideal
of harmony and balance strongly influenced future directors.
In terms of repertoire he did not escape the public demands
for light French entertainment or the melodramas of Kotzebue,
but Raupach, Iffland, and the fate-tragedies so popular in
Berlin had little representation in his program.   Under one
of the most rigorous censorships in Germany he managed to
present the widest range of drama, from the German classics to such moderns as Kleist and Grillparzer along with
an important selection of foreign works.   To all this he added
his own considerable abilities as director, critic, and translator.   Over his grave, Grillparzer said: "If anyone approached the stature of Lessing, it was he. "

Since the Theater an der Wien served during Schreyvogel's directorship as the experimental annex to the Burgtheater, the Leopoldstädter Theater and the Josefstädter
Theater served as the homes of the Old Viennese Popular
Theatre.   Though the Leopoldstädter was the more prestigious of the two major private theatres, their fare was
essentially interchangeable and the same authors wrote for
both.   They offered Kotzebue, Iffland, and translations of
modern French vaudevilles, but the greatest part of their
repertoire was from native Viennese authors, and the most
popular genre the Lokalposse, a realistic comedy in the
Hanswurst tradition.   The other genres most performed were
parodies and the Zauberstück, a spectacular fairy or ghost
play. The most popular authors in the early 1800's--Joseph
Gleich, Adolf Bäuerle (1786-1859), and Carl Meisl (1775-
1853)--were prolific producers of all three types.   Gleich
was the first to gain public attention, with a knight play,
Elizabeth, Gräfin von Hochfeld (1791), and he continued to
specialize in historical drama, converting Burgundians,
Franks, Vandals, Lombards, Prussians, and Venetians all
into standard Viennese types.   In addition to fairy plays such
as Der Mann von Kahlenberg, parodies such as Fiesko, and
Lokalposse such as Die Musikanten am Hohenmarkt, he created a number of popular moral dramas, or thesis plays such

as Der Eheteufel auf Reisen.

Carl Meisl, the most prolific of the three, created over two hundred plays, making his debut in 1801 with an outlaw melodrama, Carolo Corolini, at the Leopoldstädter. His ghost play Das Gespenst auf der Bastei was so popular as to inspire several sequels, but Meisl's particular specialty was parody, in a period when parodies and counterparodies formed a surprisingly large portion of theatre offerings. Any popular success was sure to inspire one or more burlesques, perhaps an entire series. In 1817, for example, Karl Franz van der Velde produced a comedy at the Burgtheater, Der lustige Fritz, which was promptly parodied, under the same name, by Meisl. Meisl's parody was in turn parodied by Franz Told von Doldenberg (1789-1849), another specialist in this genre, as Der traurige Fritz. Doldenberg's parody was parodied as Der närrische Fritz by Fritz Wimmer, an actor at the Josefstädter, and Wimmer's play was parodied in a ballet created by Paolo Rainoldi.

Adolf Bäuerle combined work as a playwright with editorship of the influential Wiener Theaterzeitung between 1806 and 1859 and achieved great success in all the standard genres. His Die Bürger in Wien (1813), at the Leopoldstädter, established the reputation of Ignaz Schuster (1779-1835), who became that house's leading actor, with the role of Staberl, a Viennese clown. Staberl was later interpreted by all the great actors of the folk tradition and his exploits made the subject of countless sequels by Bäuerle and others. Doktor Fausts Mantel (1820), with music by Wenzel Müller, was a major contribution to the spectacle play tradition. His two most popular parodies were Der Mann mit Millionen, schön, jung, und doch nicht glücklich (1829), based on Kabale und Liebe, and Aline oder Wien in einem anderen Weltteil (1822), which was in fact considerably more popular than the minor opera by François Berton which it parodied.

The Viennese popular theatre first achieved literary distinction with the arrival of Ferdinand Raimund (1790-1836), who, inspired by the example of Ochsenheimer, decided to devote his life to acting. After several appearances in minor theatres in Austria, he was hired by Josef Huber at the Josefstädter in 1814. He appeared both in comic and tragic parts, copying Ochsenheimer, as Bäuerle observed in the Wiener Theaterzeitung, in every detail. By 1816 he had evolved a somewhat more personal style and a reputation which earned him an invitation to appear as guest artist at

the more prestigious Leopoldstäter. His success was such
that he was invited permanently in 1817 and he remained at
this theatre until his retirement in 1830.

Gleich, now the leading author of the Josefstädter, admired the new arrival's comic ability, though Raimund himself still considered his greater skill to lie in tragedy. For
him Gleich wrote Die Musikanten am Hohenmarkt, with a new
Viennese Hanswurst, Adam Kratzerl, a part which made Raimund famous. A whole series of Kratzerl plays naturally
followed, and by the time Raimund went to the Leopoldstädter,
he was a serious rival for Schuster, that theatre's leading
actor. The administration capitalized on this rivalry by offering the actors on alternate nights. The public and newspapers
warmly took sides, but the supporters of Raimund, headed by
Ludwig Costenoble from the Burgtheater, were soon clearly the
larger party. Raimund turned to playwriting in 1823 when a
promised play from Meisl was not completed in time for a
benefit. Like most of the popular folk actors of the period,
Raimund was quite accustomed to inserting material of his
own into other works, and he had little difficulty creating
under this pressure a complete play, Der Barometermacher
auf der Zauberinsel. Its success then encouraged him to
write Der Diamant des Geisterkönigs (1824), an even more
popular offering which brought influential members of the
aristocracy to the Leopoldstädter, was widely produced in
Germany, and was eventually even adapted by Hans Christian
Anderson for the Danish stage.

This success led Raimund to aspire to the creation of
a folk drama of real literary significance. After long discussions with Grillparzer and assiduous study of Shakespeare,
Calderon, and the Greeks, he wrote the first of his "original"
plays, Das Mädchen aus der Feenwelt (1826). The background
plot, of the trials of a daughter born to a fairy and a mortal,
is traditional enough, but the "real" world of the play had an
honesty and naturalness quite different from traditional folk
theatre offerings. The interpenetration of fairy and peasant
worlds in this charming play is reminiscent at times of A
Midsummer Night's Dream. The key figure is the peasant
guardian of the fairy child, Fortunatus Wurzel, which Raimund played. Suddenly and undeservedly made a millionaire,
he loses all his peasant good nature and compassion and cuts
as ridiculous a figure as Molière's M. Jourdain. The play
was a great success, and its new richness of tone was widely
praised. One Berlin critic observed:

Both as an actor and an author, Raimund is abso-
lutely serious, but those who are not so themselves
never notice it. He never relaxes, and where he
seems to, only a thin gauze curtain separates his
humor from a view of the end of all things, humor
among them. [24]

In his next two plays, Moisasurs Zauberfluch (1827)
and Die gefesselte Phantasie (1828), Raimund continued to
show both an idealized supernatural world and a realistic one
with a conflict between good and evil developed in each. Despite the simplicity of this contrast, Raimund's public was
confused and intimidated by these works. The folk theatre
had always relied on trivial plots with standardized fairy sequences used more for spectacle than for any intellectual
reference. Now Raimund was constructing elaborate alle-
gories on unfamiliar myths. Moisasurs Zauberfluch tells of
an Indian queen cursed by a demon who travels to Austria
seeking a way to break the curse. Die gefesselte Phantasie,
set in the pseudo-classic land of Flora, demonstrates by
allegory how a queen triumphs over Evil and Arrogance to
make her kingdom a haven for Poetic Art. Later critics
have pointed out Raimund's place in the tradition of baroque
drama and linked his allegorical world to that of Goethe in
Faust II. [25] Later dramatists found Raimund an important
source of inspiration; Anzengruber's peasants are direct de-
scendents of Raimund's and Wagner used Die gefesselte
Phantasie as part of his inspiration for Die Meistersinger
von Nürnberg. But to Raimund's own audiences, these rich
works were complicated, even annoying puzzles, and neither
Zauberfluch at the Wien nor Phantasie at the Leopoldstädter
was well received.

Finally in Der Alpenkönig und der Menschenfiend
(1828) Raimund achieved a fusion of reality and fantasy,
poetry and philosophy, which was also a great and immediate
popular success. The play's servants are excellent examples
of the buffoonery and wit of the Viennese folk tradition, but
the central character, Herr von Rappelkopf, is a richer and
darker creation, closer to Molière's Alceste or even Shakespeare's Timon, and his depiction in an isolated charcoal-
burner's hut, where his intolerance of all human society has
driven him, has been called a precursor of naturalism in the
German theatre. Still, Rappelkopf is more fortunate than
Alceste or Timon, whose compatriots lack the power to reconcile them with the world. A higher order and harmony
in nature is represented in Raimund's play by the mountain

king Astagalus, who by creating a double for Rappelkopf
proves to him his disappointments are all his own making
and sends him back to mankind cured. The play, after a
great initial success, became a standard revival piece; one
of its songs, "So leb' denn wohl, " became accepted as an
Austrian folk melody.

The great success for Raimund was undermined, however, by a series of quarrels with Rudolf Steinkeller, who
became director in 1828. Steinkeller was apparently a difficult administrator, since he ultimately lost not only Raimund,
his artistic director and major author, but also such key
members of the company as Ignaz Schuster and Therese
Krones. Raimund announced his departure shortly after the
failure of Die unheilbringende Krone (1829), a work which
returned to the ambitions of Moisasurs Zauberfluch and Die
gefesselte Phantasie and aroused almost identical protests.
The play's hero, Phalarius, who receives a magic crown
from Hades that makes him all-powerful, owes a literary debt
to Macbeth and a historical one to Napoleon, but around
these specific references Raimund wove a mixture of classic
antiquity and German folk tales, tragedy and comedy, realism
and fantasy that was simply too complex for his audience to
assimilate.

After leaving the theatre, Raimund traveled in Germany until 1832, then returned to Vienna and to the Josefstädter, where he presented his final play, Der Verschwender
(1834). Ghosts and fairies have almost disappeared from
this last work, the story of the rich Flottwell whom fortune
reduces to beggary, of his loyal, Kent-like servant, and the
evil secretary Wolf who inherits his treasure. Der Verschwender enjoyed a greater success than any play Raimund
had written, and was his first work performed by the Burgtheater. Still, Raimund realized that his style of acting and
playwriting was passing, and his audiences turning to a rival
who had recently appeared on the Viennese scene--Johann
Nepomuk Nestroy (1801-1862). Raimund looked back to the
baroque and romantic era, Nestroy forward to realism, and
the gentle and naive humor of the former was soon considered quaint and old-fashioned beside Nestroy's keen and sar-
castic wit. Raimund's acting style was more persistent.
Though he last appeared in Hamburg in 1836, his tradition
was carried on by Schuster and by several younger actors:
Johann Baptist Lid, Eduard Weiss, and most importantly
Franz Wallner (1810-1876) and Moritz Rott (1797-1867). Rott
was the first to attempt to play Raimund's works in other

than their original style, but the Raimund interpretations remained dominant for a full generation after his departure
from the stage. After 1830, however, as Raimund correctly
anticipated, Nestroy became the dominant literary figure in
the Viennese popular theatre.

5. The Lesser German Stages

By the beginning of the nineteenth century every major
German city and many minor ones had permanent theatre
buildings. Some of these provided temporary shelter for
traveling companies, of which there were still a great many,
but approximately forty cities during this period possessed
permanently established companies. Theoretically, established
organizations were divided into "private" theatres, managed
by entrepreneurs and presumably self-supporting, "state" or
"national" theatres, subsidized by public funds, and "court"
theatres, subsidized by the local Duke, Prince, or Count,
though still generally open to the public. In practice the
politics and the social situation of the period were so unstable
that every theatre evolved a somewhat different financial and
organizational structure, titles were loosely applied, and
many houses were in fact private at one time, state or court
theatres at another according to who could be found to pay
the bills. The repertoire of most German theatres between
1800 and 1830 was much the same. The more ambitious
produced Shakespeare, Schiller, Goethe, and Lessing, with
perhaps a bit of Kleist, Grillparzer, or Calderon, but the
standard fare everywhere was translations from the popular
contemporary French authors such as Picard and Duval, and
the light comedies and melodramas of the contemporary Germans Kotzebue, Iffland, Houwald, Müllner, and later Raupach.
Most theatres also had native playwrights who supplemented
this fare with local comedies and parodies.

An important extra attraction was the guest artist, and
most of the major actors of the period, even those with an
established home theatre, spent a significant part of their
careers appearing for a few months or even for several seasons at other houses. Iffland, for example, though settled
from 1784 until 1796 at Mannheim and from 1796 until 1812
at Berlin, appeared during these years as a guest artist in
Lübeck, Hamburg, Bremen, Braunschweig, Magdeburg, Potsdam, Dessau, Leipzig, Gotha, Weimar, Dresden, Breslau,
Prague, Frankfurt, Manau, Darmstadt, Dürkheim, Saar-

brücken, Karlsruhe, Pressburg, and Vienna, and in many of
these cities several times. He would normally remain for
four to six weeks, playing fifteen or twenty roles. Such
touring not only allowed theatre audiences throughout Germany
to observe the best actors of the time, but in many towns
where local companies feared to attempt classic works, gave
them their only exposure to such authors as Schiller and
Shakespeare.

Naturally the major touring artists came from the
most important theatre centers, but several theatres during
this period are of interest only because of their contribution
of an important touring star to the rest of the country. From
Karlsruhe came Amalie Morstedt, a popular soubrette.
Frankfurt produced Karoline Brandt, later an important member of the Prague theatre. Carl Ludwig Paulmann (1789-
1832), an outstanding character actor and one of the period's
most popular interpreters of Lear, came from Hannover.
Karl Seydelmann (1793-1843), an important pioneer in the
development of realism in acting, came from Kassel.

Certain other theatres, while clearly not rivals of
Weimar, the Vienna Burgtheater, or the Königliches Schauspielhaus of Berlin, still made important general contributions
to the period. Breslau, Dresden, and Hamburg have already
been mentioned. To them should be added Prague, Leipzig,
Munich, Braunschweig, and Bamberg.

In the early years of the century, the Hoftheater in
Munich was directed by Josef Marius von Babo (1756-1822),
a popular writer of bourgeois dramas and chivalric spectacles which dominated the repertoire here. Schiller was
played little, Goethe not at all, and Babo submitted without
protest to the censorship of Count Seenau, who found even
most of Kotzebue too strong for the Munich stage. In 1811
a second royal theatre was founded, the Isartortheater,
modeled on the successful Leopoldstädter and Josefstädter
theatres in Vienna and with a similar repertoire. The most
important actor of the Isartortheater was Karl, who after
1818 served also as its director. He made his fame in the
folk role of Staberl, but his interpretation was quite different
from Schuster's in Vienna. Besides the predictable changes
of Viennese references to Munich ones, Karl showed Staberl
as a comic servant, much closer to the old Hanswurst, with
a rich English master. Karl's personal popularity in Munich
was great, but the folk comedy he presented did not take
root there as it had in Vienna, and the Isartortheater was

forced to close in 1825.

Neither Babo nor any of the three administrators who followed him between 1815 and 1824 contributed much to the theatre, but they were fortunate enough to have the services of one of the outstanding actors of the period, Ferdinand Esslair (1772-1840). He first appeared in Munich with a traveling company in 1797, and was so popular with the public and with Babo and Seenau that he returned frequently thereafter. About 1820 he settled more or less permanently in Munich, while making lengthy guest appearances in other cities like most major actors of the period. During his early years his most noted roles were Orindus in Müllner's Schuld, Meinau in Kotzebue's Menschenhass und Reue, and Schiller's Ferdinand and Karl Moor. After 1815 he shifted his attention to more mature roles, becoming a popular interpreter of Lear, Macbeth, Wallenstein, Tell, and Nathan. His most famous roles were those favored by German romantic actors, but Esslair was a restrained, technical artist, with only occasional touches of the passion or emotional truth of the romantic style. His contemporaries considered him closer to Talma in interpretation than to such emotional actors as Kean or Devrient. "Esslair made Lear a hero fallen into misfortune, " reported one observer,

> ... but he always remained a hero. Thus the mad scenes produced a violent effect. Devrient played a weak but wilfull old man, who is really no longer quite in his right mind when the play opens. Thus his change to complete madness had an unsurpassed honesty. [26]

This should have made Esslair the ideal partner for Sophie Schröder, and it is therefore not surprising that Schreyvogel made a great effort to win him for Vienna. Esslair did come as a guest, but eventually returned to Munich when both he and Schreyvogel became convinced that after all, Esslair would not fit into the Burgtheater ensemble. Esslair clearly preferred the more casual and individualistic emphasis of the Munich stage, while Schreyvogel had little interest in keeping an actor who, as he complained, was "nothing but mannerisms. " Certainly in his later years Esslair was often ridiculed by young romantic actors for his stress on technique and his habit of portraying gestures literally (the most notorious example being measuring off small units on his staff to accompany Lear's line "Every inch a king. ") "Esslair had beautiful tones, but no tone, " Zelter

complained. "I often had the impression when I saw him
that he was speaking some other part."[27]

In Munich Esslair's usual partner was Charlotte Birch-
Pfeiffer (1800-1868), a powerful young tragedienne similar in
style to Sophie Schröder. The lovely young Charlotte von
Hagn (1809-1891) came in 1828 and achieved great success
opposite Heinrich Moritz (1800-1867), a veteran from the unfortunate Isartortheater. Esslair and Wilhelm Vespermann
(1784-1837), a specialist in the dramas of Iffland, served
during these years as regisseurs, and made no attempt to
bring the scattered talents of the Munich theatre into any sort
of ensemble. What would later become known as the virtuoso approach was followed here, with the spoken theatre dependent upon the personal popularity of various actors and
holding its own with difficulty against the opera and ballet.

The golden age of the theatre in Prague began in 1806
with the arrival of Johann Carl Liebich (1773-1816). During
the Napoleonic wars, Prague was a peaceful haven for artists
and intellectuals, and Liebich was able to rely upon an audience to support a more ambitious repertoire than that of
most German theatres. He took advantage of his opportunity
by presenting relatively little Werner, Houwald, Kotzebue,
and Iffland, and instead introduced to Prague Shakespeare,
Goethe, and Schiller. Few directors were more solicitous
of their company than he. He introduced the first complete
pension plan in the German theatre, and his home was always
open to his troupe, which became a kind of artistic family,
calling him and his wife Papa and Mama Liebich. Most of
his company eventually appeared also in Vienna. Strong
cultural ties existed between the two cities, and Prague's
theatre was modeled on Vienna's with a National house and a
smaller folk theatre, the Kleinseitner (which presented plays
both in German and Czech).

The leading man of the company was Franz Rudolf
Bayer (1780-1860), an actor the Wiener Theaterzeitung of
1817 called comparable only to Esslair. He was supported
by Ferdinand Powlawsky, who played the Fool to Bayer's
Lear and specialized in knights and bonvivants. Liebich's
wife was the leading heroine. More important, however, was
the younger generation discovered and trained by Liebich, including the soubrette Augusta Brede, who became a leading
player in Stuttgart, and several later stars of the Vienna
Burgtheater: Juliane and Ludwig Löwe, Friedrich Wilhelmi
(1788-1852), and Sophie Schröder. The popular Wenzel

Müller was music director.

After Liebich's death in 1816 his widow carried on his administration, aided after 1819 by Powlawsky. The company declined during these years, with important members leaving for Vienna and elsewhere. By 1819 only Powlawsky, Löwe, and Wilhelmi remained of the original leaders of the troupe. They were supplemented, however, by important guest artists, and Frau Liebich continued her husband's policy of offering important modern German works, particularly the plays of Grillparzer and Raimund. In 1818 Löwe created his greatest role, Jaromir in Die Ahnfrau. The prosperity of Carl Liebich's era was briefly restored by Franz von Holbein, who came from Bamberg and Hannover in 1819 as regisseur and who served as director of the Prague theatre from 1823 until 1825. He brought in new talents, most notably Carl Seydelmann, who had been playing young lovers in the provincial Austrian theatre of Graz but who began in Prague the character roles which established his reputation. Holbein restored the sort of ensemble approach Liebich had developed and encouraged a new interest in design by bringing Antonio Sacchetti from Vienna to serve the theatre. When Holbein left, this brief renaissance was over. Löwe and Wilhelmi soon followed him, then Seydelmann, and the generally weakened troupe was taken over by a triumverate of the faithful Powlawsky, his treasurer Stěpánek, and a singer, Kainz, who managed it until 1834. Little of the distinction of Prague's golden age now remained. The company was small and weak, scarcely able to hold its own against the ballet and opera. The major dramatic genres were now parody, Posse, and Scribean comedy, the most frequently performed authors the undistinguished Holbein, Töpfer, and Raupach. Sacchetti left Prague for Poland, so that the theatre in this period of decline could no longer boast even of having a creative designer.

Before his arrival in Prague, Franz von Holbein had brought to temporary prominence the minor theatre in Bamberg. He assumed direction of it in 1809 and with considerable theatre experience already behind him as a singer in the Berlin opera, an actor and designer in Regensburg and Vienna, and most recently as a machinist in the Viennese Burgtheater and Opera. His close co-worker during his four years at Bamberg was the romantic author E. T. A. Hoffmann (1776-1822), who served as music director, composer, dramatist, scenery and lighting designer, architect, and regisseur. The two artists were similarly concerned with stimu-

lating romantic imagination in their audiences, with widening
the bounds of experience and discovering the inner man.
Calderon seemed to Holbein particularly well suited to these
purposes, and the translations just completed by Schlegel
made him readily available. In 1811 Holbein did The Bridge
of Mantible, followed in 1812 by The Constant Prince and
Devotion to the Cross. The productions stressed pictorial
and evocative elements and Hoffman designed striking though
not historically accurate costumes, subtle lighting effects,
and spectacular romantic scenery. The Weimar Journal des
Luxus und der Moden of 1812 describes a typical setting:

> The bridge passes between two towers on the banks
> and over a colossal bronze dwarf that stands in the
> middle of the river, holding a kind of citadel on
> his head in the manner of a caryatid. The gates
> to it are lowered by huge chains held by two
> bronze lions, within which one may see enormous
> machines working. As the gates lower, they be-
> come a gallery resting on a bronze beam, opening
> and forming the bridge (by uniting the citadel and
> the two banks)--a bridge so huge that it fills the
> entire background.

Similar spectacular staging was developed for various Shakespearian plays, such as Hamlet in 1811, and for Kleist's
Käthchen von Heilbronn in 1812.

The actors were distinctly subordinated to the physical
effects in Bamberg, but the theatre possessed a popular
creator of character roles, Karl Friedrich Leo; a charming
comedienne, Marie Renner (1782-1824); and one of Germany's
most popular interpreters of Kotzebue's heroines, Karoline
Lindner (1797-1863). The 1812 wars put an abrupt end to
the Bamberg theatre, dispersing actors, director, and designer. Holbein, as we have seen, went on to Prague,
Hoffmann to Berlin to devote himself to composing and non-
dramatic writing (though he collaborated with Schinkel there
on several settings). The company scattered to several
other theatres, but most went to Kassel, where Feige built
up a company headed by Seydelmann.

Just at the time the Bamberg theatre was dissolving,
another minor stage came into prominence. This was the
theatre at Braunschweig under the direction of August Klingemann (1777-1831). Klingemann, a native of Jena, married
the actress Elise Anschütz (1785-1862) and toured German

theatre cities with her before settling in Braunschweig in 1815. For three years he served as resident playwright, his most important work being Doktor Fausts Leben, Thaten, und Höllenfahrt (1815). He had no desire to promote this version at the expense of Goethe's; indeed, it was Klingemann's theatre which first offered a public performance of scenes from Faust I, in January, 1819. This cutting, composed of the prologue in the theatre, the Walpurgisnacht, the spring scene in Gretchen's room, and the scene at the well, was subsequently presented in Dresden, Leipzig, and Frankfurt as well. After Klingemann became full director in 1818, he also presented plays by Grillparzer, Schiller, Calderon, Shakespeare, Kleist, Heine (whose Almansor in 1823 caused a considerable scandal), and the operas of Auber, Rossini, Spontini, Weber, and Spohr. His own minor plays were soon forgotten, but his theoretical work, Kunst und Natur (1823-1828), a clear and pragmatic analysis of the theatre art of the time, is a still-useful source of information. The company's leading serious actors were Auguste Haake (1793-1864) and Frau Klingemann, while Carl Günther (1786-1859) and Frau Schmidt did lighter roles, but Klingemann enjoyed a great reputation as a trainer of actors, and many young talents were attracted to Braunschweig during his regime. His most noted pupils were Ludwig Devrient's two nephews, Carl (1797-1872) and Emil (1805-1872). Despite its fame, the Braunschweig theatre was never a financial success. In 1826 it converted from a National to a Hoftheater. This allowed Klingemann to achieve some stability, though his freedom of action was considerably restricted. He remained director of the Hoftheater, with steadily diminishing success, until his death in 1831.

Leipzig also possessed a theatre administered by a private speculator, here Theodor Küstner (1784-1864), who established a permanent theatre in the city in 1817. Leipzig was sufficiently near to Weimar and Jena for Küstner to feel the influence of the classic and romantic schools, and Goethe, Schiller, Calderon, and Shakespeare were predictably well represented in his repertoire. As a commercial venture, however, the theatre relied most heavily on Raupach, Iffland, and Kotzebue. Küstner's major contribution was not in the works he presented, but in the excellent ensemble company he built. Gustav Wohlbrück (1793-1847) from Munich proved an outstanding interpreter of middle-class drama, Ferdinand Löwe played young heroes opposite the Böhlet sisters-- Christine as sentimental heroines and Dorothea as soubrettes. Major tragic roles were taken by Eduard Genast (1797-1866),

son of the Weimar regisseur, aided after 1823 by Emil
Devrient from Braunschweig. By the mid-1820's the Leipzig
school of acting began to rival the declining Berlin school.
Then came a period of financial crisis and in 1828 Küstner
was forced to close. The actor Friedrich Sebald Ringlehardt
(1785-1855) reopened the theatre in 1832 and directed it until
1844, but without ever regaining the level of excellence
achieved by Küstner.

6. Opera During the Weber Period

        The Napoleonic wars brought to an end the great Mo-
zartian period which occupied the closing years of the eighteenth century, and prepared the way both for the development
of a native German operatic tradition and for a shift in predominant outside influence from Italy to France. Only in
Vienna, as we have seen, was opera developed in its own
theatre totally separated from the spoken drama physically
and financially. Elsewhere the same organization produced
both opera and drama, and in many cities, most notably in
Berlin, Munich, Stuttgart, Darmstadt, Karlsruhe, and
Prague, it produced ballet as well. In almost every case,
this worked to the disadvantage of the spoken stage. Operas
were considerably more costly to produce, and so placed a
serious financial strain on the theatres, making them generally fearful of experimentation. New theatres, as at
Munich, were built for the demands of opera and were frequently unsuited for a more intimate drama. Finally, opera
tended to dominate the repertoire. Since opera was a traditional court entertainment, it is not surprising that the many
theatres relying on court subsidy were expected by their
sovereign to favor this form, but independent directors found
it was also preferred by the general public. Doubtless the
major reason for opera's popular success during this period
was its concern for spectacle, but another important feature
was that, due to its greater complexity, it was much better
planned and rehearsed than the spoken drama. By 1820,
opera was unquestionably the dominant theatrical form in
Berlin, Munich, Darmstadt, Prague, Stuttgart, and a number
of less significant cities.

        During most of this period Vienna was the major
German center for opera, followed by Dresden, Prague, and
Berlin. The century opened with Italianate influence still
strong. Salvatore Vigano and his wife Maria Medina domi-

nated the dance, as they had since their arrival in Vienna in
1793, Schikaneder's new Theater an der Wien placed its major
emphasis on Mozart, the royal opera composer was Salieri
(who died in 1825). Yet a certain French influence was already present and grew steadily stronger. The popular
Singspiels of the late eighteenth century, spoken comedies
with interspersed songs, were distinctly influenced by French
vaudevilles and comic operas both in form and subject.
Early evidence of French romantic themes, the use of fairy
tales and legends, could be seen from the 1790's on in such
fanciful works as Sylphen (Berlin, 1806) and Der Kobold
(Vienna, 1811) by Friedrich Heinrich Himmel (1765-1814) or
in plays of local color such as the popular Schweitzerfamilie
(Vienna, 1809) of Joseph Weigel (1766-1846). The Theater
an der Wien began to present, along with Mozart and Cherubini, such works as Henri Méhul's Joseph et ses frères in
1809 and Boieldieu's Jean de Paris in 1812.

The Italian ballet continued in the early years of the
century under the direction of Pietro Angiolini, whose most
popular work was Achilles auf Skyros (1808). The leading
role in this, as in most of Angiolini's works, was performed
by Filippo Taglioni (1777-1871), future author of the greatest
of the romantic ballets, La Sylphide. Taglioni, his wife,
and his daughter, whose fame in France was later to surpass his own, remained in Vienna until 1813, but after their
departure, French influence began to dominate the ballet as
well. Pierre Gardel, ballet master of the Paris Opéra,
came to Vienna to direct a program for the Congress of
1814, and the following year Jean Pierre Aumer (1776-1832)
settled in Vienna for five years as ballet master and composer. His most popular work during this period was Les
Pages du Duc de Vendôme (1815), based on a Singspiel by
the Viennese Gyrowetz presented in 1808. Of course, with
the rise of the romantic ballet in Paris, French influence
became even stronger.

After 1812, on the other hand, there was in the opera
as in the spoken theatre a noticeably greater interest in
German authors, not only as a reaction to the Napoleonic invasions, but as a part of that nationalist spirit which grew
up with the romantic movement almost everywhere. The
early romantics were divided in their opinion of opera.
Schlegel feared it would lead to artistic anarchy, with various
elements warring among themselves, while Matthäus von
Collin argued on the contrary that only opera could achieve
a total harmony of artistic design. Collin's view was de-

veloped by Ignaz von Mosel in his Versuch einer Aesthetik
des dramatischen Tonsatzes (Vienna, 1813), which clearly
anticipated Wagner, arguing that music could regulate all the
arts to achieve a total aesthetic effect. Mosel's own Salem
(1813) and Cyrus und Astyages (1818) were not notably successful in achieving this goal, but he and others of his generation prepared the way for the composer who would bring
the full tide of romanticism to the German stage, and in so
doing would also satisfy the demand for a distinctly Germanic
opera--Karl Maria von Weber (1786-1826).

Several key members of Mosel's generation prepared
the way for Weber. The romantic Hoffmann in Undine (Berlin, 1816) added a seriousness and psychological depth to the
traditional Singspiel that brought it a step closer to romantic
opera. Ludwig Spohr (1784-1859), who was called by Palffy
to Vienna to direct the Theater an der Wien in 1813, made
this a major operatic stage and contributed to it an important
series of works including Faust (1816) and later, when the
romantic movement was more clearly established, Jessonda
(1823). The major composers of the period, Schubert, Mendelssohn, Schumann, all attempted opera without success.
Beethoven's Fidelio, given in a censored form in 1805 and in
complete form at the Kärntnertortheater in 1814, was a unique
achievement standing outside the trends that would develop
into romanticism. Beethoven scorned the fanciful and "magic"
subjects dear to most pre-romantics and dismissed such
works as Don Giovanni and the operas of Rossini as immoral.
He therefore sought a theme of high seriousness, an expression of the idealism of the Enlightenment more than of the
passion of the Romantic period. His libretto, drawn from
Jean Nicolas Bouilly's Léonore, ou l'Amour Conjugale (1798),
placed the work in the tradition of the melodramatic rescue
operas of Cherubini and Grétry, transformed, of course by
Beethoven's soaring music. After Fidelio, Beethoven turned
away from opera, though he composed music for an 1810
production of Goethe's Egmont at the Burgtheater and cele-
brative choruses for Treitschke's Singspiel Die gute Nachricht
(1814) and Die Ehrenpforten (1815), paeons to freedom and the
human spirit suggestive of the Eroica.

Karl Maria von Weber was the son of a theatre director and began his career as a conductor in Breslau. His
first works, such as Das stumme Waldmädchen (1800), Peter
Schmoll und seine Nachbarn (1803) and Abu Hassan (1811)
were typical examples of the Singspiel, but he established a
reputation as leader of Germany's patriotic youth in 1814 with

his musical setting of ten songs from Körner's Leyer und Schwert. Weber was now serving as director of the Opera in Prague under Liebich, who had been the first to break away from exclusively Italian works there. The first opera given in German in Prague was Cherubini's Faniska in 1807, though there was little Germanic about it but the language. Cherubini, a native of Italy, was now settled in Paris and had written Faniska during a visit to Vienna as guest artist the previous year. The same year Liebich committed himself much more strongly to German presentations by calling Welzel Müller (1767-1835) from Vienna to serve as Chapelmaster and composer. Müller, who had already created Singspiels such as Das neue Sonntagskind and Zwei Schwestern von Prague and operas such as Das Sonnenfest der Braminen and Zauberzither, presented works like these along with the more predictable Rossini, Mozart, Méhul and Grétry before returning to Vienna in 1812. There his musical accompaniments contributed much to the success of Raimund's plays. This period also saw the first local operas, beginning in 1808 with Josef Rössler's Elisene, Prinzessin von Bulgaria, done in the style of Rossini. The company had two excellent Italian singers, the tenor Radicchi and the primadonna Caravoglia, but was otherwise generally undistinguished.

Müller helped to organize a Conservatory in 1811 to remedy this situation, but progress was slow, and when Weber arrived in 1813 he found almost everything had to be rebuilt--company, orchestra, costumes, and scenic stock. Still he achieved an impressive success almost at once with Spontini's Fernand Cortez, and followed it with many others. He presented seventeen new works in the first half of the following year, Italian, French, and German, among them Fidelio. He gradually improved the company and developed one primadonna of future international reputation, Henriette Sontag (1806-1854). Disturbed by the musical conservatism of the Prague public, he undertook to educate his audiences through his Dramatischmusikalischen Notizen, begun in 1815. Like so many others, however, he considered Prague only a stepping-stone to the more prestigious theatre in Vienna, and departed thence in 1816, the same year Liebich died. Sontag followed him in 1820, and though the great romantic operas were still to be introduced in Prague under Holbein and his musical director Triebensee, the great years of opera in that city were over.

In Vienna Weber found operatic interest divided between the Theater an der Wien and the Kärntnertortheater,

although the designation of the latter in 1810 as the city's
only theatre devoted exclusively to opera and the financial
support of the court made it unquestionably the dominant
musical house. After 1815, indeed, the Theater an der Wien
virtually gave up opera and emphasized ballet, particularly
the popular children's ballets directed by Friedrich Horschelt.
Between 1815 and 1821, when a scandal involving some of the
children and a Viennese aristocrat forced the enterprise to
close, Horschelt produced some twenty ballets. Among the
young dancers were Fanny Elssler and her sister, who entered the corps de ballet of the Kärntnertortheater (now
called the Hofoper) in 1819. Her debut in 1822 immediately
established Fanny as the major dancer of the theatre, a position she held until she departed for Paris in 1834 to challenge Marie Taglioni for the position of major interpreter of
the romantic ballet.

When Weber arrived the Hofoper was under the control of the Italian impresario Barbaja who scorned German
opera and worshipped Rossini. All the major offerings of
the years 1815 to 1820 here were Rossini works: Tancredi,
Otello, Barbiere di Siviglia, La gazza ladra. Since Barjaba
had assembled one of the best companies in Europe, his position was almost impregnable. His primadonna was Isabella
Colbran, later Rossini's wife, his bass Luigi Lablanche, his
baritone Antonio Tambuini, his coloratura Josephine Fodor.
Fortunately Weber was able to convince Barbaja to present
Der Freischütz (1820) to show his broadmindedness, and at
a stroke the German romantic opera was launched.

Der Freischütz was almost an anthology of romantic
motifs; its setting was a rustic village against an evocative
natural background, its major characters were a persecuted
heroine, a noble but perhaps too trusting hero, an unscrupu-
lous villain and a magnanimous prince. It offered picturesque
folk songs and dances and chilling supernatural sequences
culminating in a Walpurgisnacht, and it coordinated all its
elements into a powerful evocation of a struggle between the
forces of light and darkness. Ultimately the success of Der
Freischütz meant the end of the hundred-year domination of
Italian opera in Germany, but this battle was not easily won.
With the appearance of Weber's work the musical world of
Vienna split into opposing camps--supporters of Weber versus
supporters of Rossini, classicists versus romanticists, patrons of Italian and French opera versus German nationalists.

Barjaba distinctly heightened feelings by inviting

Rossini himself to Vienna and for a time there was a veritable Rossini cult in the city, with Rossini styles offered in
fashionable shops and Rossini dishes in the restaurants. But
at the same time Barjaba, who found the controversy extremely profitable, encouraged Weber to direct his next
opera, Euryanthe, at the Hofoper in 1823. Spontini, whose
Olympie had been quite overshadowed by Der Freischütz in
Berlin, and other rival composers had complained that this
work was really closer to Singspiel than to opera, and Weber,
always sensitive to criticism, tried to answer such charges
in his next work. Euryanthe did away with all dialogue and
used music throughout, not in the dominant fashion of Italian
opera but as an emotional unifying element looking forward
to Wagner, who in fact used the structure from Euryanthe in
Lohengrin. The opera was probably the most ambitious created in Germany between Beethoven and Wagner, but it was
not popular, and Rossini's dominance returned with the production of William Tell which shortly followed. Weber's
final work, Oberon (1826), was a step backward, a rambling,
oriental fantasy whose music was almost incidental. Even
so, Weber had so clearly established himself as the foremost German operatic composer of his time that his early
death brought the development of the genre to a sudden end,
and it was another generation before a work comparable to
Der Freischütz appeared.

Two of Germany's most popular primadonnas during
the early nineteenth century were closely associated with
Weber's works, Henriette Sontag and Wilhelmine Schröder
(1804-1860). Sontag, whose early years in Prague have already been mentioned, came to Vienna in 1820 and, although
only fourteen years of age at her arrival, had soon attracted
sufficient attention to lead Weber to create his Euryanthe for
her in 1823 and Beethoven to give her the solos in his 1824
mass. She gained much greater public acclaim in Berlin
between 1825 and 1827 and her Paris tour of 1826 made her
an international celebrity. She retired from the stage in
1830 to marry Count Rossi, but a decline in her husband's
fortunes brought her back in 1849. Her public found to their
surprise and delight that her talent had scarcely diminished,
and she toured Europe and America with great success until
her death in 1854.

Wilhelmine Schröder, daughter of the famous Sophie,
began her career as a child actress in Hamburg, and when
her parents came to Vienna in 1815 she joined Horschelt's
children's ballet. She appeared on the stage of the Burg-

theater with her mother in 1819 and then surprised her public
by suddenly and successfully turning to opera at the Hofoper
as the leading role, Agathe, in Der Freischütz. She equalled
this triumph with her interpretation of Fidelio in 1822, then
left Vienna for the Dresden stage, the opera nearest to
Vienna in significance at this time. The Dresden opera had
been directed at the opening of the century by the French
composer Ferdinand Paër, who was called to Paris in 1807
by Napoleon. His successor, Francesco Morlacchi, a champion of Italian opera, steadfastly refused to present in Dresden the works of Weber, or any of his German predecessors,
though he did allow Wilhelmine Schröder to revive her Fidelio there. This policy changed abruptly in 1823 when
Morlacchi was replaced by Heinrich Marschner (1795-1861),
a disciple of Weber. Der Freischütz and Euryanthe were
given as soon as they could be prepared, along with Marschner's own works, most of them, like Der Vampyr (1828)
studies of the supernatural with grotesque comic elements.
Wilhelmine Schröder remained in Dresden for twenty-four
years, though like Sontag she toured widely, to great acclaim. Unfortunately she did not preserve her ability in her
later years as Sontag did, and her popularity and fame departed long before her death in 1860.

After 1830 the emphasis in both opera and ballet
shifted gradually but steadily toward Paris. Ludwig Spohr
continued for a time the tradition of Italianate opera, and in
the 1830s Donizetti appeared to fill the void left by Rossini,
but it was the French, such as Herold, Adam, and then
Meyerbeer, who dominated the German opera stage of the
1830s and 1840s, while Marschner and other native composers
were ignored. It seemed until the appearance of Wagner that
Weber had succeeded in driving the Italians from German
opera houses only to make way for the French.

Notes to Part I

1. A. Genast, Aus Weimars klassischer und nachklas-
    sischer Zeit (Stuttgart, 1904), I, 89-90.

2. But when we consider that harmony
    In the whole performance is the only thing that will serve
    To stimulate your approval, that each actor,
    Each voice, all working together
    Should present to you a beautiful whole,
    Then fear springs up in our breasts.

3. "Eröffnung des Weimarischen theaters, " Werke, XL
    (Weimar, 1901), 11.

4. "Einige Scenen aus Mahomet nach Voltaire, " Werke,
    XL (Weimar, 1901), 67.

5. J. Wahle, Das Weimarer Theater unter Goethes Leitung
    (Weimar, 1892), 166.

6. K. von Holtei, Der Salon für Literatur, Kunst, und
    Gesellschaft, III (Berlin, 1870), 679.

7. Moon-besplendoured magic night,
    Holding the senses captive,
    Fairy world, filled with wonder,
    Arise in your ancient glory.

8. See his Kritische Schriften und dramaturgische Blätter
    (Leipzig, 1850), II, 208-32.

9. J. Eichendorff, Werke (Stuttgart, 1957), III, 243-44.

10. E. Devrient, Geschichte der Deutschen Schauspielkunst
    (Berlin, 1905), II, 99

11. Letter to Goethe of September 7, 1803, Briefwechsel
    zwischen Goethe und Zelter (Berlin, 1833), I, 84.

12. A. Klingemann, Kunst und Natur (Braunschweig, 1828),
    III, 344.

13. Devrient, Geschichte, II, 185.

14. G. Altman, Ludwig Devrient (Berlin, 1926), 194ff.

15. A. von Wolzogen, Aus Schinkels Nachlass (Berlin,
    1862-63), II, 209.

16. Koller, Aphorismen für Schauspieler und Freunde auf
    dem damaligen Kunst (Regensburg, 1804), 245.

17. Schreyvogel, Tagebücher (Berlin, 1903), II, 42.

18. Kunst und Natur, I, 345.

19. C. Costenoble, Aus dem Burgtheater (Vienna, 1889),
    II, 133.

20. "Selbstbiographie, " Sämtliche Werke, I, 16 (Vienna, 1925), 127.

21. Letter of Feb. -March, 1818, Sämtliche Werke (Vienna, 1909-1952), III (Briefe und Dokumente), I, 98.

22. Letter of August 3, 1818, K. W. F. Solger, Nachgelassene Schriften (Leipzig, 1826), I, 653.

23. Schreyvogel, Tagebücher, II, 364.

24. K. Kahl, Raimund (Velber, 1967), 49.

25. See H. Kindermann, Ferdinand Raimund (Vienna, 1940), 319ff.

26. G. Parthey, Jugenderinnerungen (Berlin, 1907), II, 378.

27. Letter to Goethe of September 17, 1827, Briefwechsel, IV, 378.

II. THE VIRTUOSO PERIOD
1830-1870

In comparison with the stimulating theatrical period
just completed, the period after 1830 provides a generally depressing picture. The great creative drive which had invigo-
rated the German stage since the <u>Sturm</u> <u>und</u> <u>Drang</u> was apparently exhausted. Most theatres were now managed by
bureaucratic appointees from conservative courts, or were
dependent entirely upon commercial success, neither alternative likely to produce innovative theatre. The public also
encouraged caution and conservatism. In Germany, as in
France, the political and social upheavals at the turn of the
century had brought new audiences into the theatre, audiences
not acquainted with the theatrical or literary tradition and inclined to view the stage only as a form of light entertainment. Still, it was fashionable to be able to discuss the
plays seen with some facility, and for a public rather unsure
of its critical abilities, an almost inevitable development was
the powerful theatre reviewer. In Paris the first such dominant figure was a stern former professor of rhetoric,
Geoffroy, but German audiences generally tended to ignore
critics with literary backgrounds such as Tieck or Schreyvogel in favor of journalists like the Berliners Saphir and
Oettinger. Such reviewers even at best were more interested
in displaying their wit than discussing the plays, and at worst
their reviews contained little more than theatre gossip and
scandal. The influence of this sort of public and this sort of
critic encouraged actors to rely on personality rather than
artistry and on employing claques to influence public opinion.

Such developments had clear financial implications.
Reviewers, their friends, and the claques all required free
seats and this appreciably decreased any theatre's income.
Any intendant was thus forced either to gear all his productions toward box office success or to find a prince or duke
who from artistic interest or the hope of future glory would
continually support an unprofitable venture. Unfortunately,
the rulers of the period were not generally more elevated in
their taste than the general public, and so were inclined to
support only the sort of offerings which would probably have

91

been commercial successes without their aid. Most theatres
therefore had no real option but to give way to popular taste,
and this raised problems not all of which were artistic.
Though the public could best be attracted by popular actors
and striking scenic effects, both became steadily more expensive. The smaller provincial houses soon realized that
they could make more profit by importing a well-known guest
artist to play with even a mediocre company than by maintaining an established ensemble with no outstanding name in
it. A fierce competition began for the popular actors, reinforced the personality cults, and encouraged the decline of
many of the quite good regional companies which had developed throughout Germany in the early part of the century.

     Once begun, this process became increasingly waste-
ful and seemingly irreversible. In the days of Iffland, a
guest artist might stay in a theatre for months, even years.
Now both the desire for novelty and the great expense of
bringing a major artist prevented this. Guest appearances
were brief, actors were expected to perform certain popular
parts, and most leading actors would perform perhaps only
three roles regularly. Even these few soon became highly
mannered virtuoso interpretations, since they would be given
with little or no rehearsal time and with a supporting local
cast as unfamiliar to the star as it was inferior to him. Not
even a major theatre city like Berlin could escape these unfortunate developments, and the situation there became so
distressing that even Seydelmann, an actor notorious for his
disregard of ensemble playing, was led to complain:

> Give us back artistic ensembles and a commonality
> of interest and we will submit to them; now, how-
> ever, when talent is totally subordinated to personal
> caprice and the only satisfaction an actor can get in
> the theatre is that of personal gain, such an un-
> profitable sacrifice would be foolish for him. [1]

     Against this generally depressing background a few
theatres nevertheless stand out either as continuing the best
traditions of the romantic period or preparing the way for
the impressive achievements of the German stage at the end
of the century. The most important of the former was the
Düsseldorf theatre under Immermann, whose work in the
1830's was probably the most important of that decade in
Germany. The same decade saw the development in literature of Young Germany, a movement which had much to do
with introducing the political and social concerns of the sub-

sequent realist theatre, but between the revolutionary years of 1830 and 1848, Metternichian conservatism still dominated the cultural life of Germany. Young Germany's passion for freedom and social change inevitably aroused official wrath. Many members of the movement were forced into exile, and until Metternich's fall in 1848, few Young Germany plays could be publicly presented. After 1848, Gutzkow, one of the leaders of the movement, became dramaturg of the Dresden theatre, which made an important contribution by presenting his plays and those of Otto Ludwig, one of the period's best dramatists.

Two other young men associated, but less closely, with Young Germany, emerged after 1850 as the major theatrical directors of Germany. Heinrich Laube and Franz von Dingelstedt stand not only historically but artistically at the pivot point of the nineteenth-century German stage. Each developed certain traditional concerns--Laube the simplified staging of Tieck and Immermann and Weimar's elevated style and emphasis on diction, Dingelstedt the Berlin concern for spectacle and pageantry along with the romantic interest in Shakespeare and Goethe's in the German classics. Both fought the bureaucracy and commercialism of the theatre of their day, and the emphasis on the virtuoso actor at the expense of the ensemble. Together they did much to prepare the way for the modern idea of the director and the unity of a theatrical production. Laube was associated primarily with the Vienna Burgtheater. Dingelstedt succeeded him there, but worked earlier in Munich and Weimar as well, where he introduced the works of Germany's outstanding mid-century dramatist, Hebbel.

Although the opera (and after 1850 the operetta) was a far more popular form in Germany at mid-century than the spoken drama, no German composer of note had appeared since Weber. Here too a major innovator at last appeared, Richard Wagner, but his departure from tradition was far more violent and shocking than those of Laube and Dingelstedt, and if his subsequent fame was far greater, the chronicle of his activities during these years is one of constant frustrations and setbacks. Only after 1870, thirty-five years after the performance of his first work, was the full force of Wagner's impact on the theatre felt.

1. Immermann and Düsseldorf

Only one German theatre director during the 1830s
attempted with any degree of success to revive something of
the spirit of Goethe, Tieck, or Schreyvogel in these un-
promising times.   This was the writer Karl Leberecht Immermann (1796-1840), who led the theatre in Düsseldorf from
1832 to 1837.   His novel, Die Epigonen (1836), gave its name
to a whole group of authors of which he was the outstanding
example, authors painfully conscious that theirs was a transitional generation.   Neither of the dominant literary schools
of the day was acceptable to them; romanticism they found
too vague and other-worldly, the patriotic Young Germany
movement seemed too inclined to artless propaganda.   They
looked back wistfully to the classicism of Goethe and Schiller,
all too aware that as epigones, "late-born ones, " their generation would never savor the joys of Weimar or Jena in
their great days.   The major contributions of this movement
to dramatic literature were Grillparzer's late plays such as
Sappho, Das goldene Vliess and Des Meeres und der Liebe
Wellen, and Immermann's Faustian Merlin (1832), Andreas
Hofer (1833) and the trilogy Alexis (1836), dealing with his
somewhat confused reaction to the revolution of 1830.

It was not as a playwright, however, but as a director
that Immermann made his major contribution to the German
stage.   He settled in Düsseldorf in 1827, a young poet with
a modest reputation and all his major works still ahead of
him.   He soon became acquainted with the city's artistic
elite, composed mainly of painters and headed by Wilhelm
Schadow, since Düsseldorf's most important cultural establishment was its notable Academy of Art.   The city had a theatre building, but no permanent troupe.   The traveling
Derossi company normally spent most of the winter there,
and presented in 1829 an early version of Immermann's
Andreas Hofer.   In 1832 Immermann wrote an epilogue for
and helped to stage a commemorative production of Goethe's
Clavigo, but in general he and his circle found the offerings
of the Derossi troupe too trivial to engage their interest.

The example of Goethe, however, stimulated Immermann to dream of establishing a theatre of more artistic respectability in Düsseldorf, and though the court showed no
particular interest in such a project, Immermann formed an
artistic society to work toward it.   When the old theatre was
condemned and a new one built in 1832, Immermann's society
managed to gain control over it.   Derossi became their

tenant, and in addition to exercising a certain control over
his repertoire and personnel, they required that each year
the theatre present up to twelve "model productions" (Mustervorstellungen), to serve as artistic guides for theatres
elsewhere. Immermann became dramaturg and regisseur for
this venture, which gained money by the selling of subscriptions. The Düsseldorf public was delighted with his first
productions, Emilia Galotti, Calderon's The Constant Prince,
Kleist's Prinz von Homburg, and Schröder's Stille Wasser
sind tief. Immermann thus demonstrated that productions of
artistic merit could also be popular, and the citizens of Düsseldorf could now boast of a theatre as significant as their
beloved Academy. Immermann invited Mendelssohn to come
to direct opera and in 1834 he produced distinguished offerings of Mozart and Cherubini while Immermann presented
Egmont, Die Braut von Messina, Nathan der Weise, and his
own Andreas Hofer.

In achieving his great initial success, Immermann
made no pretense of establishing anything new, but said he
was continuing the tradition which had begun with Neuber and
led through Goethe's work at Weimar. He insisted that the
rebirth of the German stage required no revolutionary insight
but simply the determination to combat the inertia, careless-
ness, vanity, and egoism which prevented its regular development. Still, the particular emphases Immermann placed on
his work, while derived from Goethe, were both novel and
significant. Most important was his concern with the primacy
of the regisseur, and in his writings we find clearly set forward for the first time the theatrical approach that would
lead ultimately to such master-regisseurs as Reinhardt. "The
poet's work springs from a single mind, " he wrote.

> Therefore the reproduction of it obviously must also
> come from a single mind. I therefore begin by
> reading the play to be given to my actors. Then
> I have a special reading rehearsal with each, out
> of which grow the general reading rehearsals. If
> disparities in interpretation appear then, the awk-
> ward places are touched up. If nothing else helps,
> I myself demonstrate how they are to be done until
> the interpretation of the whole is correct. [2]

The emphasis on carefully prepared line readings
shows a clear influence from Goethe, but the next step in
preparation, the "room rehearsals" (Zimmerproben) was Immermann's own:

I set the action in room rehearsals of a single act
or even a pair of scenes. This is done in an
empty room where the bare walls challenge the
actor to exert his imagination and escape the ghosts
which haunt every German stage--those demons
bombast, rhetoric, and artificiality. After the
work is prepared here, without illusionistic crutches,
I take my actors to the theatre. The play is not
given until everyone, down to the butler who does
the announcing, has established his role as well as
nature and industry allow it to be done. [3]

The goal of the room rehearsals was a complete immersion
in the part which anticipated techniques of Stanislavsky, but
the lengthy preparatory work used in the Moscow Art Theatre
would have staggered Immermann. For Emilia Galotti, one
of his most carefully prepared offerings, there was one reading of the play, several individual reading sessions with leading actors, one general reading rehearsal, four room rehearsals and two rehearsals on stage before performance.
That this was considered unusually extensive preparation by
Immermann's contemporaries is an indication of the general
state of rehearsal practice at the time.

      For his early productions, Immermann followed the
usual practice of importing leading actors, Franz Grua (1799-
1867) for The Constant Prince, Karl Seydelmann for Nathan
der Weise, Carl Weymar (1803-1839) for Andreas Hofer. By
1834, however, he had developed a company which he worked
into an ensemble dedicated to the plays they presented rather
than to personal aggrandizement. The key members were the
tragedienne Frau Lauber-Versing (1811-1879), the leading men
Friedrich Schenk (1825-1858) and Karl Jenke (1809-1886),
Wilhelm Henkel (1788-1853), who did older men, and the
character actors Wilhelm Reger (1804-1857) and Franz Hoppé
(1810-1849). This company under Immermann's direction
presented a total of 355 productions in four years, and though
his own interest was in plays of literary significance, almost
every sort of drama available to a theatre of the time was
represented. One-third of the offerings were opera, though
Mendelssohn quarreled with Immermann after a single season
and left, to be replaced by the less notable Julius Rietz.
Only sixty-five productions were of classics or major modern
works. The rest were the standard light fare of the times,
including such popular new forms as the horror play (Schau-
erdrama), imported from France, and the native German
Liederposse. There were even programs of living pictures,

concerts, French dancers and actors, and public balls.

Most of the major plays Immermann gave had been
given before in Dresden, Weimar, or Vienna; here too he
was the epigone, keeping alive the old tradition rather than
breaking new ground. Among the few new works he presented were three by Calderon, an author particularly well
suited to his interpretations, which tended to favor literary
values over mimetic ones, and the symbolic over the real.
Immermann saw the theatre as a kind of illustration of a
text, contending that one of the major weaknesses of the
German stage of his day was that actors placed themselves
above the text and sought to make something out of it when
on the contrary they should let the text make something out
of them. Given too much freedom by indulgent directors and
public, actors had changed from "interpretative organs for
the thoughts of the poet into independently producing gen-
iuses."[4] This concern led Immermann frequently to break
with traditional interpretations, not to gain new values from
the text, but to present its surface meaning more clearly.
No German director before him treated authors with such
respect. He restored most of the magical and musical scenes
which Klingemann had cut from Faust I in 1829 and presented
parts of Hamlet, most notably the pantomime in the Players'
scene, which had never before been seen on the German stage.

Schadow and Theodore Hildebrant, Immermann's
friends from the Academy, aided him in achieving striking
effects in staging and lighting. The posed scenes so important in eighteenth century production were central to Immermann's theatre as well, and he speaks proudly in his
diary not only of the tableaux created for him by prominent
Düsseldorf artists, but of others based on famous paintings:
a Rembrandt in Faust, a Raphael in Calderon's Wonderwork-
ing Magus. It is therefore not surprising that he considered
evenings of living pictures posed by his company as excellent
training. Given this painterly inclination, Immerman's productions varied widely in technique, since he believed in
suiting the staging to the style of the play as he conceived it.
His Shakespearian productions were spare and severe, his
Calderon ones as elaborate and ostentatious as his painters
and machinists could make them. The battle scene in Macbeth was suggested by off-stage noises, that in The Constant
Prince by a chorale, but for Die Räuber and Wallenstein he
created realistic and detailed mass scenes which anticipated
the Meininger:

I saw to it that every one of my Wallensteiner was
in the right spot at the right time. ... I showed a
man now from the front and now from the rear, now
in this position and now in that, now in relationship
to this comrade, and now in a group with others. ...
I developed for the various scenes a formal stra-
tegic plan which allowed groups and crowds to move
naturally yet which were based upon the poetic moments in the script. Thus it happened that the
spectator's eye would be drawn to the person speaking, the bearer of the plot, while in the background
other soldiers could be observed moving to and
fro. [5]

Immermann's most famous production actually came
after his official retirement from the Düsseldorf stage, but
it was a culmination of interest pursued all during these
years. In the late 1820's he became involved with the presentation of single Shakespearian scenes for the Academy
circle and through these was led to a study of Tieck's theories of simplified Elizabethan staging. In 1831 he sketched
a modified Shakespearian stage based on Tieck's ideas which
was essentially a semi-circular playing area thrust out
among the spectators with a simple relief stage behind. Such
a stage fitted in well with his conviction that one of the reasons for the decay of theatre in Germany was the belief of
theatre directors that all plays of every sort had to be given
spectacular and costly productions to attract audiences. The
idea of simplified staging influenced all eight of Immermann's
Shakespearian productions, though he made no attempt to build
a special stage for them until he came out of retirement to
direct a special private performance of Twelfth Night just before his death in 1840. The stage for this production, created by the architect Wiegmann, actually suggested a Roman
theatre more than an Elizabethan, but it followed Tieck's
vision in being architectural rather than illusionistic, suitable
for a variety of scenes, and united with the auditorium. Two
steps led from the audience up to the main acting area, a relief stage with arch entrances at either end. In the center
was a small inner stage with a door and archway at either
side.

Despite the support of a faithful public and the favorable attention Immerman was drawing to Düsseldorf from outside, his theatre had to close in 1837. He had manged to
demonstrate that a major theatre could in fact operate on an
artistic and literary rather than a purely financial basis, but

the struggle was wearing and the absence of even token support from the court discouraged him.

He probably could have kept his experiment going for some time beyond 1837, but by then he had presented most of the scripts which interested him from the tradition, and without some relief from financial concerns he was disinclined to continue his efforts. He expressed a willingness to do so elsewhere in Germany, but was met by indifference everywhere, and so disbanded his society. Derossi resumed his irregular possession of the Düsseldorf stage and Immermann devoted himself full time to his writing. A few months after his departure from the theatre, however, this sole major director of the decade wrote bitterly:

> Now winter has come and I first truly suffer the loss of my fine theatre. What sorrow it is to see something go under to which one has given years of devotion and for which one has struggled until his hair turned grey. How furious I become when I consider that among the thirty-six ducal stages of Germany there is not one that is willing to give modest support to a well-equipped theatre with a classic repertoire and an established tradition and organization. Yet everywhere inferior royal theatres are supported at enormous expense. [6]

2. Dresden and Young Germany

The literary generation which emerged in Germany in the 1830's was widely varied in taste, talent, and temperament, but certain forces and events turned the thoughts of the entire group in similar directions. Some of these forces had little to do with the specific situation in Germany. Travel and communication were becoming noticeably easier through much of Europe; presses proliferated, new daily journals replaced the old almanacs, monthlies, and weeklies, resulting in a greater feeling of immediacy and contact with political and social events locally and nationally. Another general force was an increasing consciousness of scientific advance, new theories and discoveries being brought to the average man in Germany regularly by such popular scientific writers as Alexander von Humboldt, Helmholtz, Dubois-Reymond, and Liebig. The schools, under the influence of Pestalozzi, laid new stress on the relation between abstract

learning and the concrete facts of daily life, so that students
began to consider the immediate relevance of all theory. The
bases of scientism and positivism were being laid even while
romanticism dominated the literary scene. Ludwig Börne's
(1784-1837) pamphlet Leben und Wissenschaft provided a representative statement of the new trend: "all perception of
truth is destined to become reality in life, and every reality
of life is destined to become the object of scientific consideration. "[7]

The drive to unite learning and life was conditioned
in a particular way in Germany by the oppressive conservatism of the Metternich period. Universities were policed and
contemporary references forbidden as rigorously there as they
were in the theatre. Many of Börne's writings were banned,
and he was forced eventually to take refuge in Paris. The
French Revolution of 1830 profoundly stirred most young
German writers of the time. Gutzkow, one of the leaders of
this generation, later confessed that although he was then an
honor student in philosophy at the University of Berlin, he
had never read a newspaper in his life until he was inspired
to do so by the events of 1830. For such students the translation of abstract learning into terms of everyday experience
and contemporary politics now became a burning concern.
Their enthusiasm reached a peak in a series of rallies and
mass meetings held in Southern Germany in the summer of
1832, but the effect of these meetings on contemporary German politics was as slight as the demonstrations which had
aroused Kotzebue's anger fifteen years before. The authorities banned further rallies and arrested many leaders of the
movement. Many frustrated liberals were forced to go into
exile, the most famous of these being Heine, who joined
Börne in Paris. Others led a more cautious existence at
home. But both carried on the struggle for a more liberal
political system through pamphlets or political statements in
the guise of poetry and drama.

A disparate group of writers emerged from this situation, but they shared a keen interest in political life, indeed in life in all its aspects, and a scorn for repression in
society and for abstraction and illusion in art. They condemned the vagueness and the medievalism of the late romantics which they felt had supported the conservative status
quo by avoiding contemporary questions. The most important
manifestos of the new writers were Ludolf Wienbarg's series
of lectures at the University of Kiel, published as Aesthetische Feldzüge (1834) and Gutzkow's essay Über Goethe in

<u>Wendepunkte zweier Jahrhundert</u> (1836). The movement was
christened <u>Das junge Deutschland</u> by the critic Adolf Menzel,
who, noting that Wienbarg's book was dedicated "to Young
Germany," applied the label to most of the politically involved writers of the time. He named as leaders of the
group Heinrich Heine (1797-1856), Karl Gutzkow (1811-1878),
Heinrich Laube (1806-1884), Wienbarg, and Theodore Mundt.

The major author of Young Germany was Heine, but
his dramatic output was slight. Gutzkow and Laube were the
most significant dramatists of this group, and by mid-century
they had moved to positions of major importance in the German repertoire, despite considerable official suspicion of
their work. Since their plays were so closely associated
with the particular political situation of the time, they were
soon forgotten. No study of the contribution of Young Germany to the theatre has ever appeared, and this is most unfortunate, for although Laube and Gutzkow's plays were undistinguished enough, they contributed significantly to the development of the realistic drama later in the century and less
directly to the politically engaged theatres of more recent
times. It was Young Germany that turned the theatre toward
modern social problems, that insisted that theatre, as Mundt
put it, become "engaged in reality," which meant in the
activities of its time. Young Germany brought to the theatre
the scientific spirit, the technical, documented, "real" use of
material, an emphasis also on "real" people. The grandiose
figures of the romantic theatre were now replaced by persons
from everyday life, presented as accurately as social and
psychological theory and observation would allow. In structure, as distinct from subject matter, the French interest of
Young Germany resulted in the introduction into Germany of
the technique of such dramatic craftsmen as Scribe, so that
the drama of social realism which evolved in both countries
at mid-century was built upon the solid technical foundation
of what the French called the <u>pièce</u> <u>bien</u> <u>faite</u>--the well-made
play.

The manifestos of the movement, as is often the case
with manifestos, did not always lay stress either on these
ultimate contributions of the movement or on the specific
practice of contributing authors at the time the manifestos
were written, but the relation between the results actually
achieved and the goals proposed is generally clear. Wienbarg made essentially three demands of contemporary literature. First it should have a "national spirit," meaning not
the mystic nationalism of the romantics, but a calculated

appeal to the liberal, democratic aspirations of the people as
a whole. This was a significant step on the path from the
rather elitist view of the German literary theatre of the
eighteenth century to the increasingly populist view of the
nineteenth. Wienbarg had no intention, however, of pander-
ing to the masses nor of artistically elevating them. Like
Brecht a century later, he aspired to make them politically
and socially aware, not to imbue them with a specific point
of view but to inspire them "to engage in the conflicts of the
time. " He insisted that the theatre be rigorous, but never
esoteric.

His second requirement was that the theatre be national in a somewhat different sense--that it deal with themes
of interest to the entire nation. He expressed strong dis-
satisfaction with the historical plays of Goethe, Schiller, and
their followers, which were national, he maintained, only in
subject matter, not in their basic concerns. This fine distinction was in fact much debated in Wienbarg's generation.
Wienbarg explained that historical subjects were possible if
they showed "the eternal in human nature the same in every
age. " Everyone could agree on dismissing Raupach's histories on these grounds, since they were virtually devoid of
content anyway, but Schiller and Shakespeare caused more
difficulty. Some participants in the movement shunned all
history plays as unfit for a theatre engaged in the contemporary scene, while others, less philosophical and perhaps
more political, used historical subjects with immediate political relevance, as a pragmatic device for avoiding censorship.

This leads naturally to Wienbarg's third requirement,
since all were inter-related, and that was that every theatre
must closely reflect its own times. Wienbarg likened his
own generation to the authors of the Sturm und Drang, engaged in the same struggle to renew art and maintain its
relevance. Gutzkow's Zeitgenossen (1837) reached a parallel
conclusion, that the task of literature was to express the
spirit of the times and to aid in the reorientation of social
issues. The concept of the Zeitgeist is found everywhere in
these writers, and expresses as well as any single idea their
diversity and their dilemma. They agreed that their duty
was to reflect their times, but they also agreed that these
times were transitional. Refusing to look back like the Epigones, and often discouraged by the barriers to the new
period of the German spirit they hoped to find ahead, they
often felt, as Wienbarg expressed it, "insecure even in their

own skins. " Few escaped the emotional stresses he graphically described: "the noblest spirits of our time so frequently feel loss of hope, restlessness, doubt, inner strife,
all those plagues of mankind, reborn in us nightly. And yet
our hope must remain greater than our fear. "[8]

The careers of the two major dramatists of Young
Germany, Gutzkow and Laube, provide interesting parallels.
Both began as students of philosophy and religion and were
struck like many of their generation by the chasm between
these abstract studies and the social problems of the time.
Both then turned to journalism and to the writing of political
novels, pleading for moral and social emancipation, which
earned them both jail sentences in the early 1830's. Finally,
both eventually turned to dramaturgy where they achieved
their major success. Their later careers sharply diverged.
Laube became director of the Burgtheater in Vienna and increasingly conservative in viewpoint, while Gutzkow, after a
rather brief connection with the Dresden stage, renounced the
theatrical establishment and remained a revolutionary to the
end.

Laube's interest in the theatre developed from his exposure to Seydelmann, appearing as guest artist in Breslau
where Laube was a theology student. He did not begin writing plays however until after serving a sentence for his political novel Das junge Europa (1833). Traveling in Paris
after his release, he found in the salon plays and the romantic tragedies of the time both inspiration and models.
His first play, Mondaleschi, was already completed when he
returned to Germany and was premiered with great success
in Strassburg in 1841. In subject it was a typical Young
Germany historical drama, purporting to tell the story of a
hero murdered by Queen Christina of Sweden but actually
bristling with references to Germany of the 1830's. What
assured its success, aside from its author's notoriety, was
its unusually careful construction. Through its example and
Laube's subsequent works in the same genre, French technique entered the drama of Young Germany. All of Laube's
plays were weak in character motivation, strong in democratic ideals, and far too burdened with contemporary references to enjoy a long existence, though Die Karlsschüler
(1846) fared somewhat better than the others due to its subject, the sufferings of the young Schiller in conflict with a
reactionary Duke over Die Räuber.

Not surprisingly, Laube's plays were banned in much

of Germany during the 1840's, but the revolution of 1848 brought an abrupt change in his fortunes.   In Vienna Metternich, the pillar of reactionary absolutism, was deposed, liberal and democratic ideals were proclaimed for every civic institution including the Burgtheater, and Laube, an obvious representative of these ideals and one of the best known theatre figures of Germany, was invited to become its director.   His important contributions to the Viennese theatre in this post from 1848 until 1867, however, led him gradually but clearly away from Young Germany.

Gutzkow's literary career began with his novel Wally die Zweiflerin (1835), a plea for the emancipation of women. This was a popular concern with Young Germany writers, though hardly their exclusive property in the 1830's.   Friedrich Halm, a popular Viennese closer in spirit to Grillparzer than to Gutzkow, launched his dramatic career in 1834 with Griseldis which reversed the ancient legend, making its heroine refuse to accept her husband's brutality and speak out instead for decency and dignity in the relationship between man and wife.   Gutzkow was much more eclectic than Laube in his early plays.   Nero (1835) was an Aristophanic tragicomedy, Hamlet in Wittenberg (1835) a Faustian fantasy, and König Saul (1839) a more traditional reworking of historical material, with David clearly representing Gutzkow's generation and Saul the old order.

Gutzkow felt a strong obligation to this generation, and his most important ultimate contribution to the German theatre during the 1830's was surely his arranging for the publication of Georg Büchner's (1813-1837) Dantons Tod in 1835.   Though Gutzkow asserted that the work showed great talent, he was probably more taken by its revolutionary sentiments and subject than by its literary merit.   Certainly he considered it unfit for the stage, a view shared by all German producers for the rest of the century.   Büchner was in many respects the Kleist of this new generation.   He stood apart from Young Germany as Kleist had stood apart from the romantics, even while submitting to some of their influence.   Like Kleist he died tragically young, before witnessing the social upheavals which his work seemed to anticipate.   Like Kleist also he went almost totally unrecognized in his own lifetime yet became eventually hailed as one of the major German dramatists of the century.

Büchner's memoires say little of any early theatrical experience and his unconcern for standard stage practice

which nineteenth century producers found so baffling suggests
that he had little. He grew up in Darmstadt, which had a
popular and productive theatre at least until the death of
Ludwig I in 1830. In his early years, however, the major
emphasis was on opera, and later, the director Küstner
offered some guest stars--Esslair, Sontag, and Seydelmann--
but relied generally on rather undistinguished light opera and
comedy presented by a mediocre company. From 1831 until
1834 when Büchner began writing, the theatre was closed entirely. He drew attention to himself in 1834 with a pamphlet, Hessischer Landbote, which thirteen years before the
Communist Manifesto outlined in similar fashion the inevitable conflict between poverty and riches. The revolutionary
implications of the work aroused predictable official wrath
and Büchner was forced to seek refuge in Strassburg. Not
surprisingly, this pamphlet caused Büchner to be associated
in official minds with Young Germany, but in fact he was far
more radical in his pessimism than such writers as the
easy-going Gutzkow. Even the Hessischer Landbote specifically condemned such typical Young Germany aspirations as
the gradual cultural uplifting of the masses, and his plays
and letters make even clearer his scorn for such social in-
volvement. "Only a total misconception of our social situation, " he observed dryly, "could permit us to believe that
current literature could result in a complete transformation
of our religious and social ideals. "[9]

It was therefore hardly surprising that Büchner dis-
regarded a suggestion from Gutzkow that he join those authors
dealing with political problems in literary terms. In his
fundamental assumptions about art, Büchner had much in
common with Wienbarg. He too insisted that it must reflect
real life and not some idealized vision. But while this implied for Wienbarg an art made relevant to social and political questions, for Büchner it meant an art which faithfully
reflected life as he saw it, the beautiful and ugly alike. His
assumptions are clearly expressed in a striking letter written
to his family in 1835:

> If someone should say to me that the poet should
> not show the world as it is, but as it ought to be,
> then I would reply that I will not make it better
> than the Good Lord, who certainly must have made
> it as it ought to be. It seems to me that the so-
> called idealist poets have given us nothing but
> marionettes with sky-blue noses and affected pathos,
> not human beings of flesh and blood who make us

feel their joy and sorrow with them and whose
deeds and actions fill us with revulsion or admiration. In short, I have great fondness for Goethe
or Shakespeare, but very little for Schiller. [10]

Such observations make it clear why Büchner was
later regarded as a forerunner of the naturalists, but if he
shared with them a determination to bring the whole range of
life under artistic scrutiny, with perhaps even a special interest in those areas hitherto considered offensive, in certain
critical ways he was as far from the naturalists as from
Young Germany. Nowhere is this more clearly seen than in
his injection of his own philosophy into his dramas, a kind
of subjectivity that naturalistic theory deplored. Clearly
Büchner himself speaks through his hero Danton, as a comparison of the play with the poet's letters unmistakably demonstrates. In this central figure of the French Revolution,
Büchner found a paradigm for his own dark view of the human
condition. While the play was still taking shape in his mind
he wrote to his fiancée:

> I have been studying the history of the Revolution.
> I feel as though I have been crushed beneath the
> fatalism of History. I find in human nature a
> terrifying sameness, and in the human condition
> an inexorable force, granted to all and to none.
> The individual is no more than foam on the wave,
> greatness mere chance, the mastery of genius a
> puppet show, a ridiculous struggle against a brazen
> law, which to acknowledge is our highest achieve-
> ment, which to master is impossible. [11]

This vision helps to explain the striking passivity of
Büchner's hero. He shows Danton in his last days, when his
role in the Revolution has been played out--all but the dying.
Danton alone sees the futility of all that has happened, the
mindless working out of forces beyond his control or com-
prehension. He stands as a contemplative commentator, surrounded by the bustle of a rich variety of characters engaged
in working out the delusion of meaningful action which Danton
has escaped. Even more than by this curious hero Büchner's
contemporaries were puzzled by his flexible dialogue and his
pattern of staccato scenes, both the result of his attempt to
capture the disjointed rhythms and the fleeting impressions
of life itself. From a later vantage point we can see in his
ironic juxtaposition of scenes and in the rich mosaic Büchner
weaves from them a sense of form similar to that of Goethe

or Shakespeare, but to the theatre directors of the 1830's these scenes seemed truncated, fitful, and arbitrary. A theatre opened in Zurich in 1834, the same year the traveling exile arrived there, but his offer of his new play was brusquely refused.

Büchner's second play, Leonce und Lena, fared no better, though it was cast in the more attractive form of a romantic comedy. The depth of characterization here never approaches that in Dantons Tod. Even the leading figures are a sort of Pierrot and Columbine, abstracted from reality and cultivating a life of voluptuous languor. The play has been dismissed as a casual etude in the style of Musset, but beneath its porcelain-doll surface there are serious concerns. Though its characters and situation are romantic, Büchner's exaggeration and ironic distancing make the play an attack on its romantic and idealistic roots. Deeper still, it continues to develop its author's fatalistic view of history. Leonce and Lena, lacking Danton's insight, blissfully assume they can exert their free will and avoid a preordained marriage, but they are pulled to their destiny as inexorably as the heroes of classic tragedy.

Büchner's final work, Woyzeck, was left uncompleted at his death, but despite (indeed in part because of) its fragmentary form, it has exerted a tremendous influence on later drama. Here Büchner returned to a serious view of man caught in and destroyed by the incomprehensible racing machine that is the world, but Woyzeck is no Danton. No trace of the insight or the stature of Büchner's first hero can be found in him. Woyzeck goes to his doom like a calf to slaughter, and his tragedy is played out not against a great social upheaval but against the everyday world of a small town and its military barracks. The abrupt individual scenes and the jagged language are far more marked here than in Dantons Tod, and each scene, as Brecht proposed for his Epic theatre, makes a striking statement on its own and yet comments on the rest. Suggestions of almost every significant subsequent dramatic movement can be found in this remarkable play. It is the first and one of the most successful attempts to achieve one of the ideals of naturalist drama, the depiction of the tragedy of a common man prevented from realizing his greatest potential by the forces of his society and environment. The striking juxtapositions, fragmented dialogue, rapid movement, and pushing of realism to the grotesque were all techniques developed by the expressionists, and later by Brecht, whose debt to Büchner was great.

Finally, in its despair and its conviction of the futility of
human action, Woyzeck prefigures the world of such modern
absurdists as Beckett. Danton, Büchner's most verbal and
perceptive character, gives to Julie a description which could
fit Woyzeck or indeed any of the inhabitants of Büchner's dark
world:

> What is this in us that lies, whores, steals, and
> murders?--What are we but puppets, manipulated
> on wires by unknown powers? We are nothing,
> nothing in ourselves: we are the swords that spirits
> fight with--except no one sees the hands--just as in
> fairy tales. [12]

Unfortunately Büchner had no Tieck to champion his
work after his death, and after Gutzkow arranged for the
publication of Dantons Tod it was virtually forgotten. Critics
who mentioned it at all generally dismissed it as a minor
precursor of the host of dramas on revolutionary subjects
produced by Young Germany after 1850 such as Gutzkow's
Wullenweber and Karl Robert Griepenkerl's (1810-1868) Robespierre (1851) and Die Girondisten (1852). Only one of
Büchner's plays was produced during the entire nineteenth
century, Leonce und Lena at Max Halbe's Intimes Theater in
Munich in 1885. Even Max Martersteig's comprehensive
Deutsche Theater im neunzehnten Jahrhundert (1904), which
devotes six pages to Kleist, gives Büchner only three sentences, and those in a paragraph otherwise devoted to the
now forgotten dramatist Michel Beer. Only with the coming
of Max Reinhardt and the expressionist movement of our own
century were the theatrical possibilities of Büchner's work
first realized.

Gutzkow's own career in the theatre began in 1839
with the striking success of his first produced play, Richard
Savage, in Frankfurt. Other stages were soon offering this
rather sentimentalized story of a preromantic poet struggling
against unjust class distinctions. The characterization was
weak and the incidents contrived, but the contemporary relevance and the honesty of its passion allowed audiences of its
own time to overlook the deficiencies. Gutzkow expressed
the aims of this and his later works most clearly in his best
comedy, Das Urbild des Tartuffe (1845), which like Laube's
Die Karlsschüler used a famous author's problems with censorship to attack indirectly Metternich's stage officials:
"The stage must connect life with art and art with life. Place
people there who are not taken from past centuries but from

the present, not from Assyria and Babylonia--no, from your
own environment. "13 Most of Gutzkow's plays are faithful to
this goal, whether they are social problem plays of the type
which Ibsen later brought to perfection, such as Werner
(1840) and Ella Rose (1856), or historical dramas such as
Patkul (1841) and Zopf und Schwert (1844). Gutzkow's best
play, and the only one to survive from the entire Young Germany movement, was Uriel Acosta (1847), a plea for religious
tolerance in the tradition of Lessing's Nathan der Weise.
Here liberal idealism is represented by a young Jew of Amsterdam whose vision is cruelly condemned by the orthodox
elders of the city.

Most of these plays had their premieres in Dresden,
where Gutzkow himself came as dramaturg in 1847. Though
his collaboration with Tieck had not been a notable success,
the intendant von Lüttichau continued his efforts to make
Dresden a major theatre center and indeed amid the undistinguished German stages of the mid-nineteenth century its
level of achievement was striking. The hiring of Wagner in
1842 as conductor and composer in residence was surely von
Lüttichau's major achievement, and will be discussed pre-
sently, but the spoken theatre also boasted major talents.
Though a major new theatre was built for von Lüttichau by
Gottfried Semper in 1841, the departure of Tieck for Berlin
left him with no dramaturg to manage it. He called upon
Eduard Devrient (1801-1877) in Berlin to assume the post.
Since Dresden already possessed the talents of the other
nephews of the great Ludwig Devrient, Karl and Emil (1803-
1872), this important acting family dominated the Dresden
stage of the next decade. Eduard was a great success in
Julius Caesar, Nathan der Weise, and Urbild des Tartuffe,
but his approach to the theatre clashed sharply with that of
Emil and most of the other Dresden actors. Eduard preferred a natural, realistic style integrated into a company
trained in ensemble work while Emil, as a virtuoso actor of
the period, focussed on his individual performance, and as a
disciple of the Weimar school stressed beauty and theatrical
effectiveness, if necessary at the expense of nature. One
sought to lose himself in the part, the other sought to make
the part a vehicle for himself. Considering Eduard's con-
demnation of virtuoso actors in his Geschichte der deutschen
Schauspielkunst, his attitude toward Emil and the rest of the
Dresden company was extremely tolerant, but a close working relationship with them proved impossible. There was
never any question as to which side would triumph. The
virtuoso approach dominated the German stage at mid-century

and the conservative and traditional Dresden stage felt little
of the political currents so strong in Berlin however much
Eduard might champion Gutzkow there. He retired from the
post of dramaturg in 1846, but remained in Dresden until
1853 when he was called to reorganize the theatre at Karlsruhe. There he worked for the next seventeen years developing a rather mediocre company into a very effective ensemble.

Whatever their theoretical differences, both Emil and
Eduard supported the appointment of Gutzkow as Eduard's
successor. The major creations of his brief administration
were his own Uriel Acosta (1847) and Der Königsleutenant
(1849), the former interpreted by Emil, the latter by Eduard.
Gutzkow also presented Shakespeare and Calderon, sought
young authors and tried to improve the company, but he resented the pressures brought on him to do minor scripts by
aristocratic authors and was disturbed by the growing tension
between proponents of realistic and idealistic acting in the
theatre. He resigned in 1849, but remained in Dresden during the 1850's and premiered most of his later works here.
His replacement was a young literary critic, Dr. Pabst.
Emil was now at the height of his powers, known throughout
Germany for his Hamlet, Tasso, Acosta, and Tell. In 1852
he traveled to London where in addition to the inevitable
Shakespeare, he gave English audiences their first experience
with German plays done in London. The departure of his
brother Eduard from Dresden should have committed the
Dresden stage to Emil's idealized and harmonious delivery,
had not a new, a more powerful and determined realist ar-
rived--Bogumil Dawison (1818-1872). His nervous, tormented, and almost naturalistic rendering of such characters
as Richard III, Shylock, and Iago rivalled Emil's most popular creations and the conflict between their approaches dominated the Dresden stage for the next decade, until the retirement of von Lüttichau in 1862 brought this major productive period in Dresden to an end.

Though the 1850s saw several Gutzkow premieres in
Dresden, the major dramatist of the decade was another
local author, Otto Ludwig (1813-1865) who sought a theoretical
middle ground between Emil Devrient and Dawison. Ludwig,
like Büchner and Kleist, was a significant dramatist who resisted association with any movement of the times. Like the
realists he condemned the classical idea of beauty, arguing
that everything was beautiful, nothing ugly if in its proper
place. He also condemned the romantics' emphasis on fate,

and called for an unequivocal causal relationship between
guilt and catastrophe. On the other hand, he condemned exaggerated realism, which he called Naturalismus, and had no
interest whatever in the problem drama or in any play designed to make an audience think instead of feeling. The
play should not illustrate some preconceived idea but bring
an impression of totality, harmony, and fulfillment to the
spectator. In all this, Ludwig stands as a key figure in the
reaction setting in after 1850 to the socially engaged literature of Young Germany. The Realismus he championed, and
opposed to both Naturalismus and Idealismus, is probably best
translated as poetic or artistic realism. In it, everything
should be real, but not particular, honest but beautiful and
harmonious. Action and characters should be elevated to
type without losing either humanity or simplicity. Ludwig
continuously went back to Shakespeare as his greatest example, but unfortunately his life-long study of the English
dramatist, summarized in his Shakespeare-Studien (1871),
exaggerated his already strong critical sense and made him
deeply distrustful of his own inspiration. He conceived
countless schemes for dramas, sketched them out, reworked,
destroyed, and constantly began again. Only two of his
efforts satisfied him sufficiently to be published and performed during his lifetime and even those in his eyes were
full of serious flaws.

        Der Erbförster (1850), which Ludwig called a declara-
tion of war against unnaturalness and conventionality in contemporary poetry and theatre, was a powerful if occasionally
melodramatic work, showing the effects of an unjustified
hatred arising between former friends. The psychological
model for Chief Forester Ulrich is clearly Othello, but Ludwig keeps the situation entirely within the framework of
middle-class tragedy. The rustic and earthy side of the
drama makes it as effective a work of local color as any
German romanticist achieved, but this blends rather uneasily
with the high tragic emotions the plot strives to produce.
The final acts, as Ludwig was all too aware, are honest and
unpretentious, but also somewhat petty and largely devoid of
the pathos he sought.

        Die Makkabäer (1854), like Die Erbförster, grew out
of repeated reworkings of a basic story, here the history of
Judas Maccabeus' revolt against Antioch. Each version
focussed on a different aspect of the story, and traces of all
can be found in the rich but diffuse final work--the personal
conflicts of Judas' family, the opposition between freedom

and authority, the interest in the dramatic psychology of the
mass, the nation itself striving to fulfill its destiny. Echoes
of Young Germany can be found, but no member of that
movement would have balanced, as Ludwig did, the people's
desire for a democratic ideal with their inertia and their respect for authority. His drama is therefore more complex
than most of its time, but he never learned from Shakespeare
the technique he so admired of giving to a complex action a
conciseness, directness and external simplicity. Once again
he was as aware as any of the defects of his work, and he
continued to pursue the elusive ideal form. Few dramatists
have ever so clearly and ruthlessly analyzed the deficiencies
in their own work, and there is a particular poignancy in his
observation: "The worst of it is that we today have to con-
sume our best powers in seeking a path, and generally
scarcely get beyond the beginning."[14]

        The revolution of 1848 freed many hitherto banned
plays of Young Germany for the stage, but at the same time
robbed them of much of the revolutionary impetus which was
their major attraction. Revolution was a popular theme after
1850, but treated as historical anecdote in the manner of
Scribe. Indeed the major legacy of Young Germany to the
next generation was its discovery of French themes and
techniques. Typical was the evolution of Rudolf von Gottschall (1823-1909), who supported liberal causes in the 1840s
with Ulrich von Hutten (1843) and Robespierre (1846), turned
to Scribean historical comedy for Pitt und Fox (1854), and
later still attempted even classic tragic form in Katherina
Howard (1868). The influence of French dramatic technique
was particularly marked in the Viennese Eduard von Bauernfeld (1802-1890) in the 1830s and 1840s and in Gustav Freytag
in Die Valentine (1846), Graf Waldemar (1850), and Die Journalisten (1853). The latter, one of the most popular German
comedies of the century, took an amused and detached view
of the various political extremes of the day. The French-
inspired structure of Young Germany plays and their suc-
cessors was summarized with high praise in Freytag's
Technik des Dramas (1893), but by this time the original
subject-matter had quite disappeared. The liberal bourgeoisie
which came to power in the 1850s had little interest in the
subject of revolution, but their daily concerns, social, financial, and personal, were explored by the dramatists of
the 1850s and 1860s through the Scribean dramatic structure
inherited from Young Germany.

3. Berlin

When Count Redern followed Brühl as intendant of the Berlin Hoftheater in 1828 there was some complaint, since he was both young (twenty-six) and inexperienced, but it was apparently hoped at the court that he would grow into the position. In fact he seems to have had little influence, good or bad. Brühl's bureaucracy managed the business side of the theatre, the experienced regisseur Karl Stawinski (1794-1866) organized the productions, and after 1831 the repertoire was controlled by a reading committee. The dramatist Raupach totally dominated the theatre as his plays did the repertoire. He headed the reading committee until 1833, and his departure from it meant no lessening in the number of his plays regularly presented in Berlin. The orgy of Raupach productions which filled the 1830s reached its peak in a cycle of fourteen spectacular history plays on the Hohenstaufens, ten of which were revived to be presented in series in the spring of 1837. Raupach had little competition during most of the decade. The other Berlin writers most represented were the actor Louis Angely (1787-1835) who in such plays as Das Fest der Handwerker (1828) drew gentle humor from Berlin society as Raimund did with the society of Vienna, and Karl Blum (1786-1844), who continued the tradition of Kotzebue with such works as Ich bleibe ledig (1835). Immermann, Halm from Vienna and Benedix from Frankfurt were represented along with three very popular women dramatists, Johanna von Weissenthurn (1773-1845), Amalie von Sachsen, and Charlotte Birch-Pfeiffer (1800-1868), who stopped acting in 1828 to devote herself to writing stage adaptations of popular novels such as Der Glöckner von Notredame (1837), after Hugo.

During these years the company developed by Iffland and Brühl steadily declined. Wolff was dead, Devrient left in 1832, Beschort in 1836, with no important new talents appearing to replace them. Eventually only Frau Stich-Crelinger and Lemm were left of Brühl's noted ensemble. Parts were distributed at random, plays poorly rehearsed and casually memorized. Berlin began to rely increasingly on guest artists like any minor provincial house. Eduard Devrient, Ludwig's nephew, founded an actors' society in 1834, with the support of Lemm and fifteen others, but the ensemble which might have grown from this society was undermined by a bitter factionalism which now plagued the theatre. In 1833 Charlotte von Hagn came to play young heroines and was an instant success in tragedy (as Juliet, Des-

demona, Ophelia, Gretchen, and Joan of Arc), in the family
dramas of Raupach and Halm, and even in character parts in
the salon comedies of the period. Karl Blum began to write
plays especially for her and the public's approbation steadily
grew. This popularity aroused the jealousy of Frau Crelinger
and of her daughter Bertha (1818-1876), who coveted the parts
von Hagn now controlled, and their anger was increased by
the fact that their rival represented a different style, more
manneristic, more concerned with theatrical effects, which
seemed to the Crelingers cheap and artificial.

This rivalry eventually divided both the company and
its public. Members of the old Brühl company and their
allies rallied around the Crelingers and dominated Eduard
Devrient's society, while important young actors, such as the
popular Moritz Rott, who had assumed many of Ludwig
Devrient's roles, sided with von Hagn. The echoes of this
bitter feud persist and color the judgements on many of these
actors in Eduard Devrient's important Geschichte der deutsche
Schauspielkunst. The opposing sides were never reconciled,
but the mannerists clearly dominated the theatre after 1838
and the arrival in Berlin of Carl Seydelmann (1793-1843), the
greatest of what came to be known as the virtuoso actors.

Seydelmann began his career in the army, and turned
to acting in 1815. He was accepted by Rhode in Breslau to
understudy Johann Kettel (1789-1862), the theatre's specialist
in youthful heroes. Apparently Seydelmann's age was his
only qualification for such roles; he was so maladroit physically and vocally that Rhode soon urged him to consider some
other profession. He therefore left Breslau, but not the
theatre, and toured about Germany working to improve his
deficiencies. He subjected his body to rigorous training and
like Demosthenes, practiced orating with stones in his mouth
to improve his clarity. He had sufficiently improved by 1822
to win a position at Kassel under Fiege which he kept until
1828, establishing there a significant reputation. When he
set out to tour again, between 1828 and 1835, it was as an
established star, and he was warmly welcomed in such cities
as Stuttgart, Berlin, and Vienna. Laube's first impressions
of him in Vienna are worth noting:

> This actor was then, it must have been in 1829,
> newly arrived from North Germany, and his smiles
> at our theoretical infallibility confounded us. We
> were struck to the heart by the simple, clear,
> assured acting of the man, by the power of his

> words. His words! They were like a sword, a
> Protestant sword thrust into our mist-enshrouded
> romanticism. [15]

The metaphor is a significant one, suggesting that Seydelmann's style, while more theatrical than realistic, was yet
clear and specific. Its opposition to Viennese romanticism
seems therefore to parallel the opposition between late romantic drama in Germany and the new competing schools of
poetic realism and Young Germany.

The Berlin theatre, which tried for several years to
obtain Seydelmann as a permanent actor, at last succeeded
in 1838. He spent the last five years of his life there, at
the peak of his power, and temporarily restored to the Berlin stage something of the enthusiasm of the Iffland era.
Many older members of the company and audience in fact
likened him to Iffland, for he placed a similar emphasis on
the building of theatrical effects. Like Iffland, and unlike
Lemm or Devrient, he played directly to the audience, usually assaulting them by a striking first entrance and a mask
and bearing which instantly established his character, then
building on this through a series of carefully chosen details.
Seydelmann much exceeded Iffland in power and agressive-
ness, however; it was said that Iffland charmed while Seydelmann imposed. His voice was generally conceded to be the
loudest in Berlin. His most popular roles were his great
villains, such as Shylock or Mephisto, which he played with
little irony or subtlety, but with tremendous power. In such
roles, his disregard of any realistic conventions could be
turned to greatest advantage. His biographer Rötscher reports of his Mephisto:

> Even in his countenance the artist seemed no
> longer a human being at all, indeed seemed com-
> pletely removed from any restrictions of human
> existence, so that we could not help marvelling at
> the virtuosity which allowed him thus to individu-
> alize the son of Hell. A slender, wasp-like body,
> his fingers curved like talons, his head covered
> with shaggy black hair, his hooded eyes, his nose
> drawn down to his chin--all this combined to give
> his figure a thoroughly demonic appearance. In
> vain we sought to relate this characterization to
> some creation in the human world; the figure ap-
> peared to be <u>sui</u> <u>generis</u>. [16]

His last new role, Iago in 1842, was one of his greatest, a
character of demonic power generally considered the equal of
Devrient's famous Franz Moor.

The closing years of Redern's directorship saw an
impressive improvement in the repertoire, too. Berlin's
major premiere of the period came in 1840 with the production of Judith by Friedrich Hebbel (1813-1863). Hebbel, who
gradually came to be recognized as the most important German dramatist between Schiller and Hauptmann, had no real
ties with Berlin, and his first major contribution was made
there almost by chance. He had begun his literary career
writing ballads, stories, and a few dramatic fragments, contributing regularly after 1832 to a Hamburg fashion journal.
Its editor, Amalia Schoppe, assumed the role of his patro-
ness, inviting him to Hamburg in 1835 and sending his first
completed play to her friend Auguste Crelinger in Berlin.
The actress was fascinated by the part, and arranged for its
presentation.

Since Hebbel was more concerned with Judith as a
woman than as a Jew or a patriot, and since her conflict
with Holofernes was developed in bold psychological and social terms, this first work had a certain similarity to the
dramas of Young Germany. Hebbel's debt to this dominant
contemporary movement was, in fact, slight. He admired
Tieck and Uhland but observed in 1838 that all literature
from his own generation was rubbish. Certainly his treatment of the Judith theme achieved a depth of social question-
ing and a realism in psychology quite impossible to find in
Gutzkow, Laube, and their followers, which helps explain
why the critic Witkowski calls the play the first modern
drama of the century. Unfortunately the play as Hebbel conceived it was not given until 1896; the version presented in
Berlin in 1840 was greatly adjusted to suit the censor. The
entire sexual element disappeared, and Holofernes' attempt
to dominate Judith was interpreted only as a patriotic or even
religious urge. Her drive to slay him was attributed to similar motives and the focus at the end shifted from the central
characters to the entrance of the triumphant Jews praising
Jehovah, their deliverer. All these changes further confused
a work which was already bearing a heavy intellectual burden, dealing as it did with a conflict of cultures, the effects
of a Schopenhauerian will to power, a struggle between reason
and passion, and the battle of the sexes. Critical reaction
to the play varied widely, and many reviewers, among them
Wienbarg and Gutzkow, were calculatedly ambiguous. Yet

even the most negative reviewers generally acknowledged that
the new work possessed real intellectual and artistic power
and that Hebbel was a dramatist who would bear watching.

His second play, Genoveva (1841), was another explo-
ration of sacrifice, developed in a manner contrasting strikingly with Judith. The story was the medieval legend already
treated by Müller and Tieck, and for it Hebbel turned from
prose to blank verse with clear echoes of Goethe and Kleist.
He submitted the new work to Frau Crelinger in Berlin, but
she refused it on the grounds that a work by Raupach on the
same subject was already in the repertoire. Genoveva was
finally premiered in translation in Prague eight years later,
but Hebbel could interest no German theatre in it until he
wrote an epilogue contradicting the original tragic ending.
The play was never particularly popular even after this adjustment, probably due to its static quality. Judith's action
precipitates her tragedy, while Genoveva's greatness is
achieved through suffering, and the structure of the two plays
reflects these different emphases in the ratio between conversation and dramatic action. Moreover Hebbel was still
himself seeking some acceptable solution to the questions
raised in his plays over the purpose of human action and the
meaning of suffering. He made the sacrifice of Judith and
Genoveva pathetic and moving, but had difficulty in justifying
it. Even the noblest deeds could not rise above the empti-
ness and vanity of earthly life, as the young dramatist then
saw it. He dealt more directly with this vanity in his first
comedy, Der Diamant (1841), wherein the fate of a royal
family depends on a magic stone which a Jewish usurer
swallows rather than give up. The peasants which surround
the Jew are amusingly drawn, and the court room scene
achieves a rustic humor recalling Kleist's zerbrochene Krug,
but the joke and the comic invention wears thin, and at last
one is led to agree with the sarcasm of the French reviewer
who spoke of Hebbel's "délicate invention; un mal d'entrailles
en cinq actes. "17

Der Diamant attracted neither directors nor a pub-
lisher, and after this disappointment, and the great fire which
destroyed most of Hamburg in 1842, Hebbel left that city to
seek a position at the University of Copenhagen (since as a
native of Schleswig-Holstein he was officially a Danish subject). He was unsuccessful in this attempt, but due to the
support of the Danish poet Adam Oehlenschläger (1776-1850)
he obtained a royal pension which at least allowed him to return to Hamburg in more material comfort. In 1843 he pro-

duced his first important theoretical work on the theatre, <u>Ein</u>
<u>Wort über das Drama</u>. The Danish critic J. L. Heiberg took
issue with the essay, raising a charge often brought against
Hebbel later--that by emphasizing suffering he had lost the
necessary element of tragic guilt and left his dramatic world
with no means for reconciliation. Hebbel replied through a
major expansion of his original essay (changing its title from
<u>Ein Wort</u> to <u>Mein Wort</u>). He reaffirmed his conviction that
a reprehensible action in the hero's past was unnecessary,
since the basis of tragedy was the thwarting of human action
by the will of the universe, and the human undertaking could
be either a noble or an evil one. He cited as evidence Antigone, destroyed for performing a sacred duty. As for reconciliation, he suggested that the most positive note tragedy
could offer was the recognition by the hero of the necessity
of his defeat and his acceptance of it. The goal was thus
not reconciliation but "satisfaction" and this satisfaction would
be incomplete "when the individual meets defeat defiantly or
sullenly, insisting that the battle will be renewed elsewhere,"
and complete "when the individual gains from the defeat itself a clearer vision of his relation to the whole and exits in
peace. "18

Hebbel's theory of drama was developed more fully in
the preface to the most important of his early plays, <u>Maria</u>
<u>Magdalena</u> (1844). Here he argued that only three periods
so far in history had involved the sort of crisis between man
and the world in relation to a central idea which he felt
could produce great drama. The first was when the Greeks
conceived the idea of fate; the second when the Elizabethans
explored the freedom of the individual; and the third was the
present, from Kant on, when men became dissatisfied with
formal morality and insisted on its examination in the light
of necessity. Thus Hebbel found the meaning he had been
seeking in human action in a kind of evolutionary process.
The tragic conflict of an individual with a world order is now
related to a conflict of systems at a turning point in history,
with the defeated individual normally an early representative
of the new order which is struggling to establish itself. The
process suggests Hegel but with the important difference that
Hegel saw conflict developing between simultaneously existing
systems of value while Hebbel placed it between a declining
order and an emerging weaker but morally superior one.
Thus at first in theory, then in the plays themselves, Hebbel
moved beyond the fatalism of a dramatist like Grillparzer.
The "satisfaction" experienced by his tragic victims grew
from their acceptance of their role in the evolutionary pro-

cess. The antagonism of the old order guaranteed their destruction, but as heralds of a superior evolutionary stage
they performed an important role in the historical process.
Thus Hebbel hoped to achieve both reconciliation and meaning.
Maria Magdalena, the first clear expression of this new
drama of social evolution, or social criticism, lays the
foundations for much of the social drama of the rest of the
century. This prose tragedy of lower middle-class German
life depicts the destruction of both Clara and her well-mean-
ing father Master Anton through his desire to uphold bourgeois respectability at all costs. By focussing on the old order
and its discredited but still powerful views, the play produces
a darker picture of life than Hebbel's theory, with its concern for affirmation and satisfaction, might suggest. Maria's
passivity and helplessness made her a more pathetic victim
than Hebbel's later and stronger sacrifices to the old order,
and involved a sense of outrage that made Hebbel seem more
of a social revolutionary than he actually was. The social
drama which followed him was far more ruthless in subject-
ing the old moral order of middle-class society to the dread
test of necessity, but Maria Magdalena's exposure of the
rottenness of society beneath its respectable veneer clearly
prefigures such works as Ibsen's Pillars of Society and
Ghosts. The similarity to Ibsen is particularly striking since
Maria Magdalena is built on the same principle of analytic
exposition which became a characteristic of the work of the
later dramatist.

Though Maria Magdalena ultimately became Hebbel's
most popular play, he suffered his usual difficulty in getting
it presented. Once again he appealed to Frau Crelinger in
Berlin without success. She spoke warmly of his poetic
talent and his improvement in technique since Judith, but
she was quite convinced that the subject was impossible for
the stage. At last in 1846 the play was premiered in
Königsberg. Hebbel did not find a truly sympathetic producer
of his work until after 1850, when he entered his productive
relationship with Franz von Dingelstedt. Most of Hebbel's
subsequent works were premiered at theatres under Dingelstedt's control and the Berlin stage, after Maria Magdalena,
neither requested nor received any Hebbel works.

Berlin's disinterest in Hebbel was to an extent balanced by an eagerness to present other important dramatists
of the 1840s, though as a rule they had to prove themselves
elsewhere first. Thus Gutzkow's Richard Savage was given
in 1840 after its success in Frankfurt and his Werner and

Patkul brought from Hamburg in 1841. Laube's Mondaleschi
came from Dresden in 1842. With these came the first Berlin productions of French well-made plays, such as Scribe's
A Glass of Water in 1841. As if in acknowledgement of the
new literary emphasis, Raupach disappeared almost completely from the theatre after his first major failure, 1740
(1840). Redern's company also provided the actors for
Tieck's important court productions of Antigone in 1841 and
Midsummer Night's Dream in 1843.

The Berlin stage showed a distinct decline under
Count Redern's successor, Theodor von Küstner, who ar-
rived in 1842. Major artists departed--Seydelmann died in
1843, Amelia Wolff retired and Eduard Devrient and the two
Crelinger daughters left in 1844--and the replacements von
Küstner found were distinctly inferior. Seydelmann's roles
were divided between the best of the new actors, Franz
Hoppé, who came from Immermann's troupe in 1844, and
Theodore Döring (1803-1878), who arrived the next year.
Hoppé was a careful and contemplative arranger of effects
whose style somewhat suggested Seydelmann's, while Döring
attempted to live in his part, so much so that his disciple
Friedrich Haase reported that audiences often had to struggle
even to hear him. His Mephisto was "not really a spirit,"
observed one critic, "but rather a gnome or a goblin."[19]
Neither had the power or the popularity of a Devrient or a
Seydelmann. Hermann Hendrichs (1809-1871), a handsome
young man of small talent, came from Hamburg in 1844 and
after Hoppé's early death in 1849 shared the leading parts
with Döring. The older women's parts which Amelia Wolff
had done were assumed by Frau Birch-Pfeiffer, an obvious
and rather crude actress, but a popular writer of domestic
comedies, such as Mutter und Sohn (1844), produced just
after she joined the company. Edwina Viereck (1826-1856),
a beautiful but untalented Viennese, played the younger
women's leads.

The repertoire showed a similar decline. Revivals of
the later works of Gutzkow and Freytag's Die Valentine were
the only offerings of any substance; the rest of the repertoire
was dominated by such authors as Birch-Pfeiffer, Benedix,
Hackländer, and Halm. Von Küstner devoted himself to
pleasing the claque and the journalists, installing seats to his
right and left in his own box for reviewers from the major
papers. All the worst evils of commercialism beset the theatre. Actors and authors turned to stereotyped devices and
easy and proven effects. Sensations and scandals were played

up to attract audiences, and the private life of a play's star or the glamor of its physical production was often the most noteworthy thing about it.

The political crisis of 1848 dominated the end of this undistinguished administration, destroying what stability the theatre had left. The revolutionary tremors of 1830 had affected a number of the smaller German states, but left such powerful centers of conservatism as Berlin and Vienna almost untouched. 1848 was a different story. Mobs of students and workers rioting in Vienna forced the resignation of that great pillar of the old order, Prince Metternich, and gained the Emperor's promise to create a liberal constitution. The revolution then swept northward, engulfing Berlin a few days later. Friedrich Wilhelm IV wavered, promising concessions to the revolutionaries but refusing to honor their demands for a united Germany. A revolutionary Assembly convened in Frankfurt but broke up in disillusionment, and most of the reforms won by the uprisings gradually disappeared.

The theatre throughout Germany suffered greatly from the upheavals of 1848. Aside from the obvious difficulties in attracting audiences or maintaining stable organizations in a period of social disturbance, most theatres suffered a corruption of their repertoire in the politically charged climate. In liberal areas, audiences often demanded exclusively political drama or insisted upon interpreting all plays politically, applauding or hissing any lines which might possibly be construed as having reference to contemporary events. In cities where conservative forces triumphed, such as Berlin, censorship became more rigorous than ever, and plays presented had to be so inoffensive as to become almost mindless. The majority of the works offered in Berlin between 1850 and 1870 were minor single efforts by unknown dramatists; the most frequently produced established authors were the insignificant Benedix and Birch-Pfeiffer. After 1848 Scribe and his school were the dominant foreign influence; aside from their works the only non-German plays presented in Berlin in the next twenty years were two by Calderon and two by Shakespeare. The presentation of major German authors was even poorer--no Lessing, no Goethe, no Schiller, indeed nothing written in Germany before 1840 except three dramas by Iffland. Among the moderns Gutzkow and Freytag were adequately represented, but Hebbel only by his last two works. The company was no more distinguished than its offerings. Only Frau Crelinger, who died in 1865, remained from the pre-Küstner period, and among younger artists only Frau

Blumauer, who arrived in 1853 to do character parts, was generally acknowledged to possess any talent whatever. Opera and ballet replaced the spoken theatre in the public interest. All vestiges of the distinction achieved by Iffland and Brühl had disappeared.

During most of this period from 1830 to 1870 the Berlin Hoftheater, which had enjoyed a monopoly earlier in the century, had to deal with rival ventures. The first and most durable of these was the Königstädtische Theater, founded in 1824 by a horse-trainer named Cerf. Though it presented all genres and thus competed directly with the Hoftheater, its specialty was folk farces similar to the offerings of the Leopoldstädter in Vienna, but with typically Berliner situations, characters and jokes. The early years of this theatre were quite unsettled--it had eight directors between 1824 and 1829 --but then Cerf returned and developed a more stable company and repertoire. Several of the members of his popular troupe were authors as well as actors--Heinrich Schmelka (1780-1837), Louis Angely, Friedrich Genée (1796-1856), Karl von Holtei (1798-1880)--but the first real master of the Berlin Posse and of the somewhat more sophisticated Volksstück was Friedrich Beckmann (1803-1866) who gave this genre for a time a popularity in Berlin equal to that it enjoyed in Vienna.

After 1834 Cerf's outstanding company gradually began to dissolve. Angely left to tour and Holtei and his young wife Julie Holzbecker departed for Vienna. Schmelka, a pillar of the theatre, died in 1837. Genée left in 1841 to direct the theatre in Danzig, and Beckmann remained almost alone to carry on the theatre's tradition. Even so, his popularity was such that he might have managed had not Cerf, discouraged by so many losses, decided to change his emphasis to Italian opera. The disheartened Beckmann retired in 1844 and his follower Wilhelmine Grobecker brought so little skill to her work that the genre was generally considered dead. The theatre closed in 1848.

This did not remove competition to the Hoftheater, however, for by the time the Königstädtische closed, Berlin had welcomed the first of several summer theatres of the sort which sprang up in the 1840s all over Germany. Since most established theatres at this time had a season of only six months, it is not surprising that other theatrical ventures developed during the rest of the year, nor that, once established, they began to extend their own seasons into the more profit-

able winter months. The major impetus for the summer theatres of the 1840's came from the popular public pleasure
gardens of Paris, those Tivolis which offered ephemeral theatrical fare along with light refreshment, open-air concerts,
fireworks, and balloon ascensions. The theatre offered was
popular but casual, and contributed little to the development
of the art. The actors were untrained, the plays the sort of
light entertainment which would not distract from beer drink-
ing or social conversation, and audiences felt free to come
and go as they wished. Stability was rarely known in these
theatres; a totally new company and director would normally
appear each summer.

Such ventures had only negative results on the established theatres. They developed neither actors nor dramatists, and when they extended their season into the winter,
as many did if they could find a heated hall, they could develop into serious rivals for audiences. Thus after 1848 the
Hoftheater was forced to compete with the Friedrich-Wilhelm-
städter Theater and the Vorstädtische Theater and after 1852
with the Callenbach'sche Theater as well. By 1858, when
these challenges were fading, Cerf's theatre was re-estab-
lished by the actor Franz Wallner as the Wallnertheater, the
Hoftheater's most important rival to date. The Berlin Posse
was revived and surpassed its old popularity in the works of
Rüsche, Helmerding, and particularly David Kalisch (1820-
1872) who filled the Wallnertheater with such creations as
Gebildeten Hausknecht and Hunderttausand Taler.

4. Vienna and Heinrich Laube

Having driven Schreyvogel from the theatre, Count
Czernin sought for his successor an acceptable but sub-
servient director who would cause him no difficulties. He
settled on Johann Ludwig Deinhardstein (1794-1859), an innocuous professor of literature who guided the Burgtheater
for nine years until 1841, largely living off Schreyvogel's
reputation and company. In 1836 the Berlin author Adolf
Glasbrenner reported that the Burgtheater still had a reputation unequalled in Germany, but the decline had begun.
Deinhardstein had little interest in resisting the censor and
his repertoire contracted rapidly. His two most important
new offerings were Grillparzer's Der Traum ein Leben
(1834) and Weh dem, der lügt (1838). The first, as its title
suggested, owed its basic device to Calderon's play, but

adapted to Grillparzer's own concerns.   Calderon's hero
Sigismundo discovers through his dream experience the illusory nature of all apparent reality in contrast to the faith
which becomes his at his final conversion.   At that point the
crimes he committed, which were crimes in the real world,
become as insubstantial as dreams.   Grillparzer, assuming
no such atonement, leads his hero Rustan into an actual
dream, where all his strivings are carried to their catastrophic conclusion.   Then he is allowed to awaken and, purged
of these strivings, adjust to an idyllic reality.   What Grillparzer has in effect done is embed the pattern of his earlier
tragedies into Rustan's dream so that his hero may work that
pattern out and then, from beyond the catastrophe, regain
equilibrium.

With Weh dem, der lügt Grillparzer had reached sufficient objectivity toward his philosophy to attempt a comedy.
The basic conflict recalls that of Des Meeres und der Liebe
Wellen, between reason's attempt to structure human life and
the refusal of life's vital energy to be constrained.   The
comedy is another "test" play; Bishop Gregory of Tours sends
young Leon off on a perilous mission with only one uncompromising demand, that Leon never tell a lie.   The mission
succeeds, but only because Leon discovers how to deceive
with the truth.   The message of the play is calculatedly ambiguous; Gregory's standard is exposed as not only impractical
but unwise, yet no plea is made for complete amorality.   The
solution is clearly to accept life as it is pragmatically, with
an inevitable measure of moral compromise.   This morally
ambiguous conclusion was considered by some critics as the
reason for the play's signal failure at the Burgtheater, but
Grillparzer's most successful works were hardly any more
doctrinaire.   Deinhardstein's productions were doubtless at
least partly to blame, for in both of these plays he focused
on the fanciful element, and while Schreyvogel had always
used visual display in an attempt to capture Grillparzer's
inner spirit, Deinhardstein created pure spectacles, subordi-
nating the poetry to de Pian's settings and Stubenrauch's
costumes.   The new genre created another problem, for to
the Burgtheater public, comedy meant the carefully plotted
and intellectually slight works of Scribe and his German imitators, and the philosophic underpinning and psychological
complexity of Grillparzer's play simply confused them.   The
actors were scarcely less confused, and destroyed Grillparzer's delicate nuances with bold strokes of characterization.   Galomire, the son of a German count but raised in
rustic surroundings, had been conceived by the dramatist as

a simple, untutored soul, but he was interpreted as a babb-
ling idiot.   This apparently calculated insult to the German
aristocracy literally drove scandalized patrons from the theatre.   In short, Weh dem, der lügt was a disaster of such
magnitude that Grillparzer never attempted to have another
of his plays produced.   His three last works were presented
posthumously, during the 1870s.

In these final plays Grillparzer, unconcerned with production and therefore with censorship, felt free to return to
historical subjects.   In Die Jüdin von Toledo, King Alphonso
is tempted from the obligations of his position by a passion
for the Jewess Rahel, but her death, for which he is largely
responsible, frees him at last from her spell and in the
presence of her body he experiences a spiritual and intellectual awakening which closely parallels that of Rustan awakening from his dream of destruction.   Ein Bruderzwist in Habs-
burg dealt with the Reformation period just before the Thirty
Years' War and reflected Grillparzer's liberal disillusionment
with the revolution of 1848.   The Emperor Rudolf II sees that
the Protestant drive for freedom and equality will paradoxi-
cally lead to conflict and chaos, but like so many of Grillparzer's heroes, Rudolf has a vision of approaching catastrophe but is powerless to change the events leading to it.
Action and inaction alike lead to the abyss.   Libussa is the
posthumous work which most fully harmonized history and
psychology, philosophy and personal belief.   Libussa and her
lover Primislaus sacrifice a Rousseauesque harmony with
nature to enter the corrupting world of history, but Libussa,
more farseeing than Grillparzer's earlier prophets, looks beyond the increasing alienation of man in history, in the city,
in his own rational structures, to a new harmony achieved at
last by a humble acceptance of history's negative processes
in their full destructive power.   To the end, Grillparzer's
vision of history remained one of decline and catastrophe, but
the last works triumphed over that dark vision by looking
forward to a new synthesis, an atonement with the eternal, on
the far side of the historical process.   In this pattern of decline, catastrophe and renewal, Grillparzer's late plays begin
to suggest a rhythm in history similar to that being evolved
by Hebbel, the great north German dramatist of the same
period.

No writer of remotely comparable vision or imagination replaced Grillparzer in Vienna after his departure.
Deinhardstein during the 1840s. relied on Raupauch, on translations of contemporary French works, and on a prolific if

generally undistinguished school of Viennese comedy writers.
The best of these was Eduard von Bauernfeld (1802-1890),
who created charming and witty pictures of Viennese life with
a dramatic technique borrowing heavily from Scribe's salon
plays. He produced an impressive series of successes for
Deinhardstein, the most durable of which were Die Bekennt-
nisse (1834) and Bürgerlich und Romantisch (1835), but he
was as aware as posterity has been of their essential insig-
nificance. "All that I have written is weak and mediocre,"
he confessed, "but I could write nothing better. Neither the
administration nor the public would have tolerated it."[20]

The Baron von Münch-Bellinghause, who wrote under
the name Friedrich Halm (1806-1871), enjoyed a great success with his first work, Griseldis (1834), and followed it
with a whole series of popular, sentimental poetic dramas.
Though these were little more than weak echoes of the sort
of play Grillparzer wrote, they were excellent vehicles for
actors, and even more, for actresses, and so were widely
produced in the virtuoso period. Frau Rettich, Sophie
Schröder's successor, was particularly well received in such
roles, but neither she, nor any actor of the new generation,
approached the fame of their predecessors under Schreyvogel.
As the repertoire declined, so did the company, and guest
appearances steadily undermined the famous ensemble. Karl
La Roche replaced Costenoble, who died in 1837, and with
Luise Neumann and Christine Enghaus (1817-1910) led the
younger talents. Under them the intellectual and poetic style
developed by Schreyvogel gave way to a less rich and subtle
interpretation just as Grillparzer gave way to the cruder
Halm and Bauernfeld.

Franz Ignaz von Holbein (1779-1855), who guided the
Burgtheater from 1841 until 1849, was somewhat more ambitious than Deinhardstein, and brought to the position a much
more varied and promising background. He had been a
painter, musician, actor, and teacher over half of Europe,
and a theatre director in Bamburg with Hoffmann between
1809 and 1812, then in Prague and in Hannover. He dreamed
of creating in Vienna a theatre which would be a model for
all Germany, but the conservatism of Vienna and the indifference of his actors worked steadily against him. The revolution of 1848 freed the repertoire near the end of his administration, but until then he relied heavily on the French--
Scribe, Bayard, Dumas, Ponsard--and on such German and
Viennese authors as Halm, Bauernfeld, Benedix, and Birch-
Pfeiffer. His major additions to the company were Amalie

Haizinger (1800-1884), who played naive and sentimental
roles, Friedrich Beckmann (1803-1866), who did comic parts
and became a noted Falstaff, and Bogumil Dawison (1818-
1872), a Polish actor who was hired as a young lover, but
who after 1850 turned to character roles and achieved great
success as Richard III, Shylock, and Othello.

The disappearance of the censor in 1848 allowed Holbein to produce plays by Young Germany authors and, more
significantly, works by Hebbel: Maria Magdalena in 1848 with
Anschütz and Christine Enghaus (who became Hebbel's wife),
Judith in 1849 with Enghaus and Löwe, and later the same
year the premiere of a new drama, Herodes und Mariamne.
Vienna had been a second home for Hebbel since 1845 and
his works were warmly praised by critics and actors here
even though they were forbidden production. During this
period, in addition to the major new work Herodes und Mariamne he wrote a one-act tragicomedy Trauerspiel in Sizilien
and a full-length tragedy Julia, which he considered a sort of
sequel to Maria Magdalena. Here he showed another well-
meaning but rigid father and innocent girl, this time involved
with a scheming ruined nobleman, Count Bertram, who has
been described as a precursor of Ibsen's Captain Alving. He
refuses a possible marriage to the young heroine, declaring
that marriage between life and death, between corrupt age
and healthy youth, "is the mother of ghosts." This striking
line, anticipating Ibsen not only in theme but in image, is
surely the single thing most remembered about this rather
undistinguished play. One other feature certainly worth noting, however, is a "discussion scene" in the middle of the
final act, a feature which Shaw later cited as the hallmark
of the modern social drama. In short, with Maria Magdalena
and Julia Hebbel seemed to have committed himself to the
path that led directly to the social drama of the 1880s and
1890s.

Yet it was left for Ibsen and others to pursue this development. Even while writing Julia Hebbel characterized it
as a work of transition, and Herodes und Mariamne saw him
working with a distinctly different emphasis. The revolution
of 1848 served as an important catalyst for this change, as
Hebbel himself noted in a letter of that year:

> My ideas are becoming much clearer, especially
> since the conflicts out of which my earlier dramas
> grew are settled in the streets, resolved by the
> process of history. The rotten conditions of the

world used to oppress me as if I alone had to
suffer them, and I felt it a worthy goal for art to
expose their rottenness by artistic means.   This
I did, without, of course, concealing from myself
for a moment the gulf between what I hoped to do
and what I actually achieved.   Now I consider myself relieved.   I will no longer depict the old
prison with no chimney or windows, for it is collapsing and we can plan a new building. [21]

Like many liberals of the period, Hebbel found the
1848 revolution a disillusioning event, but it did not turn him
from a radical to a conservative, as some of his contemporaries claimed.   He frequently spoke of Herodes und Mariamne as the beginning of a new artistic period for him, but
this involved more a shift in focus than a change in philosophy.
Probably none of his works illustrates so clearly the moment
of change between two antagonistic historical epochs as this.
King Herod represents the old order, energetic, powerful,
and courageous, but totally self-centered and ruthless.   He
therefore cannot comprehend the new order's ideals of devotion and self-sacrifice when they appear in Mariamne, and
thus assents to her destruction.   At the end of the play the
Three Magi appear and Herod orders the massacre of the
innocents, the last futile attempt of the dying order to maintain itself.   The clarity with which this drama illustrates
Hebbel's evolutionary idea of history in no way detracts from
its richness of characterization, and the dramatist was surely
justified in having great hopes for his new work.   He was,
however, disappointed, for the play totally failed to impress
its Burgtheater audience and was withdrawn after a single
performance.   A much less substantial fairy-play, Der Rubin
(1849), did no better.   It was clear that, whatever its ultimate worth, the new direction Hebbel was taking had little
appeal for the Vienna public.

During the period from 1830 to 1850, with the Burgtheater generally in decline, the suburban theatres assumed
the dominant position in Vienna, and these were in turn dominated by the dramatist Nestroy and his director Karl Bern-
brunn (1787-1854), whose professional name was Carl Karl.
Karl's career as actor and director of the Isarthortheater
has already been mentioned.   In 1825, when that venture
closed, he brought his company as a guest troupe to the
Theater an der Wien where he and his wife Margarethe had
already achieved considerable success as guest artists. Karl,
always an opportunist, set to work immediately making this

temporary position permanent. Carl Hensler, the director
of the Josefstädter, died in 1825 and Karl immediately entered into negotiations with Hensler's daughter to gain a partial control over that theatre. At the same time he made
arrangements with Palffy, then in financial difficulties, to
take over the Theater an der Wien. Within a year, two of
the three major private theatres of Vienna were under Karl's
control.

He remained manager of the Josefstädter only until
1828, when he decided he could more profitably concentrate
on a single venture. He gathered at the Theater an der
Wien, therefore, the best actors from its original company,
from the Josefstädter, and from his own earlier Isarthortheater. From the Josefstädter came Karl's first important
discovery in Vienna, Wenzel Scholz (1787-1857), who made
his debut as Klapperl in Meisl's Die schwarze Frau (1826).
From the Palffy company came the leading man Moritz Rott
and an important character actor, Franz Meyerhofer, who
shared key roles with Karl's own leading man Wilhelm Kunst
(1799-1859), and character actor Franz Gämmerler (1804-
1876). Although the first offering under Karl's direction
here was Hamlet, with Kunst as the Prince, classic plays
were few. Karl found it much more profitable to rely on the
same magic comedies, chivalric plays, and Lokalpossen that
had always formed the bulk of the suburban repertoire.

Though the plays he offered were thus similar in type
to those offered by his competitors, Karl established almost
at once a position of superiority for his theatre which it re-
tained until his departure in 1845. There were many reasons
for this superiority, but Karl was given a great advantage at
the outset by the weakness at this time not only of the Burgtheater, but more importantly, of his two major suburban
rivals. The Leopoldstädter was collapsing under the disas-
trous leadership of Steinkeller. In 1829 its major dramatist
Raimund left Vienna and two years later the bankrupt director
closed the theatre and fled the country. Though it reopened
soon after under Franz von Marinelli, the theatre possessed
a diminished and demoralized troupe, and its major authors,
Eduard Gulden and Josef Kilian Schickh, were but poor imitators of Raimund. At the Josefstädter Karl was followed by
Johann August Stöger (1772-1846), a conductor from the
Hofoper and an operatic composer who naturally favored that
genre. Though he welcomed Nestroy in 1831, he gave much
more encouragement to Conradin Kreutzer, who arrived in
1833 and whose Das Nachtlager in Granada (1834) was one of

the most ambitious Josefstädter productions of the period.
It is hardly surprising that Nestroy within a year had been
won over by Karl, who produced Nestroy's first original
Viennese play, Der gefühlvolle Kerkermeister in 1832. Thus
Karl gained the author who was to become the most popular
Viennese writer of the period, and he was shrewd enough not
to lose him to anyone else. They remained together for over
twenty years, until Karl's death, during which time Nestroy
produced more than fifty parodies and comedies (most of
them with leading roles for himself) which formed the basis
of Karl's repertoire.

Nestroy was a native son of Vienna, but his theatrical
apprenticeship took him to Amsterdam, Graz, and several
German stages before he returned to his home in 1829. He
began almost at once his double career of actor and playwright, achieving his first major success with Der böse
Geist Lumpazivagabundus (1833). In this work the fairies
Amorosa and Fortuna argue over which can exert the most
influence on human lives, with the evil spirit of the title sid-
ing with Amorosa. A test is imposed on three of this
spirit's humble followers, a cobbler, a tailor, and a carpenter, who are made rich in a lottery. The first two dissipate
their wealth, but the third is saved by falling in love. He
and his wife attempt in vain to reform the others, but Amorosa and the king of the fairies must at last force them to
accept mates and stable lives. At first glance we seem to
be still in the world of Raimund with this mixture of fantasy
and realism, the conflict of good and evil, and the happy
ending, but closer examination reveals that Nestroy's cynicism
has in fact created almost a parody of the earlier dramatist.
He is willing enough to join Raimund in undermining foolish
dreams and fancies, but while Raimund does this in the name
of a higher stable order, based either on a benevolent supernatural power or the simple goodness of mankind, Nestroy
removes illusions to show us what he sees as the essential
man--charming and amusing perhaps, but also somewhat
pitiful and certainly unregenerate. The cynicism which runs
through Lumpazivagabundus is not cancelled but confirmed by
its totally unbelievable happy ending, just as the unbelievable
happy ending puts the capstone on Bertolt Brecht's Dreigro-
schenoper. As if to remove any possible doubt as to his in-
tentions, Nestroy showed his two weak vagabonds falling from
virtue in a sequel, Die Familien Zwirn, Knieriem, und Leim
(1834), and taking their previously virtuous companion down
with them.

The keenness of Nestroy's wit, the richness of his
language, the exuberance of his comic imagination and the
brilliance of his interpretations delighted his public even when
his shafts were at their own expense, and few pretensions of
his society were spared. In vain critics complained of the
lack of any moral or edifying dimension in his works; Nestroy became the most popular author and actor in Vienna.
He was an inspired adaptor. Of his approximately fifty major
plays, scholars have found only two which were apparently
not taken from the dramas or novels of others--mostly the
French. He changed his plots remarkably little, but his
genius for dialogue and characterization was such that he
made French vaudevilles, German farces, and English novels
seem not only totally Viennese, but perfectly conceived for
the talents of his own company. There was always a leading
role for the author, whose comic range was great, and for
his partner Wenzel Scholz, a short, fat actor who perfectly
set off the tall, thin Nestroy. Other parts were ingeniously
fitted to the stock members of the company--the villain, the
dashing young man, the soubrette, the foolish servant, and
so on.

As early as 1833 Meisl, reviewing Lumpazivagabundus,
wrote that the play "contained only enough magic to motivate
the plot, " and that "the author will deserve more praise when
he gets rid of this device entirely, since it is now no more
than useless decoration. "22 By 1835 Nestroy had indeed
moved entirely into the contemporary world. Fairy background had served him only as a means of relating to a
tradition and as a cover for his satiric attacks. His developing technique opened many other possibilities to him
now. Farce replaced fancy, and whenever his caricatures
threatened to get out of hand, his jests cut too sharply, he
knew how to soften them with unexpected turns, masquerades,
verbal flourishes or comic misunderstandings that would divert possible antagonism into laughter. The play which
marked a definite break with the fairy tradition for Nestroy
was Zu ebener Erde und im ersten Stock (1835), developed
entirely in a realistic idiom. As the title suggests, the play
concerns the relations between a ground floor family, that of
the rag-merchant Schlucker, and their prosperous first-floor
neighbors, the family of the banker Goldfuchs. In the course
of the play the fortunes of the two families are reversed, but
a happy ending is achieved by the marriage of the families'
children, to whom fortune is no concern. The work was so
great a success that most Viennese critics for the first time
began to consider Nestroy superior to Raimund.

One of the most ingenious aspects of Zu ebener Erde
was its setting, which showed both apartments simultaneously,
one above the other.   This scheme was carried a step further in Das Haus der Temperamente (1837), which offered
four apartments with a family head of a different humour in
each.   Nestroy and Scholz played rival marriage brokers
with access to all four apartments, arranging a tangle of
farce misunderstandings and mismatching of incredible complexity.

The Wien's other major resident playwright of the
1830's was Friedrich Kaiser, who wrote a small book on the
career of Karl in 1854.   After the success of his first play,
Hanns Hasenkopf (1834), Kaiser signed a five-year contract
with Karl, which he soon had reason to regret.   Karl recognized Nestroy was his most valuable dramatist and treated
him accordingly, but with lesser figures he was ruthless.
Kaiser's contract forbade him to submit plays to other theatres unless they were first rejected by Karl, and then they
had to be passed on without any changes.   He was committed
to producing a full-length play every two months, and to replacing at once any refused by the censor.   Karl reserved
the right to make any changes in the scripts, and these had
to be kept in any published versions.   Finally, Kaiser was
to receive a flat sum of 25 Gulden for every play, whatever
its success.   After the great popularity of Wer wird Amtmann? (1836) Kaiser was able to argue Karl into a rate of
40 Gulden per play for the next year and 50 for the year
after, but a play as successful as Wer wird Amtmann? could
bring profits of 10,000 Gulden into the theatre.

Karl showed the same parsimony in physical presentation.   Nestroy could request such elaborate settings as the
multiple Haus der Temperamente, but no other writers fared
so well.   Karl ruthlessly cut, rearranged, and even rewrote
Goethe, Schiller and Grillparzer just as he did Kaiser, both
to cut down their scenic requirements and to improve, so he
thought, their theatrical effectiveness.   Since he had no
humble reed hut for the opening scene of Der Traum ein
Leben, he unconcernedly substituted a comfortable bourgeois
interior with a huge tiled oven.   For Die drei Eichen (1837),
Kaiser asked the designer de Pian for three ancient trees,
which must appear more than a century old.   Karl insisted
that the production make do with a set of young fruit trees
which were already in stock, none of them more than a few
inches across.

Authors like Kaiser tolerated such exploitation because
they had almost no other outlet.   Folk comedies and farces
were not welcome at the Burgtheater.   Marinelli proved ultimately no more successful at the Leopoldstädter than his
predecessor Steinkeller had been, so that Karl was able to
buy him out and once again, after 1838, control two of the
suburban stages.   The Josefstädter under Stöger's successor
Dr. Ignaz Scheiner continued to place its greatest emphasis
on operas such as Kreutzer's Melusina (1835).   At last an
alternative to Karl appeared in Franz Pokorny, who became
director of the Josefstädter in 1837.   Pokorny had an eclectic
taste in theatre, and broadened the repertoire to include
English tumblers, concerts, and a variety of dramatic genres.
Pokorny even encouraged Franz Xavier Told (1793-1849), who
in Der Zauberschleier (1842) and other works gave the Viennese stage its last examples of baroque machine plays.

Grand opera was not neglected.   Pokorny invited
Berlioz, Meyerbeer and Felicien David to direct their works
in his theatre.   He won the popular singer Josef Staudigl
(1807-1861) from the Hofoper and brought to Vienna such
major artists as Jenny Lind.   At the same time, however,
he reopened the theatre to popular comedy and thereby became Karl's first serious rival.   When Karl refused Kaiser's
Der Krämer und sein Commis (1838), the dramatist exercised
his contractual right to submit it unaltered to Pokorny.   It
was accepted, and achieved great success, but Kaiser's pleasure was increased by finding Pokorny as reasonable and
self-effacing as Karl was egoistic and autocratic, and as
open-handed as Karl was miserly.   From the beginning of
his directorship Pokorny shared profits with his authors, the
first director in Germany to do so (though Holbein at the
Burgtheater and Küstner in Berlin, who both began several
years later, have been given credit for the innovation).   He
gave Kaiser 100 Gulden upon acceptance of his play (as
against 25 to 50 from Karl), half the income after twenty
performances and a regular share thereafter.   In this way,
Kaiser was able to realize a profit of some 1000 Gulden on
play, and it is hardly surprising that a few months later,
when his contract with Karl expired, he joined Pokorny.   The
Josefstädter extended the same terms to authors less well
established than Kaiser, and had Karl not been able to rely
on Nestroy to support his theatre, he would presented few
new Viennese plays in the 1840s.   Pokorny offered not only
far better terms, but a company which in comedy and vaudeville was not greatly inferior to Karl's.   It was headed by
the popular Friedrich Beckmann and his wife Adele, Moritz

Rott, and Karl Treumann (1823-1877). Karl managed to win
Ida Brüning (1817-1867) away from the Josefstädter to play
opposite him in the French vaudevilles which enjoyed a considerable vogue in the 1840s, but Nestroy continued to be his
only really reliable attraction.

The writings of Young Germany were now receiving
great attention in intellectual circles and not even the suburban comedy theatres of Vienna escaped the passion of the
time for subjects of relevance and social engagement. Nestroy had done much to prepare the way for the new emphasis
by purging the folk play of its magical, other-worldly elements, then Kaiser took the next step, by writing plays of
political and social "uplift." He began this phase of his
career with thesis comedies such as Dienstbotenwirtschaft
(1840) concerning dishonest domestics and Der Rastelbinder
(1844), on the bourgeois love of luxury, then he went on to
more complex character studies such as Die Schule des
Armen (1847) and Männerschönheit (1848). The influence of
Nestroy can be seen in certain plays on words and couplets
on human folly (the striking couplet was a particular Nestroy
specialty), but the tone of all these works, social message
and all, is nearer sentimental comedy, or even drama.

Whether Kaiser exerted any influence on Nestroy is
more difficult to determine, but Nestroy did apparently attempt some accommodation toward those critics who urged
him to join Kaiser in presenting a more sympathetic picture
of humanity. His plays of the 1840's are still composed of
complex intrigues and sudden theatrical turns, but there are
more realistic and even sentimental touches, particularly of
an "edifying" nature, than in earlier works. Der Talisman
(1840), dealing with the Austrian prejudice against red-heads,
allowed its hero, Titus, to employ a fantastic variety of dis-
guises to cover his liability, but it also provided him with
an opportunity to speak penetratingly and movingly on social
prejudice and man's reliance on lies. He is a great comic
creation, but also Nestroy's first real raisonneur. Das
Mädl aus der Vorstadt (1841) featured Nestroy as a modest
and sympathetic lawyer, Schnoferl, opposed to the cynical intriguer Kautz. There was much wit and buffoonery in this
popular piece, but the rehabilitation by Schnoferl of a falsely
accused cashier was developed clearly for its sentimental and
uplifting qualities. Nestroy occasionally returned, as in
Liebesgeschichten und Heiratssachen (1843), to a free-wheel-
ing and unsentimental attack on bourgeois respectability and
the delusions of love, fortune, and happiness as unqualified

as in any of his early plays, but his general evolution was
toward a kind of comedic thesis play. The concern for
social justice which occupied so much German thought in the
years just before the revolution of 1848 clearly left its mark
on Nestroy's characters. The sort of pure comic he played
in Zu ebener Erde changed gradually to the superior raisonneur shunned by society like Titus, then to an intriguer
working actively for a better social order like Schnoferl or
Peter Span in Der Unbedeutende (1846).

Most of these plays were presented in both of Karl's
theatres, since the director made no attempt to maintain two
separate established companies but simply toured productions
back and forth. This pattern of production lasted until 1845
when the Theater an der Wien, where Karl was only a tenant,
was put up for sale and purchased by his rival Pokorny.
Karl then attempted to compensate for this loss by rebuilding
the Leopoldstädter into a house that would clearly outshine
either of Pokorny's. The result was the lavish Renaissance-
style Karltheater which opened in 1847. He also took advantage of Nestroy's more serious approach to elevate his
repertoire, banning the old Kasperl plays and many of the
magic plays in the Raimund-style which now seemed rather
quaint and old-fashioned. The new theatre scarcely had time
to establish itself, however, before Vienna was plunged into
the political turmoil of 1848.

Nestroy's reaction to the events of 1848 was similar
to that of many other dramatists. Of a generally liberal
inclination, he had responded to the drift of events in the
1840s by reflecting social concerns more and more clearly
in his work. Then, when the social conflict came to a head
in 1848, he was shaken by the extremes of both sides. Some
authors reacted to 1848 by turning from liberal to conservative, but Nestroy retired to a position much more suitable to
him, that of ironic detachment. He expressed equal disillusionment with the new order in 1848 and with the counter-
revolution in 1851, and as a result had some of his comedies
banned under both regimes. His only unqualified success
during these last turbulent years was Kampl (1852), which
returned to the gentle social satires of the previous decade.

The critical assessment of Nestroy has undergone
striking changes since his own time. During most of his
career he was beloved by the theatre public but scorned by
many critics for his cynicism, his indifference to social
problems, and his crudeness. Nestroy himself belittled his

gifts as an author, and for a generation after his death he
was remembered only as a popular and versatile actor. Indeed the legend grew up that his plays were of no significance
whatever, that only his interpretation made them such great
successes. The plays remained unprinted, his career relegated to scornful passing mention in literary histories. Then
fifty years after his death, in 1912, he was rediscovered by
the Viennese critic Karl Kraus, who almost singlehandedly
aroused a public demand for the author that eventually led to
his assuming a significant place in the traditional repertoire.
More than thirty of his works have been revived in Vienna
since 1945. After 1912 Nestroy suffered another half-century
under another myth, that his plays were untranslatable, even
into German. After World War II his reputation in Germany
has steadily grown, however, and bold translators and adap-
tors have found that something of his comic vitality can still
leap the language barrier. The American theatre is particularly indebted to Nestroy for his comedy Einen Jux will er
sich machen (1842), which served as the basis for Thornton
Wilder's The Matchmaker and in turn for the major musical
comedy Hello, Dolly.

Although Nestroy wrote for fourteen years after the
revolution of 1848, the changing theatrical situation removed
him from the prominence he had hitherto enjoyed. The open-
handed and accommodating Pokorny died, burdened with debts
and amid general sorrow, in 1850. Karl died a millionaire
in 1854, praised and honored, but apparently very little
mourned. With new directors came a new public and new
interests. The old popular comedy began to give way to the
operetta and Nestroy found himself overshadowed by the young
Karl Treumann as he had once overshadowed the aging
Raimund.

At the Burgtheater a vital new director appeared,
Heinrich Laube, who between 1849 and 1867 restored to that
theatre the European reputation it had enjoyed under Schreyvogel. He was invited to come as dramaturg, but he insisted on the more comprehensive title of director, with almost total freedom in casting, rehearsal practices, and repertoire. He judged rightly that much had to be done to revivify the Burgtheater. The actors were old, the ensemble
weak, the classics given only rarely and then in mutilated
versions, the public bored and indifferent. The new director's first concern was developing a repertoire which

every cultured man could totally accept. It should

> contain every play in the German theatre since
> Lessing with any vitality, plus all those plays of
> Shakespeare which are truly theatrical in the power
> of their composition and which can still engage
> one's sympathy; then from the romantics those few
> works which are most characteristic, such as, for
> example, Phaedra, Donna Diana, or Life is a
> Dream; and from the modern French all the salon
> plays which are well constructed and not contra-
> dictory to our own customs. 23

Naturally along with them went the building of a company
sufficiently large and flexible to interpret such a repertoire.
Laube was extremely interested therefore in discovering and
developing new talents, and he aroused much resentment
among the older Burgtheater actors by his willingness to
place untried youths in major roles which could have been
adequately filled by some proven member of the company.
A saying went around Vienna that while before Laube audiences used to characterize Burgtheater actors as good, but
too old, the complaint had now changed to young, but no good.

In fact Laube had a keen sense for developing talent,
and the actors which he encouraged and trained had a great
effect on the German theatre for the rest of the century. An
indication of what was to come could be seen in his first
production, Faust I, in which Faust and Gretchen were played
by new recruits to the theatre, Joseph Wagner (1818-1870)
and his wife Bertha (1822-1858). Wagner proved a useful
leading actor for Laube, who cast him in a wide variety of
roles, from the subdued creations of modern realistic authors
to Hamlet and the passionate young heroes of Schiller. His
subdued emotionality was generally praised in modern roles,
but there was some difference of opinion as to its effectiveness in Schiller and Shakespeare. In Wagner's necrology
Laube especially praised these parts, saying "He knew how
to make the Ideal believable, " but fellow-actor Ludwig
Gabillon felt Wagner robbed the traditional heroes of all
stature. Laube, in his opinion, was too susceptible to the
reasoning "I create actors; I have coached Wagner as Wallenstein; therefore Wagner is a great Wallenstein. "24

Julius Caesar gave the more colorful Bogumil Dawison
his first major role, as Antony, though he achieved a far
greater success in his next role, Andreas in Der Erbförster.
Ludwig's play, with Anschütz in the leading role, introduced
Burgtheater audiences to the new poetic-realist theatre.

Laube was accused by conservatives of encouraging the liberal
movement by offering the first Viennese production of Schiller's Die Räuber in 1850, though ironically Laube's fellows
in the Young Germany movement were condemning him at the
same time for his conservatism.   In fact he was more interested in expanding his repertoire than in taking political
positions.   In 1850 alone he did thirty premieres, among
them Grillparzer's Medea, Minna von Barnhelm, Emilia
Galotti, Nathan der Weise, Romeo and Juliet, Braut von
Messina, Fiesco, and Don Carlos.   Eventually he produced
nineteen of Shakespeare's plays, all of Schiller, four plays
by Goethe, three by Lessing, four by Kleist, and representative works by Ludwig, Gutzkow, Freytag, and himself.

His major oversight was Hebbel, whose talent Laube
apparently never recognized.   When he became administrator
the Burgtheater had just accepted a version of Julius Caesar
by Hebbel, created at Holbein's request.   One of Laube's
first official actions was to return this version to Hebbel,
explaining that he would rather present a version of his own,
a gesture which indicated clearly enough what the future relations between these two men would be.   Laube somewhat
grudgingly presented occasional revivals of Judith, but soon
gave up on Maria Magdalena, which he remarked was so
morally offensive that it had driven all women from the Burgtheater.   He frequently repeated the old charge that Hebbel's
tragedies lacked reconciliation and added to this the more
pragmatic concern that they were deficient in stagecraft.   In
fairness to Laube, it should be noted that a majority of
critics shared his assessment.   In the early 1850s, after the
failures of his most recent works, Hebbel's supporters were
few.   With Laube's power at the Burgtheater almost absolute,
the dramatist realized that he could achieve little more in
Vienna.   He discharged some of his disappointment in a
pleasant but minor work, Michel Angelo, which took as its
theme the inevitable opposition encountered by genius, and in
1851 returned with his wife to Berlin.

Though his repertoire was certainly more distinguished
than that of any other German theatre of his time, Laube
still presented more works by the usual popular authors Benedix, Bauernfeld, Halm, Birch-Pfeiffer, and so on than by
such authors as Schiller and Shakespeare.   He had a strong
personal inclination toward the contemporary French theatre
almost every new work by Scribe, Sardou, Labiche, Girardin,
Feuillet, Augier, and Dumas fils found its way quickly to the
stage of the Burgtheater.   Out of 363 new productions during

his administration, 95 were translations from contemporary
French authors. This naturally had a distinct influence on
the acting style and scene design of the theatre. Like Mon-
tigny in Paris, he found in the new social dramas the inspiration for a more realistic, seemingly more casual interpretation. He sought ordinary, unaffected conversation and
specialized in such realistic business as the use of a newspaper or tapping one's finger on a table. New emphasis was
placed on the ensemble, not only in the search for artistic
unity, but as a means of aiding every actor to create the
illusion of reality. Actors like Dawison who were accustomed
to elevating their own character were discouraged, and for
the first time the actors with minor parts were required to
be familiar with the entire play.

Laube's rehearsal period was longer and differently
organized from that of his predecessors. Previously a play
had at most one reading rehearsal and three or four rehearsals on stage, supervised but not truly directed by the
regisseur. Laube began with a series of reading rehearsals
followed by "orientation" rehearsals on stage. For the latter, actors had not yet memorized their lines, but practiced
merely moving and speaking in the actual set. Lines were
gradually added with Laube always willing to change them to
make delivery more relaxed and true to life. He insisted on
clarity of diction and gesture, however, and worked with each
actor on this before moving on to the ensemble rehearsals
which unified the whole. Constant personal work with his
actors was central to his vision. He argued,

> A theatre today should no longer be directed by a
> bureaucracy because the director's most important
> work must be done on the stage. Three-quarters
> of a play's success depends on this. Companies of
> actors grow and are stimulated only when their
> leader is always with them. [25]

Thus Laube, like Immermann, anticipated the modern director.

The same concern for realism and unity could be seen
in settings and the use of music, but a kind of poetic realism
was the goal, never the photographic realism which appeared
later in the century. After de Pian's death in 1851, Laube
called the gifted designer Moritz Lehmann from Dresden.
Laube worked closely with him and with Johann Kautsky, who
came ten years later, to achieve suitable visual effects, but

scenery never received the sort of detailed attention Laube
gave to his actors. He was fond of stating that the ear and
not the eye was the most important organ in the theatre. In
his own appraisal of his Don Carlos of 1850 he admitted:

> the chambers were rather tacky and I should pro-
> bably have provided something better in the way of
> tapestries and furnishings. But the public was then
> still under the influence of Goethe and quite con-
> tent with a shabby Spanish interior so long as they
> could hear Schiller's poetry ... and I admit that I
> myself preferred to spend money for a good actor
> rather than for a beautiful set. [26]

Even so, Laube made at least two distinct contributions to stage design, one in poetic and another in realistic
drama. The French salon plays naturally interested him in
the box set, and it was under his administration that this
was first generally used. His other experimentation was less
common, since it was associated with the poetic and symbolic
plays which formed a much smaller portion of the repertoire.
Still, in productions such as Grillparzer's Des Meeres und
der Liebe Wellen (1849) he went a step further than Schinkel
in Berlin toward settings based on internal visions rather
than on conventional architectural or natural elements. A
single example from that production will give an idea of the
kind of effect he sought:

> For the climax I built a flight of stairs in the
> temple, in order to achieve a painter's effect at
> the end which would help to suggest the upward
> striving of Hero's soul in search of the departed
> soul of Leander. I never bothered with the ques-
> tion of whether such a stairway might really be
> found in an ancient Greek temple--what do we know
> in any case of the architecture of that ancient time,
> mythologic even for the Greeks? And since we
> know nothing definite after all, why should we be
> inhibited, since the Idea is the decisive concern
> for me in a work of art, certainly more important
> than any question of archeology. [27]

With such settings, Laube prepared the way for the symbo-
lists at the end of the century. Such productions as Reinhardt's Pelléas und Melisande in 1903 had an almost identical
concern with the emotional meaning of the setting.

Laube apparently gave less attention to the symbolic possibilities of costume, probably because Stubenrauch had built up a huge stock of historically accurate costumes even before Laube's arrival. Between 1849 and 1859 this collection was further developed by Girolamo Franceschini (1820-1859) with such success that one traveler reported: "The costumes were as a rule based on historical exactitude throughout, as I have seen on no other stage. It was as if the portraits of Titian or Van Dyke had stepped from their frames."28 In many historical productions Laube was more careful in this respect than any German director of his time. He alone presented Die Räuber in authentic dress from the period of the Thirty Years' War while throughout the rest of Germany it was given in traditional rococo costume.

Several of the key actors present when Laube arrived remained with him during most of his administration: Löwe, La Roche, Anschütz, Beckmann, and the actresses Haizinger, Luise Neumann, and Wildauer, but the emphasis remained generally on his new discoveries. Joseph Wagner in tragedy was balanced by Karl Meixner (1818-1888) in comedy. A powerful and imaginative creator engaged in 1850, he knew how to inject an occasional tragic touch into his interpretation with great effect. His most famous role was Adam in Kleist's Der zerbrochene Krug. Laube's interest in modern French drama naturally led to the development of several actors specializing in that genre. Bernhard Baumeister (1828-1917) came in 1852 and became one of the best representatives of Laube's realistic style, playing engaging characters of simple hearts and warm dispositions. In his later years, he was a memorable Falstaff. Ludwig Gabillon (1823-1896) began as a young lead, supporting Emil Devrient in London in 1853. He came to Vienna the following year and remained there until his death, playing more than 300 roles, the great majority of them in salon plays. Adolf Sonnenthal (1834-1909) began as an extra at the Burgtheater, worked for a time in Königsberg, and returned in 1856. His first important success was as Don Carlos, but he worked to perfect himself in the interpretation of modern French works, studying Parisian actors and guest artists Rossi and Salvini from Italy to attain the necessary elegance. As a result he eventually became known as the greatest German interpretor of salon drama. Two important later additions to this influential group of modern realistic actors were Ernst Hartmann (1844-1911) from Hamburg and Friedrich Krastel (1839-1908), who had trained with Eduard Devrient in Karlsruhe. Laube's interest in psychological analysis of characters was developed

in another direction by the intellectual Josef Lewinsky (1835-
1907), who gained a European reputation by his rich studies
of such classic roles as Mephisto, Iago, and Richard III.

Amalie Haizinger, Luise Neumann, and Fräulein
Wildauer were all adequate in comedy roles, but Laube at
first lacked a tragic heroine.   In 1850 he obtained Marie
Bayer from Dresden, but was unable to keep her.   Not until
the arrival in 1862 of Charlotte Wolter (1833-1897) did he
have an actress strong enough to balance his leading men.
She was a natural rather than intellectual actor and had an
astonishing range, with every new role quite different from
the rest.   Her first part in Vienna, and one of her greatest,
was Iphigenie, and she asked to be buried in that costume.
She was as powerful, however, in historical dramas and salon
plays as in the classics.   Though for thirty-five years the
Burgtheater was her home, she toured widely abroad and was
Vienna's contribution to that group of international actresses
including Rachel, Bernhardt, and Duse that dazzled the theatre world of the late nineteenth century.   Among her most
famous roles were Hermione in The Winter's Tale, Phaedra,
Lady Macbeth, Adelheid in Götz, Grillparzer's Sappho and
Medea, and Sardou's Cleopatra, Feodora, and Madame Pom-
padour.

With all Laube's success and popularity, and despite
his freedom from bias for any political position, the conservative elements in the Viennese aristocracy never forgave
him for his early ties to Young Germany.   They strongly resented the freedom he had demanded and obtained in his position as director, but were unable to abridge it until 1867,
when a new and strongly conservative Court Minister, Prince
Hohenlohe, became general supervisor of the theatre.   Doubts
were planted in his mind concerning the advisability of Laube
retaining his almost complete autonomy, and the result was
the appointment of the dramatist Halm as general intendant
over Laube with final authority on repertoire and casting.
Laube refused to submit to this erosion of his position and
gratified his enemies by resigning almost at once.   So ended
the second great period of the Burgtheater.

The years of Laube's directorship at the Burgtheater
were transitional years in Vienna's suburban houses.   After
1848 a new public with new tastes and interests appeared
here.   The old popular drama did not engage them and
gradually disappeared, despite the ability of such authors as
Nestroy and such actors as Scholz.   In its place came a new

form which after 1870 dominated these theatres, the operetta. Pokorny's son Alois inherited his father's theatres, but soon gave up the more expensive Josefstädter. In 1851 he presented at the Theater an der Wien an occasional play celebrating its half-centenary, Papageno und der Zeitgeist by Haffner, with a one-act operetta as a curtain-raiser. This work, Das Pensionat, by the theatre's resident composer Franz von Suppé (1820-1895) was Vienna's first contribution to this genre. Despite its popularity, Suppé did not produce another operetta until Die Kartenschlägerin in 1862. This was apparently due to Alois Pokorny's mistaken conviction that the old folk farce could be revivified. Such authors as Kaiser, Langer, and Alois Berla dutifully produced Raimundstyle comedies for him, while Karl Elmer carried on the tradition of the magic play. Audiences steadily dwindled, and the financial problems which Alois had inherited from his father grew worse. A Viennese monetary crisis in 1863 drove him at last into bankruptcy. The Josefstädter under the direction of Johann von Mühlfeld (until 1855) and Josef Hoffmann, presented most of the same authors with the same lack of success. Hoffman diminished his losses for a time by opening a second house, the Thaliatheater, for the presentation of spectacle plays, but at the end of the decade his administration also collapsed.

At the Karltheater Nestroy followed Karl as director, and it was ironically this company, with the best actors and authors remaining from the old tradition, which gave the new operettas their first important encouragement, thereby avoiding the catastrophe which overtook its rivals. Nestroy of course presented his own plays as well as those of Kaiser and others in the old tradition, but he also welcomed as guest artists in 1856 actors and singers from the Parisian Variétés-Palais-Royal and Gymnase. These brought samples of the operettas just then being introduced in Paris by such writers as Hervé, and the public interest was as great in Vienna as it had been in France. Karl Treumann, now the theatre's leading actor, appeared in 1858 in the first full-length operetta on the Viennese stage, Offenbach's The Marriage by Lantern. Four more operettas were offered the following year, and in 1860 the great Orpheus in the Underworld, with Nestroy himself as Jupiter.

In 1861 Treumann left the Karltheater to establish a theatre devoted entirely to operetta, the Kaitheater. Works by Offenbach and by Suppé in imitation of Offenbach formed the basic repertoire and Treumann and his leading lady, Marie

Geistinger (1828-1903), became the first stars of the new
genre. After Nestroy retired in 1861, his successor Anton
Ascher attempted to increase the popularity of the Karltheater by turning to operettas, reviews, and spicy and scandalous burlesques from Paris. Treumann's company and
orchestra was clearly superior in this sort of offering, but
fortunately for Ascher the rivalry did not last long. In 1863
the Kaitheater burned and Treumann, Suppé, and the rest of
the company returned to the Karl.

Friedrich Strampfer restored prosperity to the bankrupt Theater an der Wien by bringing Offenbach himself to
direct his major works there between 1864 and 1867. So enthusiastic was his reception that the composer reported himself more at home in Vienna than in Paris. Strampfer won
over Marie Geistinger to play leading roles opposite Albin
Swoboda (1836-1901) and the comic Karl Blasel (1831-1901).
This forced Treumann at the Karl to develop a new leading
lady, but Josefine Gallmeyer (1838-1884) proved quite capable
of assuming Geistinger's roles with no loss in public interest.
In addition to Suppé, still the major Viennese operetta composer of the time, Treumann now had the services of a popular new composer, Carl Millöcker (1842-1899). Together
they prepared the way for the leading figures of the golden
age of Viennese operetta, Alexander Girardi and Johann
Strauss.

5.   Franz von Dingelstedt

Franz von Dingelstedt (1814-1881) was the only other
director of Laube's generation to rival him in importance.
His contribution complemented Laube's so strikingly, moreover, that their contemporaries remarked that a combination
of the two would produce the ideal director. This specula-
tion proved to an extent prophetic, for the influential productions of Georg, Duke of Saxe-Meiningen, later in the century in fact showed clear influence from the practice of each
of these imaginative theatre leaders.

Dingelstedt, like Laube, was associated in his youth
with Young Germany, publishing radical pamphlets and striking up a friendship with the exiled Heine in Paris. Then in
1843, to the chagrin of his liberal friends, he accepted a
position as librarian and private reader for the King of Württemberg in Stuttgart. His position involved him in the selec-

tion of plays for the court theatre, and having been a frequent
patron of the theatres of London and Paris, he became quite
interested in the process of dramatic production. The Stuttgart Hoftheater, then under the intendant Ferdinand von Gall,
was fortunate enough at that time to possess three talented
regisseurs, each of whom made a distinct contribution to the
formation of Dingelstedt's ideas: Heinrich Moritz (1800-1867),
who shared Laube's interest in the nuances of speech and in
realistic box settings; Karl Grunert (1810-1869), who brought
to his productions the concerns of historical realism; and
August Lewald (1792-1871), regisseur of the opera, who was
involved in developing the power and effectiveness of crowd
scenes.

In 1850 Dingelstedt wrote his only successful play, the
tragedy Das Haus Barneveldt, which was so popular in Munich
that it earned him an invitation to become intendant of the
theatre there. Thus he joined a group of North German intellectuals headed by the Prussian historian Wilhelm von
Döniges that surrounded King Maximilian and were working
to make Munich a new Weimar. Dingelstedt's association
with the "foreign colony" at court was inevitable, but it
gained him automatic enemies among the clergy and the old
Bavarian aristocracy who resented the Prussian influence on
Maximilian.

Despite a certain opposition, Dingelstedt was able to
raise the Munich theatre to major importance between 1851
and 1857. He erected a new home for it in 1854, equipped
with gas lighting to give him greater control over the optical
effects which he considered of primary importance to his
productions. He sought to build a new repertoire with more
classics and such moderns as Laube, Grillparzer, and Hebbel
along with the usual Halm, Mosenthal, Birch-Pfeiffer, and
Benedix. He was able, after some difficulty with the conservative Bavarian elements at court, to present Schiller's
Wallenstein, Tell, Braut von Messina and Turandot, but
Nathan der Weise's religious theme made it impossible, and
Minna von Barnhelm was banned as being "too Prussian."

One of the first important successes of Dingelstedt's
Munich administration was Hebbel's Judith with Marie Dam-
böck and Friedrich Dahn (1811-1889). Like Immermann,
Dingelstedt relied heavily on local painters for stage compositions and the Munich "Formkunst" school left a distinct
mark on this and subsequent productions. It was a school
whose artistic goal was close to Dingelstedt's own, a realism

which yet reflected an ideal of beauty. Kaulbach, the leading
historical painter of this school, not only designed the costumes and properties for Judith, but even suggested stage
groupings. Dingelstedt reported with great pride that the
noted painter "took an active part in the rehearsals, adjusted
the folds of the lovely Miss Dambôck's gown, and even showed
Holofernes' servants the proper way of waving the peacock-
feather standards he had designed for them. "29

     The success of Judith led Dingelstedt to invite Hebbel
to premiere his next play in Munich. Hebbel therefore came
down from Berlin to attend the rehearsals and performance
of Agnes Bernauer here in 1852. Once again Hebbel depicted an innocent victim to a declining social order, this
time illustrated from German history, but the evolution of
the dramatist's thought caused him to give the familiar story
of Agnes a new interpretation. All previous versions had
presented Agnes, a barber's daughter who marries a Duke
and then must be killed so that the Duke may ascend to the
throne, as a victim of a barbaric code of value. But Hebbel,
viewing with a suspicious eye the "democratic" results of
the revolution of 1848, was willing to find some justice in
the state's cruel demand. The message of this play, he
said, was

>   ... that the individual, however good and great,
>   noble and beautiful he may be, must yield to so-
>   ciety under all circumstances, because in it and
>   its necessary formal expression, the state, all
>   human nature lives, while in the individual only
>   the single phase comes to development. 30

     The play recalls Maria Magdalena in its well-knit con-
struction and clarity of conflict, but suffers from a certain
ambiguity in Hebbel's own attitude. Intellectually he had
come to a conviction of the validity of Duke Ernst's demands
in the name of the state, but emotionally his sympathies remained with the sacrificial victim. Thus despite the clarity
of its conflict, the play received a confused reaction. The
dramatist's friends called the premiere a triumph, his enemies a disaster. The most balanced appraisal is probably
Dingelstedt's own, in his Literarisches Bilderbuch, where he
reports that the first two acts were received with enthusiasm,
the third (which dealt most directly with class conflict) created a sensation, and the last two had little effect at all.
The only group which seemed clear in its reaction was the
conservative Bavarian critics, who assumed automatically

that nothing worthwhile could come out of north Germany. Agnes Bernauer was not repeated, reportedly because of illness in the cast, but Hebbel assumed, rightly, that opposition to his works would continue in Munich. He therefore refused Dingelstedt's urging that he remain, and thereby avoided the embarrassment of being present when his Michel Angelo and Genoveva were refused production here.

Hebbel's next major work, Gyges und sein Ring, was completed in 1854. It sold well as a book, but attracted no producers. Munich, Berlin, and Vienna remained disinterested in a new Hebbel play and Gyges was not performed until Förster finally offered it at the Burgtheater in 1889. Nevertheless many critics consider this to be Hebbel's best work, and it is surely the one which most successfully balances his theory of historical evolution with a sympathetic view of the past. The story of Kandaules, King of Lydia, his wife Rhodope and his best friend Gyges is taken from Herodotus, who tells how Kandaules precipitated his own destruction by inviting his best friend to gaze on his wife's exposed beauty. In revenge she convinces the friend to kill the King and take his place. Hebbel in the King and Queen repeated certain features of Holofernes and Judith or Herodes and Mariamne. Kandaules is similarly intolerant of his wife's personal rights and thus places her, at least to begin with, in the role of martyr. Hebbel qualifies all this, however, by making the King the visionary of the new order and the ultimate victim and Rhodope the bastion of tradition. Her modesty is intrinsically understandable, but Hebbel takes it to extreme lengths and relates it to an unyielding and unthinking committment to a rigid code of behavior. She thus demands and obtains her husband's death in part simply because her system requires it, just as Herodes' system demanded the sacrifice of Mariamne. Sympathy and blame is thereby divided equally.

There is, moreover, another source of balance. The destruction of both of these opposing forces (for Rhodope kills herself in Hebbel's version) does not leave the stage world empty, or with only a hint of a better order to come. Gyges lives on, partaking, as the Queen's lover and the King's friend, of the best qualities of both, and serving as a specific embodiment of the forward movement of history. In his letters from this period, Hebbel felt obliged to stress his commitment to tradition:

Agnes Bernauer shows that the state is the basis

of all human prosperity, <u>Gyges</u> reminds us of the
eternal necessity of custom and tradition. These
plays have great faults, but the general spirit expressed in them is not to be despised during a
time when people want to upset everything and re-
make the world. 31

Yet there is a certain exaggeration in this view, as there
was in Hebbel's expressed conviction before 1848 that the
world's problems lay in a conflict between freely developing
personalities and unjust, outmoded laws. Clearly his view
of history became more conservative during the 1850s, but
in his plays this resulted not in a reversal of sympathies,
but in the more balanced view of the tensions between tradition and innovation which we find most clearly expressed in
<u>Gyges und sein Ring</u>.

Hebbel's decision to return to Berlin was a great disappointment to Dingelstedt, but he had no difficulty in apply-
ing the unity of poetic, musical, and scenic elements which
he had sought in <u>Agnes Bernauer</u> to the work of other dramatists. The Munich company was not distinguished, and
Dingelstedt devoted little time to seeking new talents to improve it. Physical production, including crowd scenes,
music, and spectacle, was normally the most memorable
aspect of his presentations. The historian Martersteig compared him to Berlioz, noting that Berlioz reformed the
orchestra by broadening the instrumentation while Dingelstedt
brought a new richness to production by borrowing heavily
from the theatre's sister arts. Inspired by Tieck at Potsdam, he presented a classic <u>Antigone</u> in 1851, followed by
<u>Oedipus</u> and <u>Oedipus at Colonus</u>. Simon Quaglio created
Greek architectural settings on a classic stage with altar and
orchestra designed by Leo von Klenze. Mendelssohn composed music for the chorus, which was arranged in artistic
groupings by the painter Kaulbach. Similar care was given
to historical spectacle in such Shakespearian productions as
<u>Richard II, Julius Caesar</u>, and <u>Macbeth</u>, and Dingelstedt's
own adaptation of <u>The Tempest</u> allowed for more fanciful display. Emil Devrient appeared as a guest artist in <u>Hamlet</u>.
The other major outlet for Dingelstedt's love of crowd
scenes and spectacle was the opera, and he emphasized such
works as Meyerbeer's <u>Prophète</u>. The great French designer
Cambon was employed to design certain operatic settings.

The high point of Dingelstedt's Munich administration
was the <u>Gesamtgastspiel</u> of 1854 organized in conjunction with

the Munich Industrial Exposition. Dingelstedt then gathered
most of the notable actors of Germany for a series of productions of Goethe, Schiller, Lessing, and Kleist which he
suggested might serve as a model for a German national
theatre. The Burgtheater in Vienna contributed more actors
to this project than any other single theatre--Anschütz, La
Roche, Haizinger, Luise Neumann, and Julie Gley. The
other stars--Marie Seebach, Döring, Hendrichs, Wilhelm
Kaiser, Theodor Leidke, Heinrich Schneider, and Emil
Devrient--belonged for the most part to the virtuoso school
and were accustomed to being the single leading player where-
ever they performed. Imposing any sort of artistic unity on
their efforts was Dingelstedt's major problem, but with the
aid of mass scenes and elaborate settings he at least put the
performances against a consistent background. The festival
was an enormous success and a model for further such experiments, opening the way to Wagner's Bayreuth and Reinhardt's Salzburg.

       After this triumph, however, Dingelstedt's fortunes in
Munich declined rapidly. A cholera epidemic forced an early
closing of the festival and a financial depression immediately
afterward wiped out most of his profits. His enemies pointed
to his deficit as proof of his extravagance in sponsoring such
a festival. Dingelstedt infuriated conservative elements still
further by offering Wagner's Tannhäuser in 1855, ten years
after its Dresden premiere. Finally a rather trivial affair,
the Bacherl scandal of 1856, sealed Dingelstedt's doom.
Franz Bacherl, a Bavarian schoolmaster, claimed that one
of the popular successes of Friedrich Halm, Der Fechter von
Ravenna, had actually been plagarized from a play Bacherl
had submitted to a contest Halm was judging. When Dingelstedt continued to present the work under Halm's name, supporters of the local author caused a riot in the theatre.
King Maximilian ordered out troops to protect the building,
and Dingelstedt cancelled the play, but the riots continued,
doubtless encouraged by those seeking only to embarrass the
director. Finally Maximilian acceded to demands for
Dingelstedt's dismissal to restore public order.

       Fortunately, Dingelstedt had gained such a reputation
by 1856 that he had little difficulty in finding a new position.
At the urging of his friend Franz Lizst he was offered the
post of intendant at Weimar, where he remained ten years,
bringing to that theatre a reputation such as it had not enjoyed since the days of Goethe. At first he left the opera
entirely to Lizst, who had built a good company and orches-

tra, and concentrated his attention on the inferior spoken
theatre, but this arrangement was short-lived. Lizst's private life and his repertoire raised protests in Weimar despite
his important contributions. The protests culminated in a
demonstration against his production of an actually rather
charming minor work, Peter Cornelius' Barbier von Bagdad
(1858). As a result of this, Lizst left the theatre and thereafter Dingelstedt managed the opera as well. He brought
Tannhäuser and Der fliegende Holländer to Weimar, which
gave him new opportunities to develop mass effects and visual
spectacle.

Freed from the prejudices of the Bavarian court,
Dingelstedt could again encourage his friend Hebbel, and the
dramatist spent the summer of 1858 in Weimar preparing a
very successful production of Genoveva. This success was
particularly gratifying to Hebbel since the same year Laube
at the Burgtheater gave up presentation of his plays entirely.
The other most notable production of Dingelstedt's early
years in Weimar was Schiller's Wallenstein trilogy in 1859,
all three parts produced during a single day. The painters
he had met in Munich had much to do with the mounting of
this production, and Dingelstedt even created something of a
scandal by basing his final tableau on a controversial modern
painting by Karl Piloty.

The high point of Dingelstedt's Weimar directorship
came in 1864 with a cycle of almost all of Shakespeare's
history plays, lasting an entire week. This major event
marked the foundation of the German Shakespeare Society,
and was attended by many of the most influential figures in
the German theatre of that time and of the coming generation,
among them Duke Georg of Meiningen. In the cycle, Dingelstedt brought to fruition Klingemann's ideal of the creation
on stage of a living but artistically unified historical painting.
Charlotte von Hagn reported that the entire cycle possessed
a unity of effect in its ingredients, a harmony in its ensemble
such as was never seen afterwards. There was not an ob-
trusive element; no isolated virtuoso exalted himself at the
expense of others; and despite the huge number of super-
numeraries required, not even one of these worked counter
to the total effect. Unlike Reinhardt, who used crowds as
undifferentiated masses, Dingelstedt sought a group of distinct
individuals, creating a harmony by blending disparate elements. He was the first modern European director of
crowds, working out every detail of their composition in his
huge promptbooks. His descriptions of the effects sought

after recall those of Charles Kean, as we may see in that for
Act I, scene 2 of Henry V:

> A London street in the Eastcheap section. At one
> side of the stage, the Boar's Head Tavern. In the
> background a military company is seen marching
> across the stage to the beat of drums and martial
> music from the orchestra. The soldiers' caps are
> decorated with twigs and flowers. There are spec-
> tators in all of the doors and windows, cheering.
> Single men, women, and girls escort the troops.[32]

Yet despite certain similarities in their results, Dingelstedt condemned Kean for "placing the scene-painter,
machinist, costumer, and property-man above the poet and
the actor."[33] He considered Kean the victim of "archeological pedantry" and sought to avoid this in his own work by
relying on painters rather than scholars and encouraging them
to seek symbolic rather than historical accuracy. Like
Wagner, he strove for a Gesamtkunstwerk, but one based essentially on visual rather than auditory elements. He scorned
such simplified staging as that used by Laube at the Burgtheater:

> Nowadays, if we leave a drawing-room wherein the
> fashions and furnishings vie with each other in
> richness and charm and are confronted with a stage
> representing, let us say, an earl's apartment, with
> four cane chairs placed symmetrically at right and
> left, a pitiful horse-hair sofa in the background
> ... then by no means do we supplement this with
> an illusion of our own, rather we are irritated or
> amused at so much poverty, least acceptable in
> the theatre of all places.[34]

In 1862 Dingelstedt premiered Hebbel's last completed
work, the eleven-act Nibelungen trilogy. Unlike Wagner,
Hebbel dispensed with all the magical elements of the ancient
story, even though he did not completely modernize the
characters as his contemporary Emanuel Geibel (1815-1884)
did in his Brünhilde (1861). Hebbel saw himself as an interpreter of the great epic, clarifying the motivations of characters without reducing their semi-mythic stature or distance.
The subject was one which attracted many nineteenth century
German dramatists, but its particular appeal for Hebbel was
easy to see. Again the background was a clash of world
views, the climax the destruction of the old pagan order with

the coming of Christianity, and such figures as Siegfried, Brünhilde, and Kriemhild could be interpreted with many of the characteristics of Hebbel's earlier assertive individuals. Yet despite its sweep and grandeur, the cycle showed no real step forward for Hebbel from Gyges und sein Ring, and the inevitable comparisons with Wagner which followed have not usually been to Hebbel's advantage. The premiere too was notably less impressive than Dingelstedt's great Shakespeare and Schiller cycles, which gave the director more opportunity to display his skill at pageantry and mass effects. The costumes and settings of the Munich professor of art Karl Döpler laid such emphasis on historical accuracy that they seriously compromised Hebbel's delicate balance between epic stature and psychologically acceptable motivation. Yet with all these difficulties, the Nibelungen's powerful characterizations and strong sense of the dramatic made this one of Hebbel's most frequently performed works. Its Weimar production stimulated such a demand for it in Vienna that Laube relaxed his opposition and offered the first two parts of the trilogy at the Burgtheater. The success of the work here was far greater than at Weimar, and when Hebbel died, two years later, he was at the peak of his fame, recognized at last both as a major poet and a great dramatist.

The departure of Laube from the Burgtheater in 1867 suggested to Dingelstedt the possibility of becoming director of that great house, far superior in facilities and company to either Munich or Weimar. Laube's place was at first filled by the popular dramatist Halm with the aid of the regisseur August Wolff, but Dingelstedt guessed correctly that the administration of these weak leaders would be short. He therefore accepted an offer to become director of the Vienna Hofoper and awaited the next favorable opportunity to move on to the Burgtheater. In the meantime, he introduced his interest in an optical ensemble to the Vienna operatic stage. He commissioned a much larger theatre, the Haus am Ring, where he moved from the old Kärntnertortheater in 1869. The much larger new stage required the restaging of all previous offerings, and Dingelstedt produced twenty such new stagings in his first ten months here. He reorganized the orchestra and demanded that the hitherto stationary chorus participate significantly in the action. Gounod considered his Faust and Roméo et Juliette superior to the Paris productions, and the crowd scenes for Meyerbeer's Huguenots and L'Africaine were generally considered to be unequalled anywhere else in Europe.

In 1870 Dingelstedt's ambition to gain the directorship
of the Burgtheater was at last realized, but the social and
financial instability created by the Franco-Prussian War in-
terfered with his activities for the next several years. He
presented works by the now aging Bauernfeld and Benedix,
along with those of a younger popular dramatist, Adolf Wilbrandt, and gave Grillparzer and Hebbel a significance in the
repertoire which they had never achieved under Laube. His
leading lady, Charlotte Wolter, entered her great years with
her interpretation of Medea in 1871. His major project during his first years at the Burgtheater was the premiering of
Grillparzer's three posthumous works, but he ran into unexpected competition. Laube, after leaving the Burgtheater,
had gone with his voice teacher Strakosch to the theatre at
Leipzig, but he found his efforts there resisted by a bureaucratic administration and by recalcitrant virtuoso actors. He
therefore returned to Vienna and in 1872 founded the Stadttheater, a home for spoken drama competing directly with
the Burgtheater. One of his first offerings was Grillparzer's
Bruderzwist, which he argued was more suitable to his theatre than to the royalist Burgtheater, since it depicted the
Hapsburgs in an unfavorable light. Dingelstedt's own production nevertheless opened four days later, and though the
Burgtheater had the advantage of the best ensemble company
in Germany, Laube had an excellent tragic hero in Theodor
Lobe (1833-1898) and both productions drew warm praise.
The next year Dingelstedt offered Die Jüdin von Toledo, but
was anticipated by several months by the theatre in Prague.
Thus from his original project Dingelstedt gained only one
true Grillparzer premiere, with Libussa in 1874. Charlotte
Wolter, as usual, took the leading role. Her reputation
grew steadily with revivals of the Hebbel Nibelungen
trilogy and Judith in 1875.

By the mid-1870s most of the negative effects of the
Franco-Prussian war and of Austria's 1866 defeat by Prussia
had passed, but a new audience had come into the theatre
during these years, a new monied class unaccustomed to the
traditions of the Burgtheater. They came not so much to
enjoy themselves as to display themselves, considering the
play something merely to be tolerated for a social occasion.
It is hardly surprising that this new public generally favored
Dingelstedt, with his emphasis on spectacle, to Laube, who
stressed language. The costumer Franz Gaul (1837-1906)
and the designer Herman Burghart (1834-1901) assumed a
prominence under Dingelstedt which had never been theirs

during the Laube administration.   Dingelstedt also continued
to work closely with leading painters, as he had in Munich.
The Viennese Makart, who specialized in voluptuous portrayals of classic scenes, proved the perfect designer for
such pseudo-classic works as Adolf Wilbrandt's (1837-1904)
Gracchus (1872), Arria und Messalina (1874) and Nero (1875).

The French salon plays so beloved by Laube were
now presented only occasionally, while the emphasis of the
repertoire returned to native writers.   In addition to the important revivals of Hebbel and Grillparzer, the theatre
offered generous selections from the Posse writers Benedix,
Moser, and Bauernfeld, and the sentimental Mosenthal and
Weilen.   In Vienna as in Weimar one of the high points of
Dingelstedt's directorship was a huge cycle of Shakespearian
histories.   The Vienna cycle of 1875, including Richard II,
both parts of Henry IV, and Henry V, was of course carried
out with a company and technical staff far superior to that of
Weimar, and was widely considered the greatest series of
productions ever seen at the Burgtheater.   Despite the enormous drain it made on the theatre's resources, the cycle's
fame was such that it was revived six times later in the
century.   As always, crowd scenes and visual spectacle were
an important part of the cycle, but Dingelstedt took full advantage of his truly outstanding company.   Sonnenthal, who
interpreted Richard, Ernst Hartmann (1840-1911), who
played Hal and Henry V, and Bernhardt Baumeister (1828-
1917), who played Falstaff, were all actors trained under
Laube, and now in their prime.

Dingelstedt inherited one of Europe's foremost acting
ensembles, but he made important additions to it.   His first
discovery was the imaginative and emotional Friedrich Mitterwurzer (1845-1897), who first appeared with Charlotte Wolter
in an 1876 production of Macbeth claimed by critics to have
achieved a level of realism unknown before then.   Dingelstedt
was unsympathetic to Mitterwurzer's claim that he could do
both comedy and tragedy, and so lost his first important discovery to Laube at the Stadttheater.   Hugo Thimig (1854-
1944) came in 1874 and became one of the great comic actors
of the latter part of the century in such plays as Freytag's
Journalisten and Gogol's The Inspector General.   Two new actresses, Josefine Wessely (1860-1887) and Stella Hohenfels
(1854-1920), provided a charming balance in interpretation, the
former specializing in young lovers, the latter in hoydenish roles
such as Georg in Götz and Puck in A Midsummer Night's
Dream.   These both however achieved their greatest success

under Dingelstedt's successor Wilbrandt, as did the Hungarian
virtuoso Emmerich Robert (1847-1899).

The most notable productions of Dingelstedt's later
years were The Vikings at Helgeland in 1876, the first Ibsen
play presented in Vienna; a new series of Mustervorstellungen
in that same year to celebrate the theatre's centenary; and
Antony and Cleopatra in 1878 with Sonnenthal and Wolter.
For the latter, huge crowd scenes were developed against
archeological reconstructions of Rome and Egypt so detailed
and painstakingly accurate that in Vienna Dingelstedt became
known as "Shakespeare's Schliemann." In order to maintain
control over such enormous productions, Dingelstedt instituted
in Vienna an important change in the regisseur system. Previously regisseurs had alternated monthly without regard for
what plays were being prepared or were in production, but
Dingelstedt in addition to his close personal supervision demanded that a single regisseur guide each work through the
lengthy rehearsal period and the first three performances
before it entered the monthly cycle. Under this system, the
Burgtheater and its outstanding company was well prepared
to continue its profitable and influential career after Dingelstedt's death in 1881. Three years later Laube died, and
the same year his Stadttheater was destroyed by fire. In
his brief directorship there, Laube had little opportunity to
create a theatre of the stature Dingelstedt, building on
Laube's own work, had achieved at the Burgtheater. No one
even proposed rebuilding the Stadttheater after the fire, and
the Burgtheater became once again Vienna's only theatre of
the spoken word.

6.   Richard Wagner

Grand opera in the French or Italian manner dominated the German operatic stages between 1830 and 1850, with
most of the major theatre centers involved in such production.
Klingemann established a respectable opera in Hamburg, and
Ludwig Spohr worked with distinction in Kassel. Munich's
operatic company was weak, but this deficiency was somewhat covered by an excellent orchestra. Darmstadt, Stuttgart, and various other cities were provided with opera by a
sovereign with a particular interest in this genre, but the
major German operatic centers were Dresden and Berlin.
In both cities an intendant had general responsibility for both
opera and drama, but the repertoire and many other concerns

of the opera were in fact controlled by the conductor. Since
this important post was held in Dresden by Morlacchi until
his death in 1841 and in Berlin by Spontini until the appointment of Meyerbeer in 1842, it is not surprising that these
major houses presented during the 1830s mostly the Rossini,
Bellini, and Donizetti tradition from Italy and the Auber,
Adam, and Meyerbeer tradition from France.

This foreign dominance was beginning to weaken by
1840. Gustav Albert Lortzing (1801-1851) achieved a major
success in Berlin with his Zar und Zimmermann in 1839.
This, with Der Wildschütz (1842) and Der Waffenschmied
(1846) established a popular new German genre, a light and
sentimental style of musical comedy with traces of Viennese
Singspiel, Mozart, and the fantasies of the romantics. The
death of Morlacchi allowed Dresden's intendant von Lüttichau
and his new conductor Karl Reissiger to open that stage more
freely to German composers, and particularly to Wagner.
Hofrath Winckler, still serving as editor of the Abendzeitung
and secretary of the theatre, as he had done in the days of
Tieck, was an old family friend of Wagner's and urged the
theatre to accept Rienzi, which Wagner had attempted, un-
successfully, to present in Paris. This request was supported from Berlin by Meyerbeer and the premiere took place
in 1842. Though Wagner himself was concerned by the length
of the work--it ran more than five hours--it was in fact a
great success. Rienzi had little of the technical novelties
that disturbed audiences in the later works and it was moreover interpreted by two of Germany's outstanding singers,
Joseph Tichatschek (1807-1886) and Wilhelmine Schröder-
Devrient.

Wagner now took up residence in Dresden, and the
Opera asked Berlin to give up its option to premiere his next
work, Der fliegende Holländer. Meyerbeer protested, but
his superiors were delighted to oblige. The sympathetic
Count Redern had retired as intendant in 1842 and his successor Küstner openly expressed his opposition to this composer whom he considered even in his first works too far
removed from French and Italian models. Dresden therefore
premiered the opera in 1843 with Wagner himself conducting
and with the same leading singers as in Rienzi. Apparently
Wagner worked well with this company, even reworking difficult sections at their request, but the public showed far less
enthusiasm than it had for Rienzi. After the historicity of
Meyerbeer, the Holländer seemed a bit old-fashioned in its
romanticism and moreover lacked Rienzi's florid grand opera

appeal. Tannhäuser (1845) was closer to the grand opera
style, but imbued with the symbolic concerns of Der Holländer, and technically much more revolutionary than either.
Here for the first time Wagner developed fully the symbolic
musical motifs which he later called Sprechgesang. Weber
and Marschner had experimented with some tonal interpretation of texts in opposition to classic phrase formation, but
nothing before Tannhäuser developed this technique so
thoroughly or consistantly. Under the circumstances, it is
a credit both to the Dresden public and to Tichatschek and
Schröder-Devrient that despite initial bafflement on all sides
the work continued to be presented and eventually won a
permanent place in the repertoire. Wagner's niece Joanna
(1828-1894), who was to become one of his major interpreters, sang the role of Elisabeth. The other operas Wagner
conducted in Dresden were important, but considerably less
innovative. He revived three works by Gluck, a composer
almost forgotten in the German theatre until Wagner and
Liszt reintroduced him at this time. Wagner's repertoire
included Donizetti and Halévy, but he placed a distinct emphasis on the Germans--Mendelssohn, Flotow, Lortzing, and
Marschner, whose Adolf von Nassau was premiered here in
1845.

Throughout his life, Wagner was prey to rapidly
shifting fortunes. After his successes in Dresden he was
invited to conduct Rienzi in Berlin in 1847. It was indifferently received. The following year Wagner aroused the suspicion of the Dresden court by his public support of the
revolutionary movement, and his works were temporarily
removed from the repertoire. With members of the community and of the theatre calling for his dismissal, Wagner
obtained a leave from von Lüttichau to visit Vienna, ostensibly
for reasons of health. Wagner hoped to obtain a position in
the Kärntnertortheater, but failed to do so, and was forced
to return to Dresden. His Lohengrin premiere was cancelled, purportedly for financial reasons. Far from being
chastened by these discouragements, Wagner plunged more
deeply into revolutionary activity, with the result that in 1849
he had to flee Dresden to escape arrest.

Wagner briefly sought sanctuary in Weimar, where
Franz Liszt (1811-1886) was conductor. Liszt, who had
come to Weimar in 1844, had for several years dreamed of
a collaboration with Wagner that would raise Weimar to musical excellence as the Goethe-Schiller alliance had raised it
to theatrical excellence a half century before. Ironically

Wagner came to Weimar not as an artistic collaborator but
as a fugitive, and Weimar had to serve him only as a way-
station on the road to exile in Switzerland. Wagner and
Liszt had a long and close association, as a voluminous correspondence testifies, but Liszt's proposal of a musical center in Weimar was now impossible. He did have the honor
of premiering Lohengrin in 1850 after Wagner's departure,
and gave also Tannhäuser and Der fliegende Holländer, but
with little support from either the court or the public.
Wagner's political radicalism turned many against him, and
Karl Alexander, who became grand duke in 1853, favored
Dingelstedt and the spoken drama over Liszt and the opera.
In vain Liszt pleaded for permission to perform the operas
of the Ring cycle. The unfortunate reception given to Cornelius' Barbier von Bagdad in 1858 was the final indignity and
after the public protests over this production he submitted
his resignation. At the grand duke's request he remained in
Weimar two seasons more, but had as little to do with the
opera there as possible.

During the early years of his exile Wagner wrote four
major essays which formed much of the intellectual underpinning of his work: Die Kunst und die Revolution (1849),
Das Kunstwerk der Zukunft (1849), Das Judenthum in der
Musik (1850), and Oper und Drama (1851). The first praised
Athenian drama as a total art work (Gesamtkunstwerk) uniting
all arts into a civil and religious celebration, and called for
a revolution to free German society to produce a similar expression. The second emphasized the importance of the
people (Volk) as the primary inspiration for this new drama.
The third blamed the Jew as the central manifestation of the
materialism which stood in the way of the new art, and the
last described the form of the art, a word-tone drama in
which verse, vocal line, and orchestra, united by certain
motifs, would convey the conceptual in terms of the musical.

After the appearance of these essays, Wagner poured
his energy into the masterpiece which they anticipated, the
Ring cycle. In the meantime Zürich, his home in exile, produced Holländer in 1852 and Tannhäuser in 1853. Certain
other cities in Germany still offered these early works, but
the major centers of German opera remained closed to him.

By the end of the decade, Wagner's reputation in Germany had distinctly improved. Though Berlin remained a
stronghold of anti-Wagner feeling, Hülsen grudgingly permitted
productions of both Tannhäuser and Lohengrin in the late

1850s. In Vienna the composer Karl Eckert began introducing Wagner to the Hofoper in 1858 with a very successful
Lohengrin. In 1860 Johann, the new king of Saxony, declared
that while he did not wish Wagner to return to Dresden, he
had no objection to his return to any other part of Germany,
if the local princes would approve. This growing acceptance
of the rebellious composer was notably speeded by the scandalous reception of Tannhäuser in Paris in 1861. The Germans closed ranks behind the victim of a French cabal, and
Wagner returned home almost in triumph. Tannhäuser, restored to the Dresden stage, was cheered as never before.

Several cities now competed for the honor of presenting the first Tristan und Isolde, and Wagner selected Vienna,
which offered the best orchestra, company, and facilities.
Here Tristan was plagued with difficulties, however. The
tenor Alois Ander (1821-1864) lacked the power of Wagner's
first great interpreter Tichatschek, and pleaded a persistent
hoarseness despite Wagner's reworking of much of the score
for him. Louise Dustmann (1831-1899), who was to sing
Isolde, became furious with Wagner for his public interest in
her disreputable sister Friederike. Finally, Wagner reopened old wounds that others were trying to heal by openly
insulting the influential critic Eduard Hanslich. Hanslich, a
friend of Brahms and proponent of Schumann, had steadily
condemned the first Wagnerian offerings in Vienna, but
grudgingly consented to attend a private reading of Wagner's
new work Die Meistersinger. For the occasion, Wagner
maliciously called the pedantic character which eventually became Beckmesser, Hans Lick. The furious critic renewed
his condemnations, encouraging other opponents of Wagner,
and a combination of this unfortunate publicity and difficulties
within the company led to an indefinite postponement of the
production.

Wagner's life was full of abrupt reversals, but none
more spectacular than those of the early 1860s. In 1862 he
was apparently well-established in Vienna, anticipating production of a major new work. The following year he was
wandering homeless over Europe, hounded by creditors, at
one of the lowest points of his career. Then almost miracu-
lously he received in 1864 an unsolicited invitation from Ludwig, King of Bavaria, to accept the royal patronage and
pursue his career free from all financial cares in Munich.
Thus began the great years of this remarkable career, and
a new era in German music. As if in confirmation of the
passing of the old order, word came to Wagner on the morn-

ing of his departure for Munich of the death of Meyerbeer in
Paris.

Though Dingelstedt had presented Tannhäuser in
Munich in 1855, he never brought to the opera there the distinction he gave the spoken theatre. Wagner found in Munich
almost nothing of what he needed to perform his demanding
works. He began at once organizing a conservatory and
training an orchestra. A temporary stage was built in
Munich's main exhibition hall to experiment with new machinery, lighting, and acoustics. Here Wagner attempted for the
first time enveloping his orchestra in a hollow area under
the stage to remove them from sight without impairing their
tonal quality. Ludwig summoned the architect Semper from
Berlin to incorporate the experiments from this stage into a
permanent opera house. The first and most important
Wagner premiere in Munich was Tristan und Isolde in 1865.
For the leading roles the composer imported Schnor von
Carolsfeld and his wife Malvina whom he had admired in a
production of Lohengrin in Karlsrühe in 1862. The orchestra
was conducted by Hans von Bülow, one of Liszt's best pupils.
Though the work was poorly attended and indifferently received, the production at least dispelled the myth that Tristan was unperformable, and so the fullest expression of
Wagner's musical ideas to date was finally launched. Like
Sacre du Printemps at the beginning of our own century, it
gained acceptance slowly, but as it did so, increasingly
proved itself a seminal force in European music.

Wagner's life in Munich was as turbulent as ever.
His relations with Bülow's wife were a public scandal, and
his intense personal friendship with King Ludwig encouraged
him to meddle dangerously in Munich politics. Bülow produced a triumphant Meistersinger in 1868, his dedication to
his position allowing him to ignore for several years the
gossip that swirled about him, but by 1869 he could keep up
the pretense no longer and left Munich, Wagner, and his
wife. Wagner's political enemies, who had already forced
the King to renounce his influence, used this occasion to
close Munich to Wagner entirely. Ludwig consented, but
maintained correspondence with Wagner, continued with work
on the still uncompleted opera house and planned for a production of Das Rheingold with its composer exiled from the
city.

The new director of the theatre was Baron von Perfall, who exerted an independence in mounting this production

which infuriated Wagner. Richter, who had replaced von Bülow as conductor, was more malleable, and Wagner encouraged him to work in opposition to von Perfall. When the elaborate scenery and machines for Das Rheingold ran into difficulties Richter blamed von Perfall for everything and resigned in protest, along with the baritone Franz Betz (1835-1900), another Wagner ally. It is probable that Wagner himself encouraged the crisis, hoping that he might be called back to set things right or at the very least that von Perfall might be replaced by Richter, but nothing of the sort transpired. With the aid of Carl Brandt, an outstanding machinist from Darmstadt, and with a new baritone and a new conductor, Franz Wüllner, Ludwig proceeded with the performance. Even demands from Wagner for its cancellation were ignored, and the production was much more favorably received than Tristan had been (though Wagnerites later claimed it to be a total failure). An even more successful Walküre followed in 1870, attracting a European audience which included such important figures from the musical world as Brahms, Saint-Saëns, and Liszt. Scarcely had this production entered the repertoire, however, when the Franco-Prussian War broke out. This provided Wagner with an excellent occasion for discharging his hatred of the French, but his lesser irritation with the Munich opera was not forgotten. Ludwig waited in vain for the next work of the Ring cycle to add to his repertoire. Wagner's vision was now to establish a festival theatre of his own, where he would at last be answerable to no one.

Notes to Part II

1. E. Devrient, Geschichte der deutschen Schauspielkunst (Berlin, 1905), 291.

2. K. Immermann, Düsseldorfer Anfänge (Berlin, 1889), 86.

3. R. Fellner, Geschichte einer deutschen Musterbühne (Stuttgart, 1888), 201.

4. K. Immermann, Theaterbriefe (Berlin, 1851), 1.

5. Immermann, Düsseldorfer Anfänge, 15-16.

6. Quoted in M. Martersteig, Das Deutsche Theater im neunzehnten Jahrhundert (Leipzig, 1904), 339.

7. L. Börne, Sämtliche Schriften (Düsseldorf, 1964), I, 110.

8. L. Wienbarg, Aesthetische Feldzüge (Berlin, 1964), 76.

9. Letter of Jan. 1, 1836, G. Büchner, Gesammelte Werke (Munich, 1948), 433.

10. Letter of July 28, 1835, Büchner, Gesammelte Werke, 426.

11. Letter of Nov. 1833 (?), Büchner, Gesammelte Werke, 405-6.

12. Dantons Tod, II, 5.

13. K. Gutzkow, Dramatische Werke (Jena, 1881), II, 13-14.

14. O. Ludwig, Gesammelte Schriften (Leipzig, 1891), V, 51-52.

15. H. Laube, "Einleitung zu Mondaleschi," Meisterdramen (Leipzig, 1908), 31-32.

16. H. T. Rötscher, Seydelmanns Leben und Wirken (Berlin, 1845), 210.

17. S. R. Taillander, "Le Théâtre Contemporaine en Allemagne," Revue des Deux Mondes, XVI (Oct. - Dec., 1852), 543.

18. F. Hebbel, "Mein Wort über das Drama," Sämmtliche Werke (Hamburg, 1867), X, 44.

19. G. Kühne, Porträts und Silhouetten (Hannover, 1843), II, 342.

20. E. Bauernfeld, Das Theater, das Publikum und Ich (Vienna, 1849), 216.

21. Letter to Kühne, June 16, 1848, F. Hebbel, Briefe (Berlin, 1906), IV, 124.

22. In Der Sammler, quoted in J. Nestroy, Sämtliche Werke (Vienna, 1924-30), II, 670.

23. H. Laube, Das Burgtheater (Leipzig, 1868), 158.

24. H. Bettelheim-Gabillon, Ludwig Gabillon (Vienna, 1900), 116.

25. Laube, Burgtheater, 162.

26. H. Laube, Erinnerungen (Berlin, 1881), 190.

27. Laube, Burgtheater, 216.

28. F. Sternberg, Ein Fasching in Wien (1851), quoted in H. Kindermann, Theatergeschichte Europas, VII (Salzburg, 1965), 138.

29. O. Liebscher, Franz Dingelstedt (diss., Munich, 1909), 67.

30. Letter to Karl Werner, Feb. 16, 1852, F. Hebbel, Briefe, IV, 358-59.

31. Letter to Baron Cotta, Oct. 11, 1857, F. Hebbel, Briefe, VI, 74.

32. F. Dingelstedt, Gesammelte Werke (Berlin, 1877), XII, 375.

33. Ibid., 475.

34. F. Dingelstedt, Eine Fausttrilogie (Berlin, 1876), 103.

III. THE REALISTIC PERIOD
1870-1900

Wagner at Bayreuth and Duke Georg II of Saxe-Meiningen are the natural introduction to the closing third of the nineteenth century in the German theatre. Each was in a certain sense the culmination of a long tradition, Wagner of the whole romantic movement and Duke Georg of the stage tradition leading from Goethe through Immermann to Laube and Dingelstedt. Each in his own way drew from this tradition a similar vision, of a unified theatrical production organized and controlled by a single creative intelligence. Each was also a major innovator, breaking the restrictive patterns of the contemporary stage and preparing the way for a new period of experiment and expansion. After the enormous success of the Meininger tours, the dominance of the virtuoso actor in Germany was over. Both in their methods and organization of production the Meininger provided a new model, not only for Germany, but for all of Europe, as they were admired and emulated by such important figures as Irving in England, Antoine in Paris, and Stanislavsky in Moscow. Wagner's contributions in the area of staging were slight, but in addition to his reinforcement of the Meininger ideal of a total production and his major contributions to musical theatre, he built at Bayreuth a theatre which revolutionized European theatre architecture.

The future of the decentralized theatre in Germany looked bright at the beginning of the 1870s. Wagner and Duke Georg proved once again, as Goethe had at Weimar, that the most obscure theatre could exercise enormous artistic influence. A Trade Law (Gewerbeordung) passed in 1869 in the interest of encouraging German economic growth removed almost all restrictions on the establishment of new theatres, and within a year and a half ninety new houses had opened in North Germany. More powerful political, social, and economic forces were working in the opposite direction, however. After the Franco-Prussian war of 1870-1871 the long awaited dream of German unification was realized, if somewhat ruthlessly, by Bismarck, who pushed aside Austria and united the rest of the German states under Prussian leadership.

Vienna and Berlin, the two political capitals of the German
people, now became unquestionably the cultural capitals as
well, the only near rival being Munich, where the traditional
distrust of North Germany and a jealousy of Berlin's new
dominance helped to maintain an important independent artistic tradition.

The many new theatres which opened in the early
1870s simply spread even thinner the public and revenue
which the older houses were already sharing with the cir-
cuses, pleasure gardens, cabarets, variety houses, and summer theatres that had steadily grown in number and popularity since the 1850s. The theatres which tried to follow
the old virtuoso system found themselves competing with many
new rivals at ever-increasing prices for the few available
stars. Those which renounced all this in favor of the new
Meininger approach found the elaborate scenery and costumes
equally ruinous. Within a few years most of the new ventures
had disappeared, and those which survived tended to become
satellites of Vienna, Berlin, or Munich, where the best of
the young actors and playwrights inevitably took their talents.

The most conservative of these capitals was Vienna,
which during this period took over from Paris the leadership
of the operetta through the works of Millöcker and Strauss.
The new realism, so important a force in much European
theatre at this time, appeared here only in muted form before the end of the century, yet its influence is clear in the
folk plays of Anzengruber and the ironic social comedies of
Schnitzler.

Munich was the most eclectic of the major theatre
cities during this period. Though the city was Ibsen's home
in exile, it never gave pre-eminence to the naturalist drama
which he more than anyone else brought to European prominence. Berlin was the German center of naturalism, and
considering its artistic independence, it is hardly surprising
that Munich encouraged alternate experiments. Both Viennese
and Berlin dramatists were presented here, along with German epigones and the early plays of Wedekind which were
preparing the way for expressionism. In staging, the Perfall Shakespeare stage was the last and most elaborate German contribution to a century of experiments in simplified
staging.

The new European forces of scientism, positivism,
and naturalism were felt most powerfully in Berlin, rapidly

growing and extremely conscious of its new role as the Paris
or London of Germany. The new German consciousness
brought a welcome new interest in the German classics so
neglected during the virtuoso period and a less praiseworthy
vogue for new patriotic and Germanic plays of little depth or
significance. The works of the new naturalist playwrights
aroused the same suspicion and hostility here as elsewhere
in Europe, and had to be introduced by the standard device
of a private dramatic society, the Freie Bühne. Once this
breach was made, Berlin showed itself remarkably willing to
accept the new works and such writers as Hauptmann and
Sudermann achieved great popular success. Brahm, the
founder of the Freie Bühne, moved on to the Deutsches, and
made it a true national theatre, with a European stature rivalling the Comédie Française or the Burgtheater. Finally,
Berlin was also the center of another major new theatrical
interest of the time, related to the rise of socialism, the
bringing of theatre to the culturally and intellectually disin-
herited working class. The Volksbühne, the first and most
successful of the many populist theatres in Europe at the turn
of the century, developed in Berlin and then gradually spread
out into the rest of industrial northern Germany. It was a
period of great expansion, not only in the themes and concerns of the theatre, but in the public to which the theatre
made its appeal.

1. The Meininger

Duke Georg II of Saxe-Meiningen (1826-1914) and his
company, called the Meininger, burst on the German theatre
suddenly and dazzlingly in 1873 when they first toured to
Berlin, but they had been developing toward this success for
years. Saxe-Meiningen, like many small German duchies,
had a long and generally undistinguished theatre history. A
court stage was built there as early as 1776, and a permanent theatre for spoken drama and opera was opened in 1831.
This had served as the refuge of traveling companies and
stars, most notably Kunst in 1839 and Ira Aldridge in 1857,
until Georg II inherited the duchy in 1866. At that time the
theatre had for six years been managed by the intendant
Botho von Hülsen, who had assembled a modest company and
given the Meiningen theatre for the first time a certain distinction. Duke Georg's plans were far more ambitious, however, and to further them he disbanded the opera entirely in
favor of the spoken drama and replaced von Hülsen as in-

tendant with Friedrich Bodenstedt (1819-1892), a well-known
poet and translator of English renaissance drama who had
been a member of the Munich circle with Dingelstedt and one
of the founders of the German Shakespeare Society.

Though Georg II was interested in the theatre long before he inherited the title, his early training and interest was
more specifically in painting, and this had a profound effect
on his theatrical vision. His early years saw the triumph in
German art and on the German stage of the Biedermeyer
style, which in its depiction of contemporary life tended
toward a rather smug and somewhat overstuffed illustration
of bourgeois domesticity. The strongest opposition to this
style was mounted by the proponents of historical realism, a
school which developed in France and England, then arrived
in Germany at mid-century in the work of Kaulbach, Piloty,
and his student Makart. Piloty's Seni an der Leiche Wallensteins, exhibited in 1852, was a kind of pictorial manifesto
for this group and, as we have seen, was actually copied on
the stage by Dingelstedt.

Dingelstedt was the only German director before Duke
Georg with a sufficiently strong interest in painting to reflect
the concerns of historical realism on the stage, but Dingelstedt's public was far smaller, and his influence compara-
tively slight. With the Meininger productions, the German
stage began to assume a striking resemblance to the vast,
crowded, historically detailed canvases of Piloty or Makart.
The visual orientation which this implied led inevitably to
conflict between Duke Georg and Bodenstedt, whose dedication
was to the literary side of the theatre. The year Bodenstedt
came to Meiningen he published an article recommending
Goethe's Rules for Actors as "the golden ABC" for every director and argued that correct diction was of more central
concern than any visual effect. As a disciple of Goethe,
Bodenstedt naturally favored stage compositions of classic
symmetry and balance. The later intendant, Paul Lindau,
collected a number of the Duke's stage directions which show
how inimical he must have been to such composition:

> If the composition proceeds from the geometric
> middle, two halves result. From this the danger
> follows that in the arrangement of groups, dispos-
> ing them to the right and left will result in a
> somewhat symmetrical balance. This will appear
> wooden, stiff, and boring. The charm of Japanese
> art rests on the avoidance of all symmetry....

> The actor should at no time stand in the middle of
> the stage directly in front of the prompt box, but
> instead he should always stand a little to the right
> or the left of the prompter. ... It is also best, if
> possible, to avoid having two persons standing at
> an exact distance from the prompt box. [1]

By 1870 Duke Georg found it necessary to request Bodenstedt's resignation, and for the next five years he served as
his own intendant.

Whatever conflicts existed between the Duke and Bodenstedt during these early years did not apparently interfere
with the developing of a strong company and an impressive
repertoire. During their first season, at a time when the
classic tradition was almost dead even in Germany's major
theatres, the Meininger presented Hamlet, Kabale und Liebe,
Don Carlos, Faust, Die Räuber, Oedipus, Oedipus in Colonus, Antigone, Lear, Medea, Iphigenie auf Tauris, Emilia
Galotti, Othello, Richard III, and Maria Stuart. To all of
these the Duke brought a new life and richness, prefigured
in the productions of Laube and Dingelstedt, but brought to
a new synthesis through the Duke's concern with ensemble
and historical accuracy. The most famous example of the
new synthesis was the Meininger Julius Caesar, which was
added to the repertoire in 1867. Here were fully developed
the two major hallmarks of the Meininger style, the imaginative and effective use of crowds and a new emphasis on
the visual details of the production, particularly on the costuming.

Modest attempts at historical costuming on the German stage had been made by Schröder and Koch, then by
Goethe and his painter Meyer, but not until the publications
of von Brühl in 1819 did most German producers attempt even
the vaguest distinctions of period. Even then, Grube suggests, most theatres recognized only five periods: antique,
medieval, Spanish, German renaissance, and rococo. Settings were equally casual, and even the box sets designed
for salon plays were formal, artificial, and generally had
tables, chairs, and other dimensional pieces simply painted
on the walls. Charles Kean's London productions in the
1850s brought a new concern for historical detail to the stage,
though the emphasis in Kean's Shakespearian offerings was at
least as much on spectacle as on accuracy. The effect of
these rich pageants was felt almost at once in the German
theatre in such productions as the ballet Sardanapal in Berlin,

which attempted a stage reconstruction of authentic Assyrian
scenes. The settings, costumes and properties were based
closely on excavations at Ninevah and on the collections of
Assyrian artifacts in the museums of Berlin and Paris.

Both Duke Georg and Bodenstedt attended Kean productions in London and the Duke also saw Friedrich Haase's
Kean-inspired production of The Merchant of Venice in Ko-
burg in 1867. The Brückner brothers, who designed Haase's
lavish settings, were later employed both at Meiningen and
by Wagner at Bayreuth. Certain of Kean's spectacular
touches, such as Jessica's flight from her father through
crowds of carnival revellers, were closely copied by both
Haase and Duke Georg in their own productions. The Duke's
artistic background naturally made him more responsive to
such display than Bodenstedt was, with a more literary concern, but certain external forces in the 1860s reinforced
this inclination. Positivism was entering the theatre as it
had already entered science and historical study, and the romantic concern with beauty was being replaced by the realist
concern with truth. The bourgeois public of the 1860s were
far better informed than their predecessors on historical
matters, not only because historians and archeologists were
bringing new facts to light, but because improvements in
printing and particularly in graphic reproduction made historical scenes and artifacts more accessible to them. Thus
while Hans Hopfen, one of the Meininger's most implacable
enemies, complained that actors and script were subordinated to the archeologist, the historian, the machinist and
the chorus leader, Gläser of the Berlin Bürger Zeitung responded that the advances of ethnography and history of
civilization and the public's awareness of these sciences made
such concern necessary.

Duke Georg's basic costume authority for Julius
Caesar was Jakob Weiss' monumental Geschichte des Kos-
tüms, the first volume of which appeared in 1856. Weiss
himself was invited to Meiningen where he instructed the
actors in the proper method of wearing togas and suggested
that the appliqué designs previously used be replaced by
stencils, which would drape more easily. Grube quotes an
amusing report on these togas by Siegwart Friedmann (1842-
1916), who came as a guest to play Cassius in 1870:

> Our Berlin togas had something of the shape of a
> middle-sized table cover. I remember the terror
> with which we unfolded the Meininger monster.

> This genuine toga, made of real wool, measured
> 30 ells and weighed--I don't know how much! We
> first had to ask the costumer privately how, by
> folding and gathering it up, one should wear such
> a toga to make it becoming--how one should adjust
> it in order to be able to move at all. [2]

A similar care went into the weapons, ordered from a crafts-
man in Paris, into the armor, made by local tinsmiths, and
into every article appearing on the stage.

Each aspect of the production was conceived in the
same spirit. The settings (reduced to seven from the original eighteen) were authentic reproductions of imperial Rome,
based on the research of Pietro Visconti, a noted archeologist, and Duke Georg urged Bodenstedt to inform the public
before the production which parts of Rome were to be represented. A concern for similar accuracy in language led him
to insert two lines into Caesar's death speech because they
were reported by Plutarch, though not used by Shakespeare.
In this Laube adaptation, as well as in Goethe and Schiller,
the Duke allowed, even encouraged his actors to interject
groans, sighs, and cries into poetic lines for greater realism, to the dismay of traditionalists. His most radical innovation was the presentation of the entire conspirators'
scene in Brutus' garden in stage whispers.

Probably the most admired aspect of the Meininger
concern with realism was the development of effective crowd
scenes, and here too Julius Caesar provided some of the
most striking examples. There had been scattered, isolated
experiments with crowds on stage for almost a century before
the Meininger. Dalberg's Mannheim production of Julius
Caesar in 1785 manipulated large numbers of people on stage
with considerable effect, but inspired no imitators. Goethe
and his contemporaries considered the problem of crowds,
but lacked the means for major experiments; Immermann's
crowd of fifty in Die Räuber was the largest seen during the
first half of the century. Dingelstedt was thus the first German director to give serious attention to the use of masses
on stage, but his experiments had little effect outside his
own theatre. In 1879 Hans Herring commented:

> Directors consider it sufficient if everyone is
> shown once or twice what his position is to be; the
> extras are taught the usual telegraphic gestures....
> They come running out of the wings like a flock of

sheep, their eyes glued to the coat-tails of their leader. [3]

Martersteig also notes that when the Meininger began touring there were very few German stages on which large-scale fluid crowd scenes, whether they were court ceremonials or battles, were not converted into grotesque parodies:

> The popular uprising before Caesar's bier which was supposed to have set fire to Rome and the world was represented by the same two dozen tired ladies and gentlemen of the chorus, familiar to every theatregoer, supplemented by half a company of the musketeers stationed in the town, all of them put into the sort of outlandish costumes which converted the whole production into a farce. [4]

Duke Georg on the other hand developed crowds which were not only full of life, but composed of carefully varied individuals--

> ... persons of sanguine or phlegmatic temperaments, unrestrained ranters and gentle peacemakers, hypocritical sycophants and rabid opponents, brazen hussies and charming matrons, individuals caught up in the events as well as curious idlers. [5]

Part of the reason for their great success in such scenes was that all Meininger actors without exception were required to serve also as extras. Crowds were separated into small autonomous groups each led by one of the more experienced actors, and these were in turn subordinate to the director, who provided them with scripts showing their positions and the lines they were to give. Suitable realistic lines were substituted for the vague "tumult" or "cries" which was usually all the script indicated. For offstage clamor, the Duke originated the practice of giving each extra a sheet of newspaper to read aloud instead of resorting to the traditional off-stage murmur of "rhubarb, rhubarb" (Rhabarbargemurmel). There was no Regiebuch--everything was planned from event to event under the Duke's personal supervision, though he usually prepared in advance a set of sketches of the stage at critical moments. Both in these sketches and in his general instructions to his regisseur we find a studious avoidance of symmetry and of obvious repetition of positions.

During the early years of the company's training and
performance, two figures grew steadily in importance. One
was Ellen Franz (1839-1923), who began her career as a
concert artist under von Bülow, then turned to acting at Saxe-
Coburg, Oldenburg, and Mannheim before she was hired by
Bodenstedt to come to Meiningen. The other was Ludwig
Chronegk (1838-1891), from the Königstädter Theater in Berlin, who made his Meiningen debut in 1866 as Guildenstern
in Hamlet. Clearly he lacked Ellen Franz's potential as a
member of the ensemble, but he had a gift for converting the
Duke's visions into stage terms, and Georg came to rely on
him increasingly as the middleman between himself and the
performers. It was Chronegk who first realized that the Duke
had created something which deserved a far greater audience
and who proposed a tour to Berlin. Duke Georg was uneasy
about so bold a step and instead invited Berlin's leading theatre critic, Karl Frenzel of the Nationalzeitung, to come to
Meiningen in 1870 to see Julius Caesar and The Taming of
the Shrew. Frenzel's review of Julius Caesar was the first
major notice that something out of the ordinary was happen-
ing in Meiningen, and on the evidence of his favorable comments, Duke Georg agreed to begin preparation for a Berlin
tour. In the meantime, two important events occured in
Meiningen. In 1873 the Duke married Ellen Franz, and
shortly after, Chronegk was officially appointed the company's
regisseur. It was he who in the coming years organized and
led the guest tours that gave the theatre a European reputation.

Frenzel returned to Meiningen in 1873 and was more
enthusiastic than before. A Berlin appearance was announced
for the following spring. New actors were engaged: Wilhelm
Hellmuth-Bräm (1827-1890) for Brutus, Joseph Nesper (1844-
1927) for Caesar, Leopold Teller (1844-1896) for Cassius,
and Ludwig Barnay (1842-1924) for Antony. All contributed
greatly to the Meininger success, though the thoroughness of
the rehearsals shocked them at first. Barnay reported:

> I was both amazed and furious with the rehearsals,
> since I felt that they wasted a great deal of time
> on absolute non-essentials: the loudness or quiet-
> ness of a speech, the way some non-speaking actor
> should stand, getting a tree or a bush in the right
> spot or effectively lighting it. The actors were
> given long lectures, virtual treatises on the mood
> of a scene, the significance of a specific incident
> to the drama, yes, even on the emphasis of a

single word. This caused the rehearsal to be
stretched out endlessly in a manner quite unfamiliar to me, since other regisseurs were satisfied with telling an actor whether he should enter
and exit right or left and on which side of another
actor he should stand. 6

Julius Caesar opened in Berlin on May 1 and ran for
a record twenty-two consecutive performances. Both the
attention to detail and the handling of mass scenes drew high
praise. Frenzel compared the crowd scenes around Caesar's
bier to the beginnings of a revolution, while others noted the
realistic fighting and dying in battle scenes, particularly as
compared with the aimless thrashing about the stage which
served for battles in other theatres.

The second Berlin production, Julius Minding's Six-
tus V, recreated Renaissance Rome as Julius Caesar had
classic Rome, but the script was too weak even for the
imaginative interpretation of the Meininger to save. The
subsequent offerings--Albert Lindner's (1831-1881) Bluthochzeit, Twelfth Night, The Merchant of Venice, and The
Imaginary Invalid with Björnstjerne Björnson's Between the
Battles as a curtain-raiser--were more successful, though
none equalled the popularity of Julius Caesar. After their
opening spectacles, the Meininger surprised their audiences
by using for Twelfth Night a single, if elaborate setting, with
two small rooms set up within it for certain scenes. They
also discarded the standard Deinhardstein version, which
collapsed Viola, Cesario, and Sebastian into a single virtuoso role, in favor of the more faithful Tieck version. A
similar simplicity in staging was used for The Imaginary Invalid, presented in a single setting without even an intermis-
sion. Every detail of the setting was authentic Louis XIV,
however, from the porcelain cups to M. Argan's enema-
syringe. Joseph Weilenbeck created in Argan one of his
greatest roles.

Lindner's Bluthochzeit, based on the St. Bartholomew's
Day Massacre, allowed the Meininger to recreate visually the
court of Charles IX, but Grube notes that it was most remembered as the first Meininger production to make extensive
and effective use of off-stage sounds:

The ringing of the bells on St. Bartholomew's night,
the victorious song of the Huguenots breaking forth:
'A Mighty Fortress is our God, ' while nearby gay

> dance music rings out from the rooms of the
> Louvre--this chaos of sound was thrilling. [7]

Similar effects were utilized in later productions--a brass
band playing offstage as Maria Stuart went to the scaffold,
and the whole paraphernalia of Gothic romances: creaking
doors, howling winds, banging shutters, for Die Ahnfrau.
The offstage crickets and barking dogs that so irritated
Chekov at the Moscow Art Theatre were doubtless suggested
to Stanislavsky by these Meininger effects.

The Meininger returned to Berlin in 1875, then
traveled on to Vienna and Budapest. The Viennese public,
accustomed to the productions of Dingelstedt, received them
rather coolly, but Berlin audiences were as impressed as
before. Von Hülsen at the Königliches Schauspielhaus presented one of their announced offerings immediately before
their arrival, Kleist's Hermannsschlacht. If this was an attempt to divert attention from the Meininger, it failed utterly.
The two productions demonstrated clearly the difference between the new and the traditional methods of staging, and
comparisons were rarely in favor of the tradition. Crowds
were of course important again, but this time Duke Georg
showed the power not of an individualized crowd, but of a
carefully directed conglomerate:

> In simple, dark grey armor and helmets of iron,
> with packs hanging from their javelins, the troops
> entered, naturally not in military step. An es-
> pecially happy directorial touch was this: the army
> flowed through that narrow lane obliquely from
> downstage up to the background, so that the audi-
> ence saw no faces, only helmets and armor-plated
> backs, as if an iron stream pressed, surged, and
> flooded its way toward the Teutoberg.

The same scene at the Königliches Schauspielhaus gave a
totally different impression:

> In rank and file they moved with a correct Prus-
> sian goose-step directly across the stage from
> right to left parallel to the footlights. No one
> could doubt that the alert Prussian National Guard,
> garbed in Roman equipment, was making a formal
> parade across the stage. [8]

A similar contrast between artifice and illusion was

to be observed throughout. Marbod's tent in Berlin was
composed of painted draperies, while the Meininger had real
animal skins crudely sewn together. The Teutoberg forest
in Berlin was represented by an open stage floor surrounded
by painted trees, while the Meininger filled the space with
dimensional underbrush and a great trunk stretched across
the stage. The Meininger also presented a more complete
version since in Kleist, as in Shakespeare, they presented
scenes previously considered too horrible for the stage. German audiences first saw in Meininger productions the murder
of the poet Cinna in Julius Caesar and of Macduff's children
in Macbeth.

By 1876 the Meininger had established a pattern which
they followed for the next thirteen years, preparing works at
home during the winter, then departing on increasingly extended tours during the spring and summer. This year they
went from Berlin to Dresden and Breslau. Not only the
methods, but the repertoire of the Meininger was beginning
to have an influence throughout Germany. The half-forgotten
classics returned to every major stage, and often in improved form. The original Käthchen von Heilbronn at last
replaced Holbein's mutilated version in a season which also
included Macbeth, Wilhelm Tell, Der Erbförster, and Ibsen's
The Pretenders. With his usual concern for authenticity,
Duke Georg made a special trip to Scandinavia to sketch
scenery for the latter production, but the play itself, or its
translation, was generally condemned as too verbose and
diffuse. The great production of the season was Wilhelm
Tell, another triumph for Meininger ensemble work and elaborate staging, but also for the leading actors Ludwig Barnay
and Josef Kainz (1858-1910) whose interpretations brought the
first influence of realism to this classic.

After a season in other German cities, the Meininger
returned to Berlin in 1878 with four new productions: Die
Ahnfrau, Der Prinz von Homburg, Die Räuber (in the most
complete version yet produced on the German stage), and
Shakespeare's The Winter's Tale, which replaced the "cor-
rected" and "improved" version of Dingelstedt with the more
authentic Tieck. During the next twelve years, the Meininger
returned to Berlin only three times. Their tours now took
them to 38 cities in all parts of Europe, exposing their
methods to the major artists of the new generation. They
even planned a tour to America, which had to be cancelled
because of Chronegk's final illness. In terms of their influence on other traditions the most important of these guest

appearances were in London in 1881, where they were admired by such leaders of the theatre as Irving, the Bancrofts,
Mme Modjeska, Ellen Terry, and Edwin Booth; in Moscow in
1885, where they made a profound impression on Stanislavsky
and Nemirovitch-Dantchenko, and in Brussels in 1888, where
despite a rather cool reception from nationalist critics they
attracted such important Parisian directors as Antoine and
Porel. The most popular of the new works added to the repertoire during these years were Maria Stuart and the Wallenstein trilogy in 1882 and Die Jungfrau von Orleans and a
reworked Merchant of Venice in 1886. In 1886 also the Duke
gave at Meiningen the first public performance in Europe of
Ibsen's Ghosts. It was planned for the repertoire, but after
a single further performance in Dresden and a police warn-
ing, it was dropped.

        A promising new dramatist was discovered in Ernst
von Wildenbruch (1845-1909) whose Die Karolinger the
Meininger premiered in 1881. A poetic idealist in the tradition of Schiller, Wildenbruch had tried vainly for a decade
to find a theatre willing to present his historical dramas
amid the farces and light comedies which made up their repertoires. Once offered by the Meininger, his works swept
the major stages, and he was as over-estimated as he had
been ignored before. German critics after 1870 were all too
willing to find in him the new Schiller to glorify the new
state. Wildenbruch, an enthusiastic patriot, obliged with Die
Quitzows (1888), Der Generalfeldoberst (1889), and Der neue
Herr (1891), celebrating the Hohenzollerns even more un-
critically than Raupach had the Hohenstaufens. This earned
him the praise of the Kaiser and an important place in the
repertoires of the major state theatres at the end of the century, but he in fact contributed little to the major development of drama during this period. The naturalists considered
his poetry stiff and outdated, his plots fantastic, his characters thin and arbitrary, and dismissed him as little better
than a creator of the trivial Possen. His one attempt at the
new style, Die Haubenlerche (1891), was well accepted by the
public, but he turned back from it to the more congenial historical pageants of his earlier years.

        The characteristics which had marked the Meininger
from the beginning were to be found in all of these produc-
tions--the careful arrangements of crowds, the emphasis on
ensemble, the elaborate and usually realistic settings, and
the evocation of mood by lighting and sound. Critics throughout Europe were impressed by these effects, but the praise

was by no means universal. The <u>London Academy</u> of June 4,
1881, wrote glowingly of the crowd scenes in <u>The Winter's
Tale</u>:

> The idea of independence in well-considered gesture
> and facial expression among the sympathizing crowd
> is so well carried through the whole scene, that
> the spectator may look in the face of every super-
> numerary in turn without having his stage illusion
> destroyed.

Others, however, found the crowds, especially in later years,
too obviously controlled, too carefully arranged, or even
simply distracting:

> Whenever it is possible in these Meininger produc-
> tions to introduce shouting, ringing, singing, chant-
> ing, fighting, jostling, pushing, these are never
> under any circumstances omitted. Two citizens
> cannot begin a conversation without the bustle of a
> market-place erupting behind them, so that we are
> willy-nilly distracted from the important dialogue.
> When Brutus and Cassius take center stage to hold
> a council of war before the battle of Philippi,
> several archers of the advance guard at stage left
> engage in an exciting skirmish--imagine!--only
> about four or five steps from the war council of
> the leading generals![9]

Duke Georg relieved the symmetry of the box set with
niches, arches, pillars, and walls placed at oblique angles,
often working with a triangular ground plan which was widely
copied after him. Doors and windows were practical with
real latches and locks, and settings were scrupulously suited
to the play. In <u>Miss Sara Sampson</u>, for example, Mellefont's
room had yellowed wallpaper, hanging in shreds, Sara's room
was in good repair, but still quite modest, while Marwood's
boudoir was rich and elegant. The traditional painted wood
wings for exteriors were replaced by perspective drops and
practical hillocks, cliffs, boulders, fences, and fallen trees,
but some compromise with artifice was inevitable, and the
Meininger concern with authenticity at times apparently only
called attention to the artifice. Antoine noted in connection
with <u>Wilhelm Tell</u> that "They abuse the idea of practical elements, cramming them in everywhere," and complained that
"the same stage carpet served for the entire play; the rocks
of Switzerland were mounted on casters; there was a squeak-

ing floorboard in the mountains. "10   The Illustrated London
News of June 11, 1881, remarked:

> ... a dais of three steps covered with green baize
> in a forest scene is bad enough ... but no tradi-
> tion can warrant the scattering about the stage of
> a number of ridiculous boulders, supposed to rep-
> resent rocks or turfy hillocks, but which look like
> so many lumps of suet-pudding with plums in
> them.

The atmospheric and symbolic use of lighting similarly
drew both praise and complaints. Gas lighting, colored if
necessary by silk screens, served the Meininger for general
illumination, as it did for most theatres of the period, but
Duke Georg was fascinated by striking and unusual effects,
which he achieved by departing from the usual lighting positions at the front and sides of the stage and by adding electric spotlights for special effects, such as the appearance of
Caesar's ghost.   Lighting, like crowd effects, could occasionally occupy an entire scene, such as the one in The
Merchant of Venice described in the Düsseldorfer Volksblatt
of June 10, 1886:

> It is twilight; night draws on; soon it falls on the
> stage, while only a few small circles are illumi-
> nated by the green or red lights of signal lanterns.
> A more powerful lantern is seen far in the back-
> ground, in another arm of the canal, through an
> opening in the wall. Its light is reflected in the
> transparent green water and shatters the thick
> darkness in the foreground as gondolas break
> through it under the high Rialto bridge. The gon-
> doliers, standing high in each bow, steer their
> crafts with powerful movements while a torch in
> each vessel shows the steersman his way, its ruddy
> light on his face deepening the darkness which
> surrounds him.

Again, Antoine balances this with his comment:

> The lighting effects, though often striking, are
> handled with epic naïveté. For example, when
> an old man has just died in his armchair, a beau-
> tiful ray from the setting sun suddenly shines
> through the window, without any gradations, to

illuminate his beautiful head--this solely to
achieve an effect. [11]

In sum, the Meininger brought to culmination several
lines of experimentation in the nineteenth century German
stage, most notably those of Laube and Dingelstedt, and at
the same time helped prepare the way for the new realist
experiments at the end of the century. Much of the ambiguity
of critical reaction can be explained by this pivotal position.
To such conservative German critics as Hopfen they were
pretentious amateurs, scarcely to be compared with the
technically proficient artists of the virtuoso period. A realist
such as Antoine, however, faulted them for not departing
enough from arbitrary, "theatrical" effects. Yet whatever
their misgivings, few directors of the next generation escaped the influence of the Meininger. Their attention to
authentic detail, though derived in part from experiments in
local color of the romantics, was far more closely allied in
practice to the growing realist movement. What Duke Georg
did for classic plays the naturalists would do for contemporary
ones. "The principal is the same, " as Georg Fuchs noted,
"whether one copies the interiors of romanesque churches or
contemporary salons, Merovingian coronation vestments or
the blouses of factory workers. "[12] There was a tendency in
the followers of Duke Georg to choose darker subjects, to
make the shift from what theatre historian Adolf Winds calls
Stimmungsregie ("staging for mood") to Dumpfungsregie
("staging for gloom"), and in such directors as Brahm and
Stanislavsky, to turn inward. Yet the staging methods of the
Meininger provided a firm base for these varied experiments.

Karl Gläser, the influential critic of the Berlin Bürger
Zeitung, pointed out another major Meininger contribution,
which he characterized as "a new principal in the German
theatre: that the total effect of a dramatic work must be emphasized above the original artist. "[13] The key word here is
total, and it is that key word which unites the Meininger with
Wagner and which most clearly separates them from the
virtuoso period which preceded them. It also necessarily
placed a new power and responsibility in the hands of the
director, whose vision assured the totality of effect. As
early as 1880 at least one perceptive critic pointed out that
what had in fact occurred was that "the virtuoso actor has
now given way to the virtuoso director, "[14] an insight the full
implications of which would not be really clear until the
twentieth century.

2. Wagner at Bayreuth

Three years after the first Berlin tour of the Meininger came another major affirmation of the ideal that all arts must work together in the theatre to achieve the maximum effect available to a script. In 1876 Wagner was at last able to produce his great cycle, Der Ring des Nibelungen, in his own theatre at Bayreuth. The difficulties in realizing this vast project had been enormous. Although Wagner was by 1870 a composer of European fame and although his plan for a festival had the antecedent of Dingelstedt's Gesamtgastspiel of 1854, the Bayreuth project was widely regarded as the insubstantial fancy of a megalomaniac. The establishment of the German state in 1870 led Wagner to hope for governmental support for his nationalistic art, but his appeals to Bismarck and the Emperor went unheeded. They apparently still considered Wagner Ludwig's responsibility.

Perhaps Wagner could have gained more Prussian support had he moved his activities to Berlin, clearly destined to be the cultural center of the new federation, but a number of considerations kept Wagner faithful to Bayreuth, his original choice. First was its location, near the center of Germany, but perhaps more important, between Berlin and Munich so that Wagner if necessary could turn to either ruler for aid. Second, despite its central location, the town was not on any major thoroughfares. Wagner wanted no crowds of casual tourists such as frequented popular resorts, but pilgrims who came to Bayreuth only and specifically for the festival. The festival could be, as it has been, all in all to this small and somewhat remote town as it could never be to a metropolitan center like Berlin. Finally, Bayreuth already possessed an eighteenth century court theatre with the deepest stage in Germany which Wagner apparently thought (until he at last tested its acoustics) might serve as a supplementary place of performance.

After the official announcement of the Bayreuth project in 1871, Wagner societies were formed throughout Germany to collect money, and the cornerstone was laid the next year, on Wagner's birthday. From the outset the project was derided by much of the German artistic world and the press, and by 1873 only 242 patrons had subscribed when 1000 were needed. Two years later this number had risen only to 404 and the festival seemed doomed. Wagner was planning to put a rough cover over the shell so far built and

abandon Bayreuth indefinitely when the faithful Ludwig stepped
in with sufficient funds to plan a production for 1876.

Both the singers and the orchestra for the festival had
to be borrowed from other theatres, so the early summer of
1875 saw artists from all over Germany gathered at Bayreuth
to begin the rehearsals.   Wagner's new idea of a unified production demanded new methods from the very beginning.
Operas normally rehearsed singers and orchestra, even
string and wind sections separately for a considerable time
before combining them.   At Bayreuth the entire 113-man
orchestra (more than double the usual size) rehearsed an act
each morning, then repeated it with singers in the afternoon.
Hans Richter of the Vienna opera conducted.   The rehearsals
were adjourned for the winter season, then resumed in June
of 1876.   The festival opened in August.

A capacity crowd appeared for the first performance
of the cycle, including kings and emperors, and representing
"every civilized country on the globe including the United
States and California" as one enthusiastic German paper
noted.   Transportation to the theatre was inadequate, food
insufficient (though a special restaurant was built nearby for
sustinence during the hour-long intermissions), water had not
yet been piped to the site, and the erratic lighting system
plunged the theatre from time to time into total darkness.
Even so the audience was deeply impressed by the presentation, and perhaps even more by the revolutionary space which
Wagner had designed for it.   Almost all of the striking innovations at Bayreuth came from a single concern--Wagner's
determination to focus the audience's undivided attention upon
the world on the stage.   Thus he darkened the house, an innovation already seen in London and Riga, but new to Germany, and once the curtain rose, no late-comer was permitted to break the spell.   The old distracting central
chandelier was banished, replaced by less obvious house
lighting from the tops of a row of pillars running along the
side walls.   Most importantly, the orchestra was placed out
of sight in a pit extending back under the stage, according to
the idea tested out by Semper in Munich.   Basically Wagner
was interested in getting rid of visual distraction, but the
softening and distancing of his heavy orchestral sound also
created a better balance between singers and orchestra.
Critics spoke wonderingly of how the new arrangement "ethe-
realized" (verklärt) the music, especially since the new theatre proved very pleasant acoustically.

The sunken orchestra, which created what Semper called a "mystic abyss" was seen by him an admirable device to combine intimacy and distance in the theatre, and he described carefully how the proscenium should be treated to create the desired effect:

> I have placed two prosceniums, separated by the sunken orchestra, one behind the other. The architecture of the narrower second proscenium is a repetition of the large anterior one, but on a smaller scale. Thus there will come about a complete displacement of scale from which will follow both an ostensible enlargement of everything happening on the stage and also the desired separation of the ideal world of the stage from the real world on the other side of the orchestral boundary. [15]

The desire to make this effect perceivable from all seats and to keep the orchestra invisible to all led to an influential new arrangement of the entire auditorium. The old boxes and galleries were forsaken in favor of ranks of seats (1300 in all) rising in semicircles and all facing the stage. Behind them was a single row of boxes surmounted by a gallery seating 300 more. The consistent rake of this house was eventually replaced elsewhere by the "dished" auditorium, but in its essential form, Bayreuth introduced to Europe the modern theatre auditorium.

Unhappily the theatre was far less innovative backstage. Josef Hoffmann of the Vienna opera designed the scenery, but since he had no studio or assistants, execution of it was turned over to the Brückner brothers of Coburg, whose pompous and heavy panoramas in the Makart tradition suited the emotional poems of Wagner much less well than the historical pageants of the Meininger. Döpler of Berlin, who did the Nibelungen costumes for Hebbel at Weimar in 1861 was commissioned by Wagner to create a new costume style, with nothing in it of either the Greco-Roman or the medieval. The result, as Cosima Wagner bitterly but accurately observed, "suggested nothing so much as Indian chiefs." The imaginative Karl Brandt again supervised the machinery, but his major accomplishment was achieving anything at all in this remote location. Materials for effects easily found in Berlin or Munich were obtained in Bayreuth only with the greatest difficulty. Some major effects were poorly carried out and only two were truly original: a dazzling electric light which played on the night scenes and a

steam machine which produced colored vapors.   Every one
of the design areas clearly suffered from the fact that Wagner
had never fully considered the visual implications of his
theories.   Eventually the impressionists created a method of
staging truly harmonious with Wagnerian music, but for many
years Bayreuth continued to mount its productions in the
ponderous Makart style.

The most successful singers at Bayreuth were the
Austrian soprano Amalie Materna (1843-1918) as Brynhild,
the tenor Albert Niemann (1831-1917) of Berlin as Siegmund
and the baritone Franz Betz, Wagner's Munich protégé, who
played Wotan.   The role of Siegfried proved most difficult to
cast, and even the most enthusiastic Wagnerites found the
final selection, Georg Unger, disappointing.   The novelty and
notoriety of Wagner's experiment guaranteed a large audience
for the premiere performance, but the rather uneven interpretation, the production problems, Bayreuth's still inadequate
transportation and facilities for guests and the open hostility
of much of Germany's cultural establishment caused a sharp
reduction in attendance for the two repetitions of the cycle.
The 1876 festival closed with so large a deficit that Wagner
virtually despaired of any sequel.   The societies had given
what they could, and the state was not interested in Wagner's
proposal to make Bayreuth a subsidiary of the national opera
in Munich.   A plan to convert the festival into a school of
drama attracted neither students nor support.   At last, in
order to pay his debts, Wagner had to give up his plan to
retain the Ring as the exclusive property of Bayreuth.   The
Munich opera assumed his deficit in return for permission
to present the cycle with the scenery from Bayreuth.   After
the Munich production of 1878, Wagner collected funds for a
new festival by releasing the work the following year to
Leipzig and Vienna, and later to Hamburg and other cities.

Wagner deplored most of these early productions.   At
Bayreuth he had selected singers and musicians from all over
Germany and no single theatre could hope to achieve a similar level of ability.   Moreover, most theatres ignored his
wish that the Ring be presented as a whole and in the original order.   Walküre was soon recognized as the most popular
part of the cycle and by 1891 had been given 823 times while
Rheingold, the second most popular, had seen only 358 productions.   Even when the tetralogy was given in its entirety,
Walküre was often presented first.   Only the Leipzig production, conducted by Wagner's pupil Anton Seidl, seemed to
satisfy the master.   He accordingly granted it permission to

tour between 1881 and 1883 throughout Germany and to Amsterdam, Brussels, Venice, Bologna, and Budapest.   This
company also had the honor of presenting the Ring for the
first time in Berlin, since von Hülsen of the Berlin Opera
had refused Wagner's conditions that in the capital at least
the work had to be performed in order and in its entirety.
Von Hülsen throughout the latter part of his administration
admitted Wagner to the Berlin stage only grudgingly, and his
death in 1886 opened a new era for Wagnerian production in
that city.   By 1890 Wagner was given five times more frequent production there as the next most popular composer.

Meanwhile the proceeds from the Ring productions
throughout Germany allowed Wagner to prepare a second
festival in 1882 for the premiere of Parsifal.   King Ludwig
placed the full resources of the Munich opera at Wagner's
disposal, which with the other artists he selected gave him
enough soloists for three companies, a chorus of 84 and an
orchestra of 105.   Ludwig hoped that Wagner would also accept Munich designers to execute the scenery designed by a
young Russian, Paul Zhukovski, but Wagner remained loyal
to the Brückners.   Karl Brandt, his machinist, had died in
1881, but his son Franz carried on with the technical side of
the production.   Parsifal was distinctly more satisfactory
both physically and vocally than the Ring.   Emil Scaria as
Gurnemanz was hailed as an ideal interpreter of Wagner, and
Materna returned to fresh acclaim as Kundry.   This time the
festival ended with a profit and its continuance was assured.
The repetitions in 1883, 1884, 1886, and 1889 met with
steadily increasing success, until by 1891 every seat was
sold out weeks in advance.   Before the end of the century
Tristan und Isolde, Die Meistersinger, Tannhäuser, and Lohengrin had also been given festival productions.   Wagner
saw the Bayreuth dream firmly established, but never saw it
grow into the national institution he desired.   He died in
Venice the winter after the Parsifal festival of 1882.

The music world of Germany managed to withstand the
force of Wagner's revolution through the 1870s.   Then the
increasing success of Bayreuth and the growing popularity of
the later works, especially Die Walküre, made Wagner into a
touchstone which defined the position of almost every other
German composer of the time.   There were some who followed Wagner almost to the point of parody, such as August
Bungert (1845-1915), whose Homerische Welt comprised two
cycles and six operas in a ponderous imitation of the Ring.
More original, and more successful disciples were Felix von

Weingartner (1863-1942), who explored Hindu themes in
Sakuntala (1884) and Heinrich Zöllner (1854-1915), who applied Wagnerian orchestration and leitmotifs to a version of
Faust (1887). In comic opera, the Wagnerian style developed in Die Meistersinger merged with the heritage of
Peter Cornelius to produce a rather heavy post-Wagnerian
style where the musical complexities quite weighted down the
libretti, producing lyric but essentially dull works such as
Hugo Wolf's (1860-1903) Corregidor (1895).

German composers were not long, therefore, in discovering that none of them were likely to surpass or even
equal Wagner in his own style, and though his influence in
the final two decades of the century was almost inescapable,
fresh approaches were constantly sought. The most effective
of these went back for inspiration to simple folk melodies
and libretti which could employ these. Thus evolved the
Märchenoper (fairy-tale opera), the greatest example of
which was Humperdinck's (1854-1921) Hänsel und Gretel
(1893), which combined the charm of a traditional tale, simple
tunes and chorals, with enough Wagnerian texture to satisfy
musical sophisticates. Among the many followers of Humperdinck was Wagner's son Siegfried (1869-1930), who in
addition to supervising the Bayreuth festivals created a series
of fairy operas beginning with Bärenhäuter (1899). The
other popular new approach of the 1890s was the folk opera,
developed in Austria by such composers as Wilhelm Kinezl
(1857-1941), whose Der Evangelimann (1895) opened the way
to a whole series of works combining a touch of Wagner with
popular songs and the ever vital Austrian folk theatre tradition.

3. Vienna

Though the Austrian economy was still subject to
periodic crises, the nation had by 1870 recovered remarkably
well from its rapid and definitive defeat by Prussia in 1866.
Looking to future cooperation, Bismarck had been generous
with his vanquished enemy once he had gained his primary
objective, the removal of Austria as a rival for the leadership of Germany. Nevertheless, Viennese society had experienced major changes in the late 1860s. The growing influence of the new monied class and the corresponding decline
in the power of the aristocracy was a Europe-wide phenomenon, but the rapid political decline of the Austrian court made
the shift particularly striking in Vienna. The new audience

which came to the Burgtheater in the 1870s was attracted not
because of the theatre's offerings, but because it was the
expected activity of a certain social level. For entertainment, they were far more likely to seek the operettas of the
flourishing suburban theatres.

Nevertheless, Dingelstedt managed to offer the new
public generally palatable fare. Light farces and sentimental
comedies made up a large part of his repertoire, and the
classics, as we have already seen, were generously enlivened
with pageantry and spectacle. The major new author of the
decade, Ludwig Anzengruber (1839-1889), was introduced by
Dingelstedt to the Burgtheater in 1873, but this was after
Anzengruber had already attracted a large following at the
popular Theater an der Wien. His first great success there,
Der Pfarrer von Kirchfeld (1870), was particularly striking
since it was in the tradition of the folk-plays of Nestroy and
Raimund, a type of play which had almost disappeared from
the suburban stages since the advent of the operetta. In
fact, much of the play's appeal came less from its form than
its subject, which capitalized shrewdly on contemporary interests. The promulgation of the doctrine of infallibility
aroused strong emotion in Catholic Europe, and Anzengruber's
depiction of the martyrdom of Hell, an all-too-fallible priest,
naturally engaged the sympathy, even the enthusiasm of
liberals of the period. Despite the protests of church officials the censor required no cutting of the play, commenting
that his office dealt with political, not religious matters.

In these days of Bismarck's Kulturkampf against Rome
the line between politics and religion was not so easily drawn
by most persons. Der Pfarrer was so generally considered
a social document that Laube felt obliged to argue that it
possessed poetic values at least equal to its social ones.
"It introduces complex thought processes and rich delineation
of character to the folk-play," he observed, "and in addition
to its undeveloped abstractions it possesses scenes of full-
blooded, genuine talent."[16] Later critics have supported
Laube's favorable assessment, finding the subtly drawn peasant Wurzelsepp ultimately a greater creation than the controversial Hell.

Impressed by the popularity of Der Pfarrer, the directors of the Theater an der Wien, Maximilian Steiner and
Marie Geistinger (1828-1903), contracted Anzengruber to write
two plays for their theatre annually, with a guaranteed eight
per cent of the profits of those produced, the highest sum

given any writer by that theatre. The theatre's best actors, Karl Matthias Rott, Marie Geistinger, Katharina Herzog (1819-1900), and Jani Szika, were given the major roles in Anzengruber's next two plays, Der Meineidbauer (1871) and Die Kreuzelschreiber (1872). Though both works kept the traditional musical accompaniment and possessed, though in diminishing amounts, a certain didacticism and anti-clericalism, in each Anzengruber moved closer to a detailed realistic picture of village life. There are echoes of Richard III in the cunning farmer Matthias Ferner as he sinks deeper into corruption first to gain, then to protect his wealth, but the world he inhabits is far closer to Tolstoi than to Shakespeare. The delightful Kreuzelschreiber also has classic echoes. The conceit of the women of a village refusing to sleep with their husbands until they make a pilgrimage to Rome suggests Aristophanes' Lysistrata not only in its theme, but in its exuberant elaboration. Yet the village scenes, especially the great brawl which closes the third act, suggest Bruegel much more than Greek comedy. Clearly Anzengruber brought realism to the folk tradition, as Raimund had brought romanticism to it. It was a realism, however, that had none of the dark and despairing tone which marked many of the followers of Zola. Anzengruber's love of life permeates every scene of a play like Die Kreuzelschreiber, and overflows from the rural philosopher Steinklopferhanns, who exalts in a revelation that came to him after a long illness:

> Nothing can harm you! Even the greatest torment does not count when it is over! Though you were lying six feet deep under that sod, or though you were to see a thousand times beyond all that stretches out before your gaze, nothing can harm you! Then for the first time in my life I was happy, and have been happy ever since, and I would have no one sad and spoiling my happy world!

Despite their popularity and poetic richness, Anzengruber's peasant plays seemed hardly suited to the Burgtheater, and Dingelstedt became interested in him only when the dramatist turned to higher class dramas, set in Vienna among the petty bourgeoisie. Here the crude and earthy backgrounds which offended the more delicate artistic tastes of the time were replaced by the more comfortable and familiar world of sitting room and salon. Unfortunately, Elfriede (1873) achieved only a modest success, though the interpretations of Sonnenthal, Baumeister, and Wolter were

warmly praised. Die Tochter des Wucherers (1873) and
Hand und Herz (1874), at the Stadttheater, were even less
popular. This judgment of Anzengruber's contemporaries
has been confirmed by posterity; it is his richer, if less
pretentious peasant plays which have survived. One of these,
the farcial G'Wissenswurm (1874) brought Anzengruber his
first lasting success at major houses, at the Stadttheater in
1884 and the Burgtheater in 1896. Its subsequent production
at the Deutsches Theater in Berlin introduced the Austrian
dramatist's work to that city.

Unfortunately Anzengruber did not live to see this
growth of interest in his work. After G'Wissenswurm his
vogue seemed to have passed. Doppelselbstmord (1875), a
merry and charming story of the uniting of a rich man's son
and a poor man's daughter, could not hold its own against the
spectacle plays and operettas of the time. The Karltheater
refused the ambitious Ein Faustschlag in 1877, accepted 's
Jungferngift in 1878 and then, when it achieved a run of only
eight nights, refused to consider any further Anzengruber
offerings. His last important play, Das vierte Gebot (1877)
was presented at the Josefstädter, its title changed to the
neutral Ein Volkstück in vier Akten in response to clerical
protests. By means of a complex multiple plot Anzengruber
managed to unite in a single work elements of the old folk
plays and the new social and psychological dramas. The
play did not escape certain of Anzengruber's usual problems
--a strong reliance on sentimentality and exaggerated pathos,
a heavy didacticism, and obvious contrivances for theatrical
effect. Yet this chronicle of the decay of the rich Hutterer
family and of the poor Schalanters proved a great success
even in the naturalistic atmosphere of the Freie Bühne in
Berlin in 1890.

In 1878 Anzengruber was awarded the Schiller prize
"in recognition of his service to dramatic art in the last
three years." Though no dramatist in Germany deserved
the honor more, it was an ironic choice. Anzengruber's
popularity in Vienna was on the wane, he was almost unpro-
duced elsewhere, and he was on the brink of giving up the
theatre altogether. "Soon there will be no actors and no
public for folk plays," he wrote, "and it will be a great
folly to create them."[17] After 1880 he had turned almost
exclusively to the novel, and the final decade of his life saw
only two minor dramas, Heimgefunden (1885) and Der Fleck
auf der Ehr (1889).

It was Anzengruber's misfortune that during the years
he was writing, the theatres which would traditionally have
been most receptive to a renewal of the folk play were involved in the development of a far more popular and thriving
genre, the operetta. After the Franco-Prussian War Offenbach seemed to disappear with the Empire which had formed
the background for his works, and Vienna replaced Paris as
the European capital of the operetta. In 1871 Friedrich
Strampfer, director of the Theater an der Wien during the
1860s, opened the Strampfertheater, an intimate and expensive
house which offered Parisian vaudeville and operetta, German
comedy, Viennese Lokalpossen, and tableaux vivants until its
closing in 1875. Thus in the early 1870s Vienna had three
major theatres--the Burgtheater, Stadttheater and Hofoper--
and three minor ones--the Wien, the Karl, and the Strampfer.
The dominant suburban theatre now was the Wien, directed
since 1869 by Maximilian Steiner and Marie Geistinger. Here
Johann Strauss (1825-1899) made his operetta debut with
Indigo und die vierzig Räuber (1871), a work so successful
that it was revived at the Renaissance in Paris, the traditional home of operetta. Geistinger, Karl Rott, and Albin
Swoboda, all distinguished operetta performers, created the
work in Vienna. Carneval in Rom (1873) was another triumph, not only for its cast and composer, but for the settings by the Russian Breslaw and the costumes by Franceschini. By contrast, Die Fledermaus (1874) was an unusual
"Operette in Zivil" (without elaborate costumes), which disturbed some critics, but did not prevent this from becoming
one of Strauss' most popular works. Alexander Girardi
(1850-1918), who became the most famous interpreter of
Strauss and who played Dr. Falke in later revivals of Die
Fledermaus, spent his early years at the Strampfertheater
and thus did not appear in these first Strauss productions.
He joined the Theater an der Wien in 1875, and played an
important role in every Strauss revival and premiere there
after Cagliostro in Wien (1875).

The same year Marie Geistinger resigned as co-di-
rector, leaving Steiner to manage the theatre alone until his
death in 1880. He turned away from both Strauss and Anzengruber to emphasize authors of farce and Posse so that the
1867-1877 season, for example, devoted 4 evenings to Raimund, 5 to Nestroy, 9 to Anzengruber, 25 to Strauss, but
39 to O. F. Berg (1833-1886) and 68 to Carl Costa (1832-
1907). During Steiner's administration only one new work by
Strauss was presented, Blinde Kuh in 1878.

Both Strauss and Anzengruber now submitted plays to
the rival Karltheater, but found little encouragement there.
Franz von Jauner, its director, accepted only one work from
each, Strauss' Prinz Methusalem (1877) and Anzengruber's
's Jungferngift (1878). The genre Jauner preferred was the
French salon play, in which he and Wilhelm Knaack (1829-
1894) were distinguished performers. As public interest in
this genre declined, he turned to operetta and spectacles,
particularly adaptations from Jules Verne. Lecocq's works
became staples here, with Madame Angot achieving an impressive 181 performances. Suppé was the favored native
composer, gaining great success with Fatinitza (1876) and Der
Teufel auf Erden (1878). Jauner, a musician, actor, conductor and regisseur who had worked for a time with Laube,
was a new sort of director for a suburban theatre. He demanded long and painstaking rehearsals, had a Wagnerian
ideal of the harmony of elements on stage, and achieved
effects in staging and lighting which were the wonder of
Vienna.

The success Jauner enjoyed at the Karl opened other
opportunities to him. In 1875 he was named director of the
Hofoper, where he gave major productions of Verdi and
Wagner, launching the years of the latter's greatest impact
in Vienna with the Ring cycle in 1877 to 1879. The popular
director then took over a recently erected theatre, the Ringtheater, and made it into a major home for salon plays and
musical spectacles. Then in 1881, scarcely a year after
Jauner had become its director, the Ringtheater suffered one
of the worst theatre disasters of the century, a fire which
claimed the lives of 383 persons. Jauner was widely regarded as guilty of negligence and threatened with prison.
He spent the next three years in clearing his name, returning at last to public life in 1884 as the new director of the
Theater an der Wien.

The Viennese operetta was now at the peak of its popularity. Die Fledermaus had by 1881 been presented 150
times at the Wien and revived in 171 other German theatres.
Internationally, Strauss was beginning to eclipse even Offenbach. Der lustige Krieg (1881) was a new international success, and Strauss was invited to Berlin to premiere Eine
Nacht in Venedig (1883). Unhappily, it was something of a
disappointment to this northern public, and Strauss was quite
willing to return to Vienna with his Zigeunerbaron (1885).
Karl Millöcker (1842-1899), the composer for most of Anzengruber's plays, added another classic to the operetta reper-

toire with Der Bettelstudent (1882), which enjoyed an almost
unheard-of continual run of two months.   After 1885, however, the impact of Verdi and even more of Wagner on the
musical world caused the operettas even of Strauss to be regarded as a minor form.   As a result, the operetta began to
turn, or return, to comic opera.   Already with Zigeunerbaron
Strauss was moving in this direction.   The staging, especially in the huge crowd scenes, suggested the operatic
offerings of Dingelstedt, and in Zsupan Girardi created a
rich character totally alien to the traditional operetta convention of caricature.   The year 1887 saw both Strauss and
Millöcker creating works of this type, the former with the
rather undistinguished Simplizius, the latter with Die sieben
Schwaben, the first work designated as a Volksoper.

   All of these plays were produced at the Theater an
der Wien, and a contemporary description of the second act
setting of Die sieben Schwaben indicated that Jauner was still
strongly interested in experimenting with striking scenic
effects:

> A curiosity such as has perhaps never been seen
> in Vienna was the new moonlight effect. . . .   The
> moon appears on the horizon and is reflected in
> the waves, blood-red and uncommonly large.   The
> higher the moon rises above the water the more
> pale and the smaller it becomes.   The moonbeams,
> turning silver, are beautifully, charmingly re-
> flected in the smooth, almost transparent surface
> of the water.   This singular picture creates a truly
> magic impression. [18]

   Millöcker's Der arme Jonathan (1890) was probably
the most extreme of the attempts to give depth to the operetta, in this case turning it to the subject and characters of
a realistic thesis drama.   Strauss after 1890 returned to
more traditional operetta subjects, but with less success.
The later works were considered memorable only for the
comic creations of Girardi--Kassim Pascha in Fürstin
Ninetta (1893), Joschko in Jabuka (1894) and Erasmus Müller
in Waldmeister (1895).   Jauner apparently felt the time had
come to break away from operetta presentation, but the tradition and the company at the Wien made this almost impossible.   Therefore he left in 1894 to return to the Karl.
Alexandrine von Schönerer, his successor, relied on revivals
of Strauss, though with little success after 1897, when
Girardi also departed.   The only important premiere of her

administration, which lasted until 1900, was the first Vienna
production of Puccini's La Bohème, in 1897.

Jauner returned to the Karl to find that it had enjoyed
little prosperity in his absence. Operettas, folk plays,
spectacle dramas had all been offered with little success.
Karl Blasel between 1889 and 1894 did somewhat better than
his predecessors by importing farces like Charley's Aunt and
guest stars such as Duse, but Jauner initiated a far more
eclectic program, presenting farce, operetta, spectacle, and
salon plays and seeking out the experimental drama of the
new generation. Ibsen's League of Youth and Hedda Gabler
had their Vienna premieres here, and Strindberg's The
Father with Emanuel Reicher as a guest artist. Jauner also
encouraged Jung Wien, a group of authors which dedicated
themselves to seeking new directions in literature while
avoiding alignment with any established movement, such as
the naturalists. From Jung Wien came Hermann Bahr's
(1863-1934) Das Tschaperl (1897), Felix Dörmann's (1870-
1928) Ledige Leute (1897) and Arthur Schnitzler's Freiwild
(1898). He also brought to Vienna a dazzling array of international stars--Duse, Antoine, Zacconi, Coquelin, Bern-
hardt--even though such appearances usually gained his theatre more renown than revenue. He was negotiating for the
tour of an entire company from Russia when he died, in his
office, in 1900.

At the Burgtheater, Dingelstedt's successor Adolf
Wilbrandt was interested in building the repertoire, but the
contemporary German and Austrian theatre offered him in
the early 1880s only such minor fare as Franz Nissel's
(1831-1893) stilted historical drama Die Zauberin am Stein
(1882). He therefore turned to the classics--Molière,
Shakespeare, Calderon, and most strikingly, the Greeks, who
had been almost forgotten on the German stage since Tieck.
One of Wolter's greatest interpretations was Sophocles'
Electra in 1822. The Cyclops was given that same year,
Oedipus in 1886 and Oedipus at Colonus in 1887. Their success, with Emmerich Robert as Oedipus, inspired contemporary dramatists such as Hugo von Hofmannsthal (1874-
1929) to turn to classic themes at the close of the century.
A premiere subscription series introduced the public to such
foreign works as Sardou's Fédora, Pailleron's Monde où
l'on s'ennuie, Ohnet's Maître de Forges, Dumas fils' Denise,
Turgenev's Natalie, Gogol's The Inspector General, and Björnson's A Bankruptcy. Native German selections ranged from such
light comic authors as Moser and Schönthan to Goethe and

Schiller. Raimund's <u>Verschwender</u> in 1885 was not a success, but was important as the first attempt at the Burgtheater to present a play directly out of the folk tradition. Like
Dingelstedt, Wilbrandt relied heavily on the ensemble he inherited, led now by Sonnenthal, Baumeister, Wolter, Robert,
and Lewinsky, but he too made important additions to it:
Katharina Schratt (1855-1940), Max Devrient (1858-1929),
Georg Reimers (1860-1936), and Rudolf Tyrolt (1848-1929).
The most noted production of this administration was a brilliant three-evening presentation of the complete <u>Faust</u> in 1883
with Sonnenthal as Faust, Lewinsky as Mephisto, and Wessely
as Gretchen. In such ambitious undertakings Wilbrandt had
the same dedication to detail as Dingelstedt, as his voluminous promptbooks in the theatre archives testify. Indeed his
concern with every aspect of the productions steadily con-
sumed his strength, and he was forced to retire, exhausted,
in 1887.

When Dingelstedt came to the Burgtheater in 1870,
one of his major responsibilities was overseeing plans for
its new home, since the ancient structure which had sheltered
it for nearly a century was becoming increasingly unsafe.
With his love for scenic display and huge casts, it is hardly
surprising that Dingelstedt insisted on a huge and excellently
furnished theatre plant. Construction began during his administration and continued all during that of Wilbrandt.

The new Burgtheater, designed by Gottfried Semper
and Carl von Hasenauer, finally opened in 1888, and was one
of the largest and best equipped in the world. The theatre
was now at the height of its reputation, its ensemble praised
throughout Europe, the tours of such actors as Lewinsky and
Sonnenthal generally acknowledged as the pinnacle of German
acting. Yet the late 1880s was a period of confusion and
marking time at the theatre, as it sought a leader to replace
Wilbrandt. Sonnenthal was serving as provisional director
when the new theatre opened, but that same fall he was replaced by Dr. August Förster (1828-1889), who had helped to
found the prestigious Deutsches Theater in Berlin five years
before. He saw the Burgtheater as another embodiment of
the same vision, a great repository of national classics on
the model of the Comédie. He hoped to develop a distinct
style of interpretation which would strike a harmonious balance between Laube's interest in language and Dingelstedt's
care for physical production. This promising program was
barely begun, however, when Förster died in 1889 and Sonnenthal again became provisional director. To add to their

problems, the company found adjustment to the new theatre
extremely difficult. The horseshoe auditorium had dead
spots, both visually and acoustically, no sight lines from the
galleries to the stage were particularly satisfactory, and the
intimacy of the old house was completely lost. Ten years
after the opening, the historian Lothar reported that audiences and actors were still adjusting to the building.

A new director, Max Burckhard (1854-1912), was
selected in 1890. Since he was a ministerial vice-secretary
with no experience whatever in the theatre, this obviously
bureaucratic appointment was bitterly resented by the company, by critics, and by much of the theatre's public. Yet
Burckhard, a genial, shrewd, and pragmatic man, rode out
the storm and eventually won over even his most bitter
opponents.

Each period during the nineteenth century at the Burgtheater produced a different emphasis in the repertoire. In
the opening decades Kotzebue and his school dominated, then
Shreyvogel introduced the Spanish, led by Calderon and
Moreto. With his departure, these were gradually replaced
by the works of Young Germany, though Laube, himself a
member of this school, shifted his emphasis when a director
to the French social drama. Halm brought his own plays
and the thin, self-consciously idealized dramas of Weilen and
Mosenthal. Dingelstedt relegated the French authors to a
minor position, offered more German and Austrian authors,
and gave a new prominence to Shakespeare. Finally, Burckhard responded to political and social pressures toward nationalism, and produced the most thoroughly Germanic repertoire the Burgtheater had yet seen. Of more than eighty
new works he presented, only three significant ones were
French--Bisson's Contrôleur des Wagons-Lits, Halévy's
Petite Maman, and Rostand's Romanesques. Shakespeare
was still well represented, but balanced by Goethe, Schiller,
Hebbel, and Grillparzer. The doors of the Burgtheater were
truly opened to the folk play at last with a series of important Anzengruber productions--Der Meineidbauer in 1893,
Stahl und Stein in 1894, Der G'wissenswurm in 1896.

The new drama was welcomed by Burckhard with
equal enthusiasm. Förster had presented Pillars of Society
in 1889, but bowed to conservative elements in the theatre
who demanded no more Ibsen. Burckhard gave not only The
Wild Duck, which Förster had dropped, but Enemy of the
People (1890), The Feast at Solhaug and The Pretenders

(1891) and <u>Little Eyolf</u> (1895). Hauptmann was introduced to Vienna with <u>Einsame Menschen</u> in 1891, and the next six years saw <u>Kollege Crampton</u>, <u>Hanneles Himmelfahrt</u>, and <u>Die versunkene Glocke</u>. Two new Austrian dramatists were also welcomed, Arthur Schnitzler (1862-1931) and Leo Ebermann (1863-1914). Ebermann's <u>Die Athenerin</u> (1896) revealed him as little more than a late disciple of Halm and his work soon disappeared, but Schnitzler gradually established a European reputation. Schnitzler, like Grillparzer, showed a distinct influence from the folk tradition, but while Grillparzer turned this heritage toward pseudo-classic tragedy, Schnitzler developed it into ironic social drama. The psychology of love was his favorite theme, treated tragically as in <u>Liebelei</u> (1895), farcically, or ironically. No dramatist was more successful than he in capturing the brittle and yet sentimental gaiety of old Vienna. In <u>Der grüne Kakadu</u> (1899), however, he created a different sort of world, anticipating a common concern of twentieth century drama with a fable of the conflict of reality and illusion set against the background of Revolutionary Paris.

Burckhard gave little encouragement to the famous ensemble of the theatre, preferring to rely on a few major actors who suited the repertoire he was developing. Ibsen, Holz, and Hauptmann gave a naturalistic emphasis to the theatre, and not many of the Burgtheater company found it easy to adjust to this style. Burckhard recalled Mitter-wurzer, who became the leading actor of his company, and, through such roles as Hjalmar Ekdal, one of Germany's most noted interpreters of Ibsen. Mitterwurzer's almost invariable partner was Adele Sandrock (1864-1937), whose tense style was at first considered distracting (some critics even characterized it as hysterical) but was gradually accepted as suitable for the new drama. "Classic parts are beyond her," observed one critic, "but no one can come near her in the interpretation of the decadent, the perverse, the degenerate, those straying in senses and nerves."[19] She in fact gained many admirers for her emotional portrayals even of such classic roles as Maria Stuart, Lady Macbeth, Juliet, and Medea. After 1893 the more usual interpreter of tragic heroines, those roles formerly taken by Charlotte Wolter, was Hedwig Bleibtrau (1868-1958). Burckhard devoted little attention to new talents, and brought only one important young actress to the Burgtheater, Lotte Medelsky. After a great success as Hedwig in <u>The Wild Duck</u> in 1897 she went on to play most of the major youthful roles-- Gretchen, Perdita, Cordelia, and Johanna. Burckhard also

brought in major guest artists, completing arrangements for
the appearance of Kainz before retiring from the directorship
in 1898.

In him the Burgtheater had found another inspired
dilettante, as Dingelstedt had been, a leader with no theatrical background who yet made a major contribution to the
great Burgtheater tradition. His major fault was his in-
sensitivity to the ensemble, but that had been sufficiently
well established by Laube and Dingelstedt to survive his disinterest. His greatest contribution was to open the Burgtheater to the moderns, most significantly to Hauptmann and
Ibsen, and by so doing, to revitalize the classics as well.
His leading players, Mitterwurzer and Sandrock, were considered by the theatre public of Vienna as the heralds of
twentieth century interpretation, though Mitterwurzer died
three years before the old century's end. It was this interest in the modern and in modernism which made Burckhard the forerunner of Mahler, who came to conduct the
Hofoper the year before Burckhard retired, and of Max Reinhardt, now a young actor in Berlin, who would revolutionize
the Viennese theatre after the first world war.

4. Munich and Lesser German Stages

Although every major German city possessed at least
one established theatre in the closing decades of the nineteenth century, Berlin enjoyed a cultural dominance over
them all which was as great as its political dominance. The
minor drama of the virtuoso period, occasionally relieved by
a revival of Goethe or Schiller, was the standard fare at
most of these theatres until the introduction of the naturalists
and of a more European interest at the close of the century.
A number of cities were fortunate enough, however, to find
during the 1870s and 1880s directors who brought prosperity
to their theatres, along with a high level of quality in production and a significant improvement in the repertoire.

Brosart von Schellendorf (1830-1913), in Hannover
from 1871 to 1887, suffered a great loss in the death of Carl
Devrient in 1872, but sought out and trained promising young
actors for his ambitious repertoire. Ibsen's Pillars of Society was presented here in 1878, and Wildenbruch, Berlin's
favored pre-naturalist, considered Hannover his second theatrical home. Hans von Bülow was conductor here in the

late 1870s and naturally brought Wagnerian works and singers
to the city.   Shakespearian production here culminated in an
1880 cycle of all the history plays from Richard II to Richard
III (except Henry VI, Part III).   After 1887 von Schellendorf
went to Weimar, where he brought similar prosperity to both
opera and drama.

Under the direction of Bernhard Pollini (1838-1897)
the Hamburg stage developed between 1874 and 1897 an excellent dramatic company which gave notable productions of
the German classics.   Even more important was Pollini's
encouragement of the musical theatre here.   175 new operas
were staged under his administration, 51 of them for the
first time in Germany.   The first Wagnerian cycle was given
here in 1880.   The Stuttgart theatre achieved distinction
under Feodor Wehl (1821-1890), who served first as artistic
director, then from 1874 to 1885 as intendant, leaving an interesting record of the duties of each in his Funfzehn Jahre
Stuttgarter Theater.   He improved the company and balanced
popular comedies and farces with original works and revivals
of Goethe, Schiller, and Shakespeare.

The Leipzig Stadttheater was directed between 1882
and 1905 by Max Stägemann (1843-1905), who achieved a success there which had eluded Laube and his followers Haase
and August Förster.   His major production was a complete
Faust, premiered in 1883 and presented regularly twice
yearly for some years thereafter.   In the late 1890s Leipzig,
like most of Germany's major cities, possessed a private
theatre inspired by the Freie Bühne in Berlin and dedicated
to the presentation of important modern plays which for reasons of censorship or financial risk could not be presented
in the established theatres.   Leipzig's Freie Bühne, fittingly
named the Ibsen Theater, was directed by Karl Martens, the
president of the Leipziger Literarische Gesellschaft.   The
usual works of Ibsen, Strindberg, Hauptmann, and Holz were
given here, and one outstanding premiere, Erdgeist (1898),
the first performance of a play by Franz Wedekind.

Wedekind (1864-1918) had by this date published four
plays, but was still virtually unknown.   Der Schnellmaler
(1889) was written while he was associating with the naturalists of Zurich and Munich, but the play was a sprawling
farce in the folk play tradition.   In its construction, Wedekind was much less influenced by any contemporaries than by
the long-neglected Büchner, whose example led him to a
striking mixture of tragedy and farce and a telegraphic style

which emphasized concepts and often reduced characters to
caricature. Hauptmann, whom Wedekind met at this time,
used the story of Wedekind's unhappy youth as the plot for
Das Friedensfest, an impropriety which Wedekind never forgave. He took his revenge in his second play, Die junge
Welt (1891), a comic satire on Hauptmann, the naturalists,
and the movement for women's emancipation. The much
more serious Frühlings Erwachen (1891) and Erdgeist (1895)
brought Wedekind to his full maturity as a playwright but
attracted no producers. Their thoroughgoing disregard for
conventional form and their strongly erotic themes made both
plays unacceptable to the established theatres and Wedekind's
feud with the naturalists closed the new experimental theatres to him as well. The Freie Bühne refused even to consider a production of Erdgeist.

Three years after this refusal came the unexpected
offer from Martens for a production in Leipzig. It was a
great success, touring to Halle, Hamburg, and Breslau, all
the more gratifying to Wedekind since at the request of Carl
Heine (1861-1927), the director, the author himself appeared
as Dr. Schön, making a simultaneous debut as dramatist and
actor. He deliberately abandoned the prevalent realistic mode
to introduce a grotesque and angular style which at first
shocked and then profoundly impressed his audience. Thus
in his interpretation as well as in his literary style Wedekind
carried on the iconoclastic heritage of Büchner and Grabbe
and looked forward to the entire expressionist movement.
Outside Germany, Wedekind's innovations may be seen as
parallel to Lunge-Poë's in Paris, where the revolt against
realism produced a different literary school, symbolism, but
a strikingly similar interpretive style. There was a parallel
also in the very extremism of experimentation: Wedekind's
Frühlings Erwachen in Germany and Jarry's Ubu Roi in
France were two of the major manifestations of a revolt
which made even the most uncompromising naturalists seem
conservative members of the nineteenth century tradition.

The success of Erdgeist at Leipzig earned Wedekind
an offer of production in Munich, which after Berlin and
Vienna was Germany's most important theatre city. He
joined the newlyopened Schauspielhaus as author, critic, and
actor, but his career there was interrupted almost immediately. Three years before, he had helped to found one of
Germany's most popular journals, Simplizissimus, a satirical
anti-establishment paper. Wedekind's mordant wit did much
to set the tone of the paper, but led in 1898 to a warrant

for his arrest on a charge of libeling the crown. Wedekind fled into exile for a year, then returned and served a nine-month sentence before being allowed, at last, to take up his position at the Schauspielhaus. His sufferings made him an avant-garde and anti-establishment hero, and after 1900 his fame grew rapidly. The first Wedekind cycle was given in Nürnberg in 1905 and the next year Erdgeist was given a major production in Berlin by Reinhardt, now Germany's outstanding director.

During the latter part of the century Berlin was the home of naturalism, the dominant new literary movement, and the center of activity for most of Germany's outstanding directors and actors. Still, Munich unquestionably offered a greater variety of theatrical experimentation. King Ludwig nationalized the old Munich Volkstheater in 1870, renaming it the Königliches Theater am Gärtnerplatz and making it the official home of folk plays, short comedies, and operetta. The old Hoftheater presented opera and those comedies and tragedies with heavy scenic demands. Other tragedy, drama, and comedy was presented at the Residenz, which had opened in 1857. Ernst Possart (1841-1921), a popular actor who had made his debut in Munich in 1864, was the director of all three houses.

Munich's leading literary school from 1850 to the mid-1880s was the Münchener Dichterkreis, which reacted to the Young Germany movement by returning, like the earlier Epigones, to the classic and romantic ideals of the Goethe and Schiller period. Paul Heyse (1830-1914) was the leading author of this group and an arch-enemy of the naturalists later in the century. As a dramatist he was best known for such historical plays as Hans Lange (1866). His colleague Adolf Wilbrandt, later director of the Burgtheater, created comedies such as Die Vermählten (1871) and Die Maler (1872) which were widely considered the best since Freytag's Journalisten and the "Roman" tragedies which Dingelstedt produced so lavishly in Vienna. On the outskirts of this circle after 1875 was a most unlikely figure who had brought his family to settle in Munich, Henrik Ibsen.

It was in Munich that Ibsen turned from his earlier poetic style to realism in The Pillars of Society, his first major success. The Hoftheater, which premiered Björnson's The Newly-Married Couple in 1875, was encouraging to Ibsen, giving The Pretenders in 1875 and The Vikings at Helgeland in 1876. The Residenz gave Pillars of Society in

1878 and A Doll's House in 1880 with Marie Ramlo (1850-
1921) as Nora and Hilmar Knorr (1847-1919) as Helmer.
Possart, the director, played Dr. Rank. The protests
aroused by this play grew to a storm here as elsewhere
with the translation of Ghosts into German in 1884. Munich
therefore did not see another Ibsen production until 1889,
when the Residenz mounted An Enemy of the People.

In the meantime, quite another sort of experimentation
was being carried out at the Hoftheater. A new director,
Karl von Perfall (1824-1907), arrived in 1887, and with the
support of the new monarch, Luitpold, carried out an extensive and revolutionary remodeling of the theatre. His
goal was to create a more satisfactory stage for producing
Shakespeare, and in the tradition of Immermann and Tieck
he sought an open and flexible space. The same year he
took charge of the theatre he explained his theory in the
Allgemeinen Zeitung:

> Modern stages with their heavy, complex machinery
> and equipment are in direct opposition to the
> Shakespearian dramas, which despite their ex-
> tremely intricate and yet clear compositions were
> conceived and written without any concern for the-
> atre mechanics. Thus we can achieve our desired
> end only if we create a stage which in its simpli-
> city allows us, through a free and unencumbered
> presentation, to find what is truly "Shakespearian"
> in these plays. [20]

Public and critics, accustomed to the lavish productions of Wagner and Dingelstedt, naturally viewed this project
with some suspicion. Von Perfall was accused of denying
three hundred years of historical development, and even of
seeking to destroy the national theatre. This made all the
more significant the unqualified success of the opening production, King Lear, in 1889. The new stage combined elements of the traditional English stage with German experiments of the early nineteenth century and some totally new
elements. Its dominant feature was a large neutral forestage
built out over the orchestra which could be approached from
all sides and even, by steps, from the front. Behind the
proscenium line was another neutral stage area enclosed by
an architectural backing in warm, dark shades that was kept
in a constant half-light. In the center of this, three steps
led up to a smaller inner stage with an opening about 25 feet
wide (the major proscenium had an opening of about 53 feet).

This inner stage, which could be closed by a curtain, contained the only changeable scenery: chairs, tables, and at the back, a painted perspective done not on a conventional drop but on a single long band of canvas which could be rolled from either end to reveal a new scene something in the manner of a comic strip. This painted backing was changed twenty-three times in Lear, but the arrangement of the stage allowed this without requiring any break in the flow of the play.

They began Lear with the inner curtain closed, opened it for Lear's palace with the throne up center before an appropriate painted background, closed it for the next scene, opened it for the next, in Gloucester's palace, and so on. The painted backings were changed, of course, while the curtain was closed. After Lear came notable productions of Henry IV (both parts), Henry V, Twelfth Night, Macbeth, The Winter's Tale, and Romeo and Juliet, which established two ideas revolutionary in Shakespearian production of the period: that curtain and act pauses should be sacrificed to the flow of the play, and that whatever machines and scenery are available, stage illusion still depends on convention and the imagination of the audience. The Munich Shakespeare stage thus provided a significant balance to the wide-spread influence of the Meininger.

Though the naturalist movement never dominated Munich letters as it did in Berlin, by 1885 it was a distinct force in the cultural life of the city. Its major organ was the review Die Gesellschaft, founded in this year by Michael Georg Conrad. No single dramatic organization comparable to Berlin's Freie Bühne emerged from this school, but a series of private societies provided Munich with similar exposure to the new drama. Student literary societies had much to do with the dramatic experimentation in Germany at the end of the century, and Munich contained one of the most noted of these, the Akademisch-Dramatische Verein. It was founded in 1890 for the reading and discussion of modern drama, but began full productions at private matinees in 1892. Their close relation to the Berlin Freie Bühne was indicated by their opening production, Einsame Menschen, the first offering in Munich of a play by Hauptmann, the major dramatist of the Berlin theatre. The next year saw Ibsen's Ghosts, Sudermann's Sodoms Ende, and Jugend, by a new author, Max Halbe (1865-1944). This naturalistic study of the psychology of adolescence proved so popular that it was moved to the Residenz for public performances.

Another new naturalist, Georg Hirshfeld (1873-1935), was introduced in 1894 with Zu Hause and achieved a great success
two years later with Die Mütter. Among the later productions of this influential society were Ibsen's Rosmersholm,
The Wild Duck, and The Master Builder, Björnson's Beyond
Human Power I with Emanuel Reicher, Hauptmann's Die
Weber and Das Friedensfest.

Though such extreme works as Die Weber or Ghosts
could not yet be attempted on the public stage, von Perfall
was willing enough to give the more moderate works a hear-
ing at the national theatres. Aside from the Ibsen and Halbe
works already mentioned, he presented Die Ehre, the first
Sudermann play in Munich, in 1891 and Hauptmann's Kollege
Crampton in 1893. Possart, who returned as director in
1893, was much less favorably disposed toward the new
movement and thus indirectly encouraged the Akademisch-
Dramatische Verein and other alternatives to existing theatres. He returned to operetta at the Gärtnertheater, where
most of these modern works had been presented, and Emil
Messthaler (1869-1927), who since 1891 had been that house's
leading actor, resigned to form the Theater der Modernen.
During the next two years he presented Thérèse Raquin,
Ghosts, Rosmersholm, Little Eyolf, Jugend, and Einsame
Menschen in Munich and on tour. A new society, the Gesell-
schaft für Modernes Leben, founded by the Hungarian actress
Juliana Déry, presented Munich's first Strindberg, Comrades,
in her home in 1895.

Possart's conservatism and the example of the new
Deutsches Theater in Berlin led to the founding of a Munich
Deutsches Theater under the director of Messthaler in 1896.
Unfortunately Messthaler attempted to please everyone, and
after a year of presenting programs indiscriminately mixing
naturalist dramas, comedies, and spectacular ballets, he was
forced to resign. The Schauspielhaus, another major new
theatre which opened in 1897 under the direction of J. G.
Stollberg, achieved more with a less eclectic approach. It
opened with Rosmersholm, produced Erdgeist, as we have
seen, in 1898, and Strindberg's The Father with Emanuel
Reicher in 1899. During these same years another Munich
stage was pioneering a major new production technique.
Carl Lautenschläger (1843-1906), a student of Karl Brandt
and chief machinist at the Residenz Theater, designed for
that house a permanent revolving stage, first used in a production of Don Giovanni in 1897. Though revolving stages
had for some time been used by Kabuki theatres in Japan

(turned by hand--Lautenschläger used electricity), the Residenz was the first theatre in Europe to install such a device.

As the century drew to a close, the naturalist movement was already giving way before other approaches, a shift reflected in the decade's last new producing society, the Literarische Gesellschaft, formed in 1897 by Ernst von Wolzogen. After opening with a classic of the naturalist theatre, Tolstoi's Power of Darkness, they presented the first Troilus and Cressida in Munich, grotesquely interpreted as a burlesque on war in the style of Offenbach. After this came two poetic works from Vienna, Hofmannsthal's Der Tor und der Tod and Schnitzler's Der grüne Kakadu. Thus Munich, lacking the theatrical pre-eminence of Berlin or Vienna, nevertheless proved more radical in production experimentation and more responsive than either to the full range of experimentation in playwriting of the period. There were no characteristic "Munich dramatists" corresponding to the naturalists like Hauptmann and Sudermann in the north or to the more poetic and fanciful Viennese from Schnitzler to Hofmannsthal, but Munich welcomed both, while supporting such late Epigones as Heyse. It was, moreover, selected as a home by the greatest of the moderns, Ibsen, who spent much of his life between 1875 and 1890 there, and by Wedekind, whose works would prove as seminal to the German theatre in the new century as Ibsen's had proven in the old.

5. Berlin

After 1870 Berlin, already established as the political center of Germany, began gradually to assume the position of cultural center as well. As the city's power grew, so did its attractiveness, and young Germans were now drawn to Berlin as young Frenchmen have traditionally been drawn to Paris. During the thirty-five year directorship of Botho von Hülsen at the Königliches Schauspielhaus (from 1851 to 1886) the population of the city grew from 483,000 to 1,500,000. Among those drawn to the new mecca were artists and intellectuals from all parts of Germany, and by the late 1880s this concentration of talent produced a period of literary activity which in its enthusiasm and productivity recalled the days of the Sturm und Drang.

Various forces both within and outside Germany during the 1870s and early 1880s prepared the way for this new

creative era, but their effects were felt slowly, and for most
sensitive observers of the theatre during this period it was a
depressing and umpromising time.   Many new theatres
opened, but they found no important new dramatists.   The
Meininger tours, beginning in 1874, made a positive contribution in presenting an alternative to the virtuoso system,
but most theatres and much of the public were most impressed in the Meininger productions by the heavy and elaborate representational settings.   A theatre involved in the presentation of classic or serious modern works was now expected to emulate these heavy Meininger offerings, which
added significantly to its already great financial burdens.
Few theatres during this period enjoyed much stability. Bank-
ruptcies were common, and the few houses which survived
normally did so by stressing physical spectacle or by relying
on fare of scarcely higher artistic distinction than that of the
variety houses and cabarets.   "Hardly ever, " says the historian Witkowski, "has there been in a highly civilized nation
in an epoch of great national triumphs a stage that was so
degenerate as the German of the seventies. "   It was the time
of the Gründerjahre, of pursuit of wealth and luxury, and the
vaudeville, the operetta, and the farce were the favored theatrical forms.

The best dramatists of this undistinguished period
were Paul Lindau (1839-1919) and Hugo Lubliner (1846-1911),
pale imitators of Dumas fils, Augier, and Sardou.   Their
pictures of contemporary society were popular for a time due
to their frivolity and facile wit, but no substance, intellectual or emotional, lay beneath these polished conversations,
and they soon passed forever from the repertoire.   Yet at
this same time dramatists outside Germany were creating the
works which would revitalize the German stage, and during
this same decade Germany felt the first influence of these
foreign masters--first Zola, then Tolstoi and Dostoevsky,
then Björnson, and finally, and most importantly, Ibsen.

The first of these great foreign authors to impress
himself on the public consciousness as a playwright was
Björnsterne Björnson (1832-1910).   His Between the Battles
was presented by the Meininger, and this in turn inspired
Berlin productions in 1875 of The Newly-Married Couple and
A Bankruptcy.   Karl Frenzel in the Deutsche Rundschau
called their realism drab and uninteresting, while Paul Lindau
in Die Gegenwart hailed them as the most impressive offerings on the Berlin stage for years.   This difference of opinion was not without its ironic side, since Frenzel had praised

Lindau's Maria und Magdalena (1872) for its "sensitivity to modern life" which placed the author "in the midst of today's movements and struggles."[21] A constant theme in Frenzel's criticism was that the theatre to develop must be based on realism and that comedy especially must be a mirror of its time, but the realist movement, as it developed, found him unsympathetic. He found its emphasis on the commonplace tedious, and was disturbed by its tendency to convert the theatre into a place of political or social instruction (Erziehungsanstalt). But the great critic's influence was rapidly waning. By the mid-1880's Björnson's dramas were in the repertoire of all the leading theatres and Frenzel's criticism was considered narrow if not outright reactionary.

Scarcely had Björnson come to the attention of the German theatre public when another and greater Scandinavian appeared, Henrik Ibsen (1828-1906), whose influence on the modern German theatre proved greater than that of any other dramatist. The Meininger production of The Pretenders, brought to Berlin in 1876, was Germany's first exposure to Ibsen, but it was generally considered merely a historical spectacle drama and made little impression. The Vikings at Helgeland, given in Munich, Vienna, and Dresden in 1876, was not even offered in Berlin. It was Pillars of Society which established Ibsen's European reputation. Five separate theatres in Berlin presented it within a fortnight in 1878, a record unequalled in Berlin theatre history. The same year the play was offered by twenty-two other theatres throughout Germany and Austria. A majority of critics still considered Björnson the superior author in terms of imagination and technique, and Ibsen a promising but not extraordinary author in the thesis play tradition.

This casual appraisal was swept aside by the storm which broke over A Doll's House. Productions in Scandinavia during the winter of 1879-1880 aroused unheard-of antagonism to play and author, condemned as an enemy of all organized society. Theatre managers and critics were in general as appalled by this apparent attack on the sanctity of home and marriage as conventional society, and only the interest of Frau Hedwig Niemann-Raabe (1844-1905) in the role of Nora brought the play to production at the Berlin Residenztheater in 1880. Though the actress requested and obtained from Ibsen an alternate ending in which Nora remains with her husband, the play created as great a scandal in Berlin as elsewhere. Frenzel and Lindau united in deploring a writer of Ibsen's apparent talent turning to subjects which

they called more repugnant and morbid than the coarsest of
the French.

The next five years saw many translations of Ibsen
into German, but few productions. Ghosts (1881) was hailed
by Ibsen's followers as a masterpiece, but its subject, even
more shocking that that of A Doll's House, made public presentation unthinkable. A group of young Munich authors
sponsored its German premiere, a private showing in Augsburg in 1886. Later that year the Meininger presented it at
their home theatre, but were prevented by the censor from
bringing it to Berlin. Then Franz Wallner, dramaturg of the
Residenztheater, obtained permission to present the play at a
single matinee for charity. The social dramas of Augier,
Dumas fils, Feuillet, and Barrière had for some years been
the particular specialty of the Residenz, but even the darkest
of these dramas prepared neither critics nor actors for
Ghosts. The leading actor Kainz flatly refused the role of
Oswald, and Wallner played it himself. Mrs. Alving was
played by the director's wife, Charlotte Frohn (1844-1888).
Critics would later look back on this performance, directed
by Anton Anno (1838-1893), as the beginning of the modern
era in German theatre, but at the time the majority of them
shared the opinion of Frenzel, who suggested that Ibsen's
only purpose was "in torturing his audience and provoking a
kind of moral seasickness. "22

Nevertheless, the Ibsen movement had been launched.
A few months later, the suburban Ostendtheater offered An
Enemy of the People. Then the Residenz presented Rosmersholm with Charlotte Frohn and Emanuel Reicher, a major
interpreter of the new drama. Neither of these works
aroused much protest, but a new storm broke over The Wild
Duck at a Residenz matinee the next year. The Norddeut-
schen Allgemeinen Zeitung poetically observed that "all the
muck of the obscure French theatre takes on the appearance
of pure water next to The Wild Duck, " while the Post complained more directly: "What we are subjected to here ex-
ceeds in naked brutality everything which occurred in the
most notorious of the French social dramas. "23

While these mature works of Ibsen were too radical
to be assimilated at once by the German theatre, they reinforced a spirit of change which grew steadily stronger
throughout the 1880s. The first major reaction against the
dominance of operettas, Lokalpossen, and thin social comedies came from within the theatrical establishment itself.

Early in the decade a group of noted actors, authors, and directors combined their efforts to establish in Berlin a Deutsches Theater which would be for the new capital what the Comédie was for Paris or the Burgtheater for Vienna, a major home for the national classics. Adolf L'Arronge (1838-1908) was the leader of this group, supported by Ludwig Barnay, August Förster, Siegwart Friedmann, Friedrich Haase, and Ernst Possart. The Friedrich Wilhelmstadtische Theater, formerly a home for farce and musical theatre, was rechristened the Deutsches and opened in 1883 with Kabale und Liebe. Works by Shakespeare, Goethe, Lessing, Kleist, Schiller, and Grillparzer followed. Before the end of the decade most of the original founders except L'Arronge had departed for other stages, but under his leadership the Musterbühne tradition and the new impetus given by the Meininger reached their fruition. His leading actors were among the best in Germany--Josef Kainz, Agnes Sorma, Arthur Kraussneck (1856-1941), and Georg Engels (1846-1907)--and L'Arronge's concern for young actors made the Deutsches an excellent training ground.

The great years of this venture were 1883 to 1888, during which time it had the classics almost to itself, since even at the Königliches Schauspielhaus the aging von Hülsen presented little except what the Kaiser called "vaterländische" plays. This meant, at best, new offerings from Wildenbruch. A new director, Bolko von Hochberg (1843-1926), a new Kaiser, Wilhelm II, and a new regisseur, Max Grube, created by 1890 a different atmosphere at the theatre. Goethe, Schiller, and Shakespeare now balanced Lindau, Blumenthal, and Wildenbruch, and even Ibsen, Turgenev, and Björnson were given occasional production. By this time other rivals in the production of classics had also appeared. Ludwig Barnay left the Deutsches in 1888 to found the Berliner Theater, with many of L'Arronge's best actors. Here he presented few new works, but important revivals of the German classics, of Sophocles and of Molière until 1893. A lesser theatre working the same repertoire was Oskar Blumenthal's Lessing Theater, which also opened in 1888.

Thus within ten years Berlin had gained four theatres significantly concerned with the presentation of the classics, while in 1880 there had been none. Yet this still provided no outlet for important contemporary dramatists most of whom in Berlin were associated with or championed by the new artistic school called naturalism. In the young generation of the 1880s the inspiration of Zola, Dostoevsky, Tolstoi, and

Ibsen, the literary heritage of the Sturm und Drang and Young
Germany, and the political and social writings of Marx and
Engels combined to produce this extreme form of realism
which was socially oriented, deeply concerned with the effects
of heredity and environment, and militantly dedicated to truth
in preference to beauty. Like Zola, whom they greatly admired, the young naturalists attempted to be scientific and
ruthlessly objective in their depiction of facts, but like him
they rarely avoided a tone of social pity, or of indignation at
the existing class exploitation.

    Berlin was the center of this new movement, and a
society, the Akademische Vereingung, was formed here in
1886 to further the efforts of young authors and artists who
called themselves simply Die Moderne. The literary members of this group formed a second society, Durch, with
goals that were set forward by Eugen Wolff at the second
meeting. Among these were that:

> All creative literature ought to clarify poetically
> the spirit of contemporary life; the author of today,
> therefore, must consider it his mission poetically
> to fashion those forces at present actually signifi-
> cant, or struggling to become so, without, however,
> purposely serving any party or movement of the
> time.... The subject matter of our literature must
> be modern; it must consider the growing interest
> in social questions.... It is the task of modern
> literature to depict men and women of flesh and
> blood, to portray their passions with inexorable
> fidelity, without overstepping the innate boundaries
> of art. Natural truthfulness of the art ought to
> enhance the aesthetic effect.... Such principles
> are hostile to the imitation of the classics, to blue-
> stocking dilettantism, and to artificial refinement.[24]

    The most important members of the new school were
the brothers Heinrich (1855-1906) and Julius Hart (1859-
1906), who began the campaign in their Kritische Waffengänge;
the critic Leo Berg (1862-1908), who became the leader of
the society; Eugen Wolff; and Arno Holz (1863-1929) and Johannes Schlaf (1862-1941), whose sketches called Papa Hamlet
(1889) were the first German work to rigorously apply the
theory of faithful reproduction of reality. A later member
of the group was the then almost unknown young dramatist
Gerhart Hauptmann (1862-1946). Though the drama was one
of the major concerns of this group, especially after the

appearance of Ibsen, the existing theatre situation showed little hope of reform. The general public seemed most interested in the light entertainment of vaudeville, operetta, and farce. The only "artistically" oriented theatre of the capital, the Deutsches, was almost totally devoted to the classics, and L'Arronge made no response to an appeal in the fourth issue (1883) of Kritische Waffengänge which challenged him to create a "modern German theatre" which would present "situations, characters, emotions as they are seen in real life." Other managers were hesitant to offend the possible prejudices of their bourgeois public. Finally, the Berlin police held power of political censorship over all public gatherings, including theatrical performances. Obviously criticisms of the state would not be permitted, but presumed attacks on religion, custom, order, and good taste were equally likely to be banned, especially when the Kaiser himself had expressed his contempt for what he called the new "gutter art" (Rinnsteinkunst).

A way around this dilemma was suggested by the example of Antoine's Théâtre-Libre in Paris--a theatre open only to members and therefore impervious to police censorship and the commercial interests of the established theatre. Wolff and the brothers Hart from Durch and seven other critics, journalists, and businessmen formed in 1889 the Freie Bühne on that model. The new society was soon dominated by two enthusiastic supporters of Ibsen and the new drama, Otto Brahm (1855-1912) and Paul Schlenther (1854-1916). These two life-long friends attended the University of Berlin together where they were deeply impressed by the works of Ibsen, Comte, Taine, and Zola. After graduation, Brahm became second in command to the dean of Berlin critics, Theodor Fontane, on the Vossische Zeitung. He held this post from 1881 until 1885, when his condescending attitude toward most of the Berlin theatres and their directors brought his dismissal. He then moved into free-lance work, and with Schlenther was instrumental in arranging the matinee performance of Ghosts in 1887. By 1889 he had established himself as a leading spokesman for the new naturalist movement. This earned him regular attacks from the epicurean Munich school and from such conservative Berlin journals as Das Kunstwerk, but it also assured him an important position in the new Freie Bühne.

In Wozu der Lärm? Genesis der Freien Bühne Paul Schlenther set forth in 1889 the purposes of the new stage:

We are united in the purpose of forming, independent of the management of the established theatre and without entering into rivalry with it, a
theatre free from conventions, theatre censorship,
and commercial aims. During this theatre year,
this group shall give in one of the first theatre
houses of Berlin some ten productions of modern
plays of decided interest which in their very nature
the established houses find difficult to undertake.
The aims of living art shall be opposed to that of
patterns and masters alike in the choice of the
dramatic works and in their presentations. 25

The founders designated themselves active members; as such
they chose plays, obtained regisseurs, and made all arrangements for the productions. The general public was then invited to become passive members by buying subscriptions to
finance the venture. Oskar Blumenthal offered the Freie
Bühne the use of his Lessing Theater for Sunday matinees,
and here the first production was given, Ghosts, on September 29, 1889. Oswald and Mrs. Alving were portrayed by
two actors who contributed greatly to the development of a
naturalist style of presentation, Rudolf Rittner (1869-1943)
and Else Lehmann (1866-1940).

For Brahm's second offering, Theodor Fontane re-
commended a new German drama, Gerhart Hauptmann's Vor
Sonnenaufgang. It was at once hailed as the first major
naturalist drama, though Fontane noted that Hauptmann could
also be regarded as a contributor to the tradition of German
realist drama going back through Ibsen to Hebbel. The play
concerned a peasant family in Hauptmann's native Silesia,
which formed the background for most of his early works.
Suddenly made wealthy by the discovery of coal on their land,
the Krause family becomes totally corrupt, sinking into al-
coholism, gambling, adultery, even incest. They are visited
by that common figure of naturalist drama, the idealistic out-
sider ("der Retter aus der Ferne"), here Loth, a young
socialist. He and Helene, the innocent daughter of the corrupt family, fall in love, but at last, fearing the taint of her
heredity, he deserts her and she commits suicide.

Vor Sonnenaufgang's debt to the earlier naturalists
was great. Each act was introduced with a little masterpiece
of description which, with the extensive stage directions,
showed that Hauptmann was well aware of the effects of
milieu and atmosphere on his drama. The alcohol-ridden

family had strong echoes of Zola, and the theme of the
hereditary taint strongly suggested Ibsen. The young re-
former also owed a great deal to Ibsen, developed with that
odd combination of intellectual sympathy, ironic detachment
and comic exaggeration which we see in such an Ibsen re-
former-manqué as Dr. Stockmann or Gregers Werle. It is
therefore hardly surprising that Hauptmann, like Ibsen, had
to deny specifically that his young idealist was also his raissoneur. The character in the play who seems in fact to
come closest to expressing Hauptmann's own ideas is the
doctor Schimmelpfennig, who admits that his patients' chance
of recovery is slight, but who seeks to alleviate their suffering as much as possible by his medicine.

     If Loth echoes Gregers Werle, Schimmelpfennig serves
as the Doctor Relling of this play, with his "medicine" replacing Ibsen's more abstract "life-lie." Such parallels receive striking confirmation in the play when in the first act
Helene asks Loth his opinion of Zola and Ibsen. He replies:
"They aren't really poets at all, but necessary evils. I for
one am honestly thirsty and ask for a clear and refreshing
drink from literature. I'm not sick. But what Zola and
Ibsen have to offer is medicine. "[26] Hauptmann made it clear
that his own position was rather different: "Alfred Loth is an
optimist, while I, on the contrary, am a great admirer of
Zola and Ibsen and really consider them great poets. "[27] The
title of the play itself ("Before Sunrise") suggests that Hauptmann felt it represented the same world of gloom which was
associated with the work of Ibsen and Zola, but the rich and
sympathetic development of Helene, played by Else Lehmann,
introduced a strong note of compassion, of affirmation, some
critics have even said of joy into this dark tragedy. Her
love scene with Loth possessed a tenderness and charm which
set Hauptmann distinctly apart from Zola and Ibsen and indeed caused some contemporary critics to complain that
Hauptmann was corrupting naturalism by the introduction of
beauty.

     These were extreme reactions, however. For most
of the theatre public, Vor Sonnenaufgang was a naturalist
drama, pure and simple, and its production therefore a crucial test of whether that genre would succeed in the theatre.
Under the circumstances, it is hardly surprising that the
opening, though officially private, occasioned a riot reminiscent of the famous classic-romantic clash at the opening of
Hugo's Hernani in Paris:

The play, in a whirling vortex of accompanying
rumors, had already circulated in Berlin society
as a book. From the beginning, the dispositions
of the factions were at the boiling point, and they
exploded on this beautiful, sunny autumn morning
into one of the wildest theatre riots that the German stage had ever witnessed. Dr. Kaston the
physician, a noted tiger at premieres, was the
leader of the offended faction, and with laughter
and whistles he gave the signal to an opposition
no less spirited than himself. This disagreement
turned to violence when, near the end of the fourth
act as the dialogue on stage was concerned with
the labor pains taking place behind the scenes, he
threw his own forceps onto the stage as a scornful
demonstration against such realism. The uproar
continued a full month as the active members of
the society decided, in view of this demonstration,
to remove the membership cards of every malicious
disturber of the peace. [28]

The controversy delighted the reformers. Brahm observed that if the Freie Bühne accomplished nothing other
than the literary discussion engendered by this work it could
be proud of its achievement. A contemporary critic marveled:

> People wanted to fight over art! who would have
> thought that possible in the home of reserve offi-
> cers? Temperatures were rising--not over new
> cannons or gun models, not over the duty on grain
> or trade agreements, not over antisemites or
> socialists--no, over a new drama that for several
> weeks after it appeared people not only bought, but
> read! [29]

Two more Hauptmann premieres soon followed, Das
Friedensfest (1890), at the end of this first season, and
Einsame Menschen the following year. The dominant influence in both works was still Ibsen, both in themes and in
technique. Both were domestic tragedies developed according
to the classic unities of time and place. The first was based
on events in the life of Wedekind, but reinterpreted (as Wedekind may be forgiven for not understanding) to stress a number of Hauptmann's (and Ibsen's) favorite concerns. A
doctor, needing money to finance some complex projects,
has, like several of Ibsen's heroes, made a "financial" mar-

riage. His wife, an uneducated girl of sixteen, has borne
him children, but now, with the children grown and departed,
the loveless marriage has broken apart. On a Christmas
eve the children return, and in a "feast of reconciliation"
all the old family disputes break out afresh. The confronta-
tion causes the father to collapse, dying (rather like John
Gabriel Borkmann, whom he in a number of ways resembles).
Still, Hauptmann opens the possibility of escape from the
past. Wilhelm, the son, is offered this opportunity through
marriage to Ida Buchner, a representative of an uncontami-
nated exterior world. The Ibsenian obsession with heredity
makes him hesitate to accept this opportunity, and Hauptmann
does not reveal his decision, but the death of the family pa-
triarch seems at least to open the possibility of a new beginning.

Einsame Menschen deals with another man who has
married, to assure his means, a woman intellectually beneath him. His wife, a simple hausfrau, cannot understand
him, nor can his parents, for he has turned from a student
of theology to a free-thinking disciple of Darwin and Haeckel.
Temptation and catastrophe come into his home in the form
of Anna Mahr, a student from Zurich who provides precisely
the companion the neurasthenic Johannes Vockerath feels he
needs. His proposal of a mariage à trois meets with such
revulsion on all sides that Anna is forced to leave and Johannes drowns himself. Ibsen's Rosmersholm seems to have
inspired the main outlines of the plot and a number of the
details, though the triangular relationship of a weak man between two contrasting women is a common motif not only
throughout Ibsen's canon, but throughout German literature.
With this drama Hauptmann began to establish an international
reputation, and Emanuel Reicher (1849-1924) created so striking and life-like a character in Johannes Vockerath that
Brahm later called him "the foster-father of the new German
acting style. "

None of the rest of the seventeen productions offered
by the Freie Bühne were as significant as these Hauptmann
premieres, but they did give Berlin a good selection of contemporary European drama, and some more conventional
earlier German plays such as Fitger's Von Gottes Gnaden
and Anzengruber's Das vierte Gebot, which had previously
been held back by the censor. Aside from Hauptmann, the
only native authors presented were Otto Hartleben (1864-
1905), whose Angele (1891) was one of the naturalists' best
studies of city life, and Holz and Schlaf, whose joint work

Die Familie Selicke, according to Hermann Bahr, "set the
idiom of the German theatre for the next fifteen years. " He
went on to explain:

> We certainly cannot today break down the Brahm
> style to determine how much of it came from Holz,
> how much from Hauptmann, how much from Reicher,
> or Rittner, or Lehmann, or finally, what Brahm's
> own share in it was. But the style began with
> Holz, and Holz originated the pattern of German
> naturalistic drama. Holz for the first time sought
> to fix in symbols the gloss shining on his words
> through which the speaker reveals himself, to
> abandon no longer the accent to the desultory reader
> or to the caprice of the actor, but to insist on a
> single, unique tone (from which this style arose) by
> means of a complete score of sounds, stops, and
> breaths at every point. [30]

This grim tale of a daughter who sacrifices her own happiness to her degenerate parents may indeed deserve the credit
for establishing the naturalist genre in drama, but if so,
Hauptmann's first work far surpassed his mentors'. After
Vor Sonnenaufgang, the production of Die Familie Selicke
passed almost unnoticed.

A much more diverse and distinguished selection of
non-German works was presented by the Freie Bühne, though
the bias toward naturalism was clear; after Ibsen's Ghosts
came Björnson's A Gauntlet, Tolstoi's Power of Darkness,
Strindberg's The Father and Miss Julie, the Goncourts' Henriette Maréchal, Zola's Thérèse Raquin, and Becque's The
Vultures.

In 1892 the Freie Bühne officially disbanded. The
authors it supported were now being accepted by commercial
theatres and in any case the rather restricted genre in which
it specialized was almost exhausted. Brahm revived it from
time to time, however, when an important new work needed
this device to evade the censor. The most important play
thus presented was Hauptmann's Die Weber (1893), the culmination of Hauptmann's social dramas and one of the greatest
plays of the naturalist movement. Except for the social concern of his subject and the attention to realistic detail, Hauptmann in this work quite shook off his previous subservience
to Ibsen. He departed from portraits of contemporary society to treat a historical theme--a famous workers' uprising

in Silesia in the 1840s. Ibsen's tight plot is forsaken in favor of a series of illustrative scenes, and despite a great deal of action, there is no traditional dramatic development in the five acts. There is instead a steady increase in emotional tension until the revolt at last breaks out. Most importantly, the focus of the plot is new--Hauptmann not only deserted the middle class which had been the subject of most previous naturalist drama, but far more radically, replaced the traditional central character with the whole community of weavers. There are many distinct individuals in the play, but it is the psychology of the mass which guides the action. With Die Weber, Hauptmann established himself as one of the major dramatists of his time, and deservedly so, for the play was a unique creation, one of Europe's few great social dramas, and one of the still fewer to make the masses a true dramatic agent.

Brahm succeeded L'Arronge at the Deutsches in 1894 and opened his administration with the first public presentation of Die Weber. Since the work was still banned in the provinces, it is hardly surprising that audiences and critics were more concerned with it as a social than an esthetic phenomenon. Yet Brahm produced it as the fullest expression of realism yet seen in Berlin, with richly detailed settings and crowds created to represent a total social milieu. The power of its ensemble was almost unprecedented in this city, for Brahm made every actor feel equally responsible for the entire production, from Rittner and Kainz to the smallest extra, and the effect of the whole was constantly stressed over any individual expression.

A distinct shift in Hauptmann's career followed the creation of Die Weber. Perhaps he felt that with the creation of this classic he had achieved all he could at this time with naturalism. In any case he now turned to comedy, and as in his first serious dramas, the development of rich and interesting characters took clear precedence over any concern with social questions. The central figure of Kollege Crampton (1892) is an imaginative but talentless alcoholic who for a time convinces his family and society that he is a great painter. The play begins to develop toward tragedy as this illusion is exposed, but Crampton is ultimately saved by the love of his daughter and the charity of a rich family whose son comes to love her. This rather arbitrary salvation weakens the play, and Hauptmann created a distinctly superior comedy the next year, Der Biberpelz. As a satire on legal malfunctionings it has certain situations which recall

Der zerbrochene Krug, but while Kleist's judge was himself
the culprit, Hauptmann's is a pompous, narrow-minded
bureaucrat who torments minor offenders and lets major
criminals and really shrewd rogues escape. The central
figure, Frau Wolffen, is one of the latter, so clever a ma-
nipulator that she arranges for the court bailiff to hold the
lantern while she steals wood. The play contains many barbs
at Prussian officialdom, censorship, and court corruption,
but as in Kollege Crampton, social commentary is far less
important than the depiction of a richly human central
character.

With Hanneles Himmelfahrt (1893) Hauptmann struck
out in a surprising new direction. His setting is again
Silesia and his topic suitable for a work of grim naturalism
--the death of an abused fourteen-year-old daughter of the
village drunkard. What makes Hauptmann's treatment of this
material remarkable is his introduction of the elements of
the old Märchendrama--dream, allegory, and supernatural
beings. In one of his letters the dramatist stressed this
fairy heritage:

> Hannele is a Märchen, and because it is a Mär-
> chen, heaven and earth flow together. If a rift
> should still exist between them, wish and longing
> have bridged it a hundred times ... in the
> Märchen early pain created heavenly blessedness
> and early poverty fairy riches. 31

The feverish visions of the dying girl endow all the figures
of her life and her limited reading with a new significance,
all the ugliness changed to mysterious beauty and harmony.
It is easy to understand the shock of Hauptmann's public
when this fanciful work was presented, but there is an understandable progression from the earlier dramas to Hanneles Himmelfahrt. The passionate search for a better
world which stimulated the hopeless rebellion in Die Weber
stimulates Hannele's vision as well; if no physical escape is
possible, the spirit has discovered one. The author as well
as his central character seemed liberated by the play; this
challenge to the doctrines of naturalism allowed Hauptmann
for the first time to demonstrate his considerable power as
a poet. Within a few years, as naturalism gave way to
symbolism and neo-romanticism, Hanneles' important contribution to this transition became clear, but at its time of
writing it was too advanced to win immediate acceptance.
Its variety in tone confused directors and its religious refer-

ences aroused the opposition of the censor (even though
Hauptmann changed the title to the less offensive Hannele).
No theatre presented it for three years, until at last Brahm
introduced it at the Deutsches.

    The Lessing Theater, which sheltered the Freie Bühne
for its Sunday matinees, was directed during this period by
Oskar Blumenthal (1852-1917), an author of popular farce-
comedies. Apparently the presence of Brahm's experiment
encouraged him to offer something more substantial amid his
own works, and so the Lessing premiered the early plays of
Hermann Sudermann (1857-1928), after Hauptmann the most
important Berlin dramatist of this period. Naturalism had
opened new subject matter in the lower classes and even in
the unconventional treatment of the bourgeoisie, and Sudermann was the most successful of those dramatists who combined this new subject matter with the old conventions of
tight plot construction and concern for theatrical effect. This
cautious mixture of old and new pleased many who found the
work of Hauptmann and the other naturalists too extreme.
The success of Vor Sonnenaufgang, as we have seen, was
bitterly contested, but Sudermann's more conventional Die
Ehre (1889) was widely considered the first clear success of
the new movement. Its stage arrangement suggested the
multiple settings of Nestroy; the front part of the stage showed
the apartment of a factory owner's family, the rear the
apartment of the family of one of his workers. The symmetrical balance of the characters also recalls Nestroy,
though the action is closer to one of the thesis plays of the
French. Each family has a son and a daughter, one corrupt, the other a sympathetic young visionary who scorns the
prejudice of class. The play arranges for the good son and
daughter to marry and even for the corrupt pair to end
happily after the predictable dramatic conflicts between class
values and between generations. The play's central thesis,
that the concept of honor varies according to situation, is
developed rather obviously if wittily by the raissoneur Graf
Trast.

    The front house of Die Ehre, which reflected the so-
cial class that supported the Berlin theatre, was drawn
amusingly but with little real bite to its satire. No such
benevolent vision informed Sudermann's second play, Sodoms
Ende (1891), a brutal and uncompromising attack on contemporary Berlin society. "Sudermann," wrote one critic, "has
laid bare the cancer of modern German civilization."[32] A
young painter, about to create his masterpiece, a depiction

of Sodom and Gomorrah, is seduced by a high-ranking lady
in Berlin society. Her debasement of him leads in turn to
his destruction and that of his innocent foster-sister. The
censor banned the play until Sudermann softened certain
parts, and this banning of a play with so piquant a title made
the work one of the most eagerly anticipated of the decade.
When it at last appeared, the public was stunned. Here was
no conventional thesis play or salacious naturalist drama, but
a savage attack on the aristocracy, the world of trade and
commerce, all polite society. As a result, Sodoms Ende
was as widely and emotionally condemned as Die Ehre had
been praised.

     This violent reaction turned Sudermann back to a
milder and more conventional social drama, Die Heimat
(1893), and he was rewarded by another major success. Its
heroine, Magda, like many of the heroines of Ibsen, finds it
impossible to reconcile individual independence with conventional morality, and must suffer the fury and rejection of her
dying father.   The theatrical turns and melodramatic arrangement of incident, however, recall Augier and Dumas fils
more than the naturalists.   Again Sudermann had demonstrated his skill in creating a successful balance between
striking effects and realistic depiction of character.   He
offered sufficient development of conflicts between passion
and respectability and between bourgeois and bohemian values
to satisfy a public that preferred intellectual dramas, if these
did not make them too uncomfortable, and added to these his
greatest creation in the character of Magda, a favored role
for the leading actresses of the time.   Not since Kotzebue
had a German drama been so widely translated and produced
as Die Heimat.

     The enormous success of Sardou's Madame Sans-
Gêne at the Lessing in 1894, greater even than in Paris,
caused many to inquire why Berlin had produced no significant comic author.   Sudermann attempted to meet this demand with Die Schmetterlingsschlacht (1894), but this dark
comedy of bourgeois life, closer in tone to Zola than Sardou,
proved as offensive to the public as Sodoms Ende.   After its
debacle at the Lessing, few other theatres would risk the
piece and only in Vienna did it achieve a modest success,
due apparently to the skill of Mitterwurzer.   This success
drew Sudermann to the Austrian capital, where he remained
to write and present his next play, a gloomy rural genre
piece, Das Glück im Winkel (1895).

The Freie Bühne, like Antoine's Théâtre-Libre in
Paris, inspired many other untraditional theatrical experi-
ments--stage societies, student performing groups, the first
of the art theatres. The most important of these in influence and popularity during the next two decades were the
people's stages, organizations closely tied to Germany's
powerful socialist party. Bismarck's anti-socialist legisla-
tion (Sozialistengesetz) between 1878 and 1890 did not weaken
the political power of the working class, but rather strength-
ened their resolve to become a recognized and significant
part of national life. When the party was banned, its aims
were carried on by hundreds of small autonomous societies,
which easily escaped detection amid the many minor societies of the period. Berlin alone possessed in 1887 some
3500 clubs registered with the authorities, and supervising
them all was obviously impossible. The socialist societies
were basically political discussion groups, but many attempted
to compensate for the inferior educational opportunities of the
working class by becoming cultural centers as well. The
regular commercial theatre was beyond the means of Berlin's
proletariat, and during the late 1880s several of the socialist
organizations made plans for a workers' theatre, some simply
to provide entertainment for the deprived class, others to
provide cultural improvement.

Two events made the climate right for the establishment of a people's theatre. The Freie Bühne's establishment
in 1889 provided inspiration and a model, and suggested a
possible repertoire; then, early in 1890, a newly elected
Reichstag voted against Bismarck's demand to continue the
Sozialistengesetz. The socialist party was thus able to
emerge from hiding, and a month later Bruno Wille (1860-
1928) published in the party paper, the Volksblatt, a "Proc-
lamation for the Establishment of a Freie Volksbühne. " Here
he observed:

> Public performances of plays possessing a revolu-
> tionary spirit have normally been prevented either
> by the capitalistic system, since they were not
> successful at the box office, or by the police cen-
> sor. A private club does not suffer such hin-
> drances. This is why the Freie Bühne has been
> able to produce plays from the new movement.
> Membership in the Freie Bühne, however, is denied
> to the proletariat for economic reasons, so it ap-
> pears to me that the time has come for the founda-
> tion of a Freie Volksbühne. [33]

Wille, a popular writer and lecturer for the socialist
cause, embarked on this project at the request of members
of one of Berlin's most active socialist clubs, The Old Aunt.
Response was enormous. A public meeting that summer,
with Wille and Brahm among the speakers, drew almost two
thousand persons, and the Freie Volksbühne opened that fall
at the suburban Ostend Theater with a membership of 1150.
This number grew to 3948 by August of 1891. Ten plays,
mostly in the realist style, were presented this season,
among them Ibsen's Pillars of Society (the opening work) and
Enemy of the People, Hauptmann's Vor Sonnenaufgang, Anzengruber's Doppelselbstmord, Sudermann's Die Ehre, and
Schiller's Kabale und Liebe and Die Räuber. The second
season saw the Berlin premiere of Ibsen's League of Youth plus
A Doll's House and Ghosts, Gogol's The Inspector General, Hebbel's Maria Magdalena, Ludwig's Erbförster and Zola's Thérèse
Raquin along with works by Fulda, Halbe, and Anzengruber.
It was a broad and unquestionably cultured selection of plays
and was well received by the public, though the necessity of
playing only on Sunday afternoons in a theatre producing its
own programs the rest of the week meant that production had
to remain quite modest.

The directors of the Volksbühne managed during these
first two years to present a united front to suspicious authorities, but serious personal and philosophical conflicts developed between Wille and certain of his co-workers. The
leader of the opposition was the treasurer Julius Türk, who
considered Wille too casual in business matters and insuffi-
ciently conscious of the theatre's obligation to the socialist
cause. An open break came in 1892, with Wille and his
supporters departing to form a rival organization, the Neue
Freie Volksbühne. For the next three years, the two groups
operated separately. The Social Democrat party considered
the Freie Volksbühne its stage, and gave it a support that
Brahm's new venture lacked. Franz Mehring (1846-1929),
Brahm's successor, still avoided establishing any open ties
with the party, recognizing that this would insure persecution
from the government. They produced in two theatres, the
Lessing and the National, with the membership, now totalling
between six and seven thousand, alternating between the theatres. At the National the Volksbühne had a free hand in
selecting their repertoire, but at the Lessing they were
forced to accept pieces selected by the theatre's management. Though this predictably caused some friction, the
repertoire at the two theatres did not in fact greatly differ.
About a fourth of the offerings were classics--Egmont,

Kabale und Liebe, Nathan der Weise, Der zerbrochene Krug.
The rest were modern German works, mostly from the naturalists, with an occasional selection from Augier, Björnson, or Ibsen. The greatest success was a revival of Die
Weber, whose royalty Hauptmann waived for the Volksbühnen.

Wille mounted a similar program at the Neue Freie
Volksbühne, though his audiences were smaller and, since
they began to be infiltrated by the petty bourgeoisie, somewhat more sophisticated in theatre experience. Die Weber
was the great success here too, and Anzengruber a favored
author. With more limited means Wille was not able to do
so many period plays, but he did present Faust I, Emilia
Galotti, Tartuffe, and Don Carlos.

Despite Mehring's professions of political neutrality
and Wille's loss of contact with the proletariat, both stages
remained linked in official opinion with the socialist movement and shared the fortunes of that party. The Volksbühne
had been created in the tolerant days of the early 1890s, but
by 1895 Kaiser Wilhelm II, disturbed by the growing power
of the party, began to regret his leniency. Restrictive laws
were again enforced and both Volksbühnen suffered. Censorship became so rigid that during 1895 and 1896 the two theatres virtually ceased operation. The Freie Volksbühne
actually dissolved in 1896, but reorganized a year later when
conditions seemed to be easing.

Chiefly by tightening their rules for membership and
filing detailed records with the authorities the societies were
able to resume fairly regular operations in 1897. A union
was explored, but feelings remained too strong between the
Social Democrats of the Freie Volksbühne and the intellectuals and Independent Socialists who had departed with Wille.
In fact a partial reunion was not achieved until 1913 and a
full union not until 1920. Through all this period the organizations brought the classics and important modern works
to an ever-increasing number of spectators. In 1913, when
the first steps toward union were taken, the two theatres together had a membership of almost 70,000. By 1925 this
had grown to 150,000 in Berlin alone, and almost 200 similar
organizations scattered all over Germany had a total membership of 480,000 more. In smaller communities the
Volksbühnen could often boast a membership of ten to twenty-
five percent of the population. Never before nor since has
a populist theatre achieved its goal so fully.

Brahm, after aiding Wille in the launching of the
Volksbühne, himself undertook a task which was to lead to
effects at least as significant in the European theatre.   In
1894 he became the director of the Deutsches Theater, which
he soon developed into Germany's major theatre.   Here he
built an outstanding ensemble, noted for the power of its
realistic presentations.   Hauptmann and Sudermann were the
favored native authors; Brahm presented major revivals of
their earlier works and premiered new ones.   The high point
of such production was the fall of 1896, which saw the premieres of three Hauptmann plays: Hanneles Himmelfahrt,
Florian Geyer, and Die versunkene Glocke.   The middle work
was a return to the methods of naturalism, applied to a more
distant historical subject than Die Weber, the Peasants' Rebellion of 1525.   The peasant leader Geyer was another of
Hauptmann's finely developed characters, but the dramatist
plunged himself into a study of period documents to surround
his tragic hero with a canvas teeming with the life of the
period--knights, burghers, and peasants, all drawn with rich
detail.   The result was a work whose length and complexity
worked against it, especially at a time when naturalism was
falling into disfavor.   For all its virtues, and its emphasis
on the popular theme of German unity, the play was a failure.
It is worth noting, however, that this original judgement was
completely reversed when the work was revived in the 1920s,
and Florian Geyer has since proven one of Hauptmann's most
popular plays.

Hanneles Himmelfahrt prepared the way for Hauptmann's fullest expression of the new romantic mood, Die
versunkene Glocke.   The hero, Heinrich, is torn between
two women, his mundane wife Magda and the elfin maiden
Rautendelein.   If this triangular arrangement recalls Ibsen
and Hauptmann's own Einsame Menschen, that is virtually
the play's only heritage from naturalism.   The entire work
is in verse, even the lines of the old witch, who speaks in
Silesian dialect.   There are long and elaborate monologues,
and a constant interpenetration of the real world with a world
of satyrs, fairies, and watersprites.   The bell-founder who
leaves men's habitation in the plain to build a temple of the
sun in the mountains has some similarity to Ibsen's Brand
or to his late artist-visionaries, but no play of Ibsen's, even
in his symbolic period, moves so completely and resolutely
into the realm of fancy and allegory as Die versunkene
Glocke.   The work exactly suited the theatrical mood of the
moment and was one of Hauptmann's greatest successes,
though later audiences, looking beyond the charming capers

of Rautendelein and the Caliban-like Nickelmann, have found
the play's elaborate and obscure symbolism less attractive.
Hauptmann's earlier and later works, more firmly grounded
in realism, have proven much more durable.

Sudermann, when he returned to Berlin from Vienna,
shifted his allegiance from the Lessing to the Deutsches,
which could offer him a clearly superior interpretation. His
plays here in the late 1890s were with one exception more
interesting as attempts to adjust to the rapidly shifting dramatic style than for any intrinsic merit. The exception was
the one-act Fritzchen, in an otherwise undistinguished cycle
of plays called Morituri (1897). Fritzchen, a young lieuten-
ant of dragoons, comes home disgraced from his regiment,
but then is allowed to return on condition he fight a duel
which will almost certainly mean his death. His acceptance
of this creates a striking blend of exultation and pathos in
one of Sudermann's most effective works. After his two
bitter failures in Berlin, Sudermann was now, if anything,
too sensitive to the wishes of his public, and he was quick
to notice and react to the decline of interest in naturalism.
Hauptmann had shown that the techniques of realism and the
concerns of the thesis drama could be turned to historical
subjects. Inspired by this, and closely imitating the technique of Hebbel, Sudermann sought in Johannes (1898) to
transfer the corrupt society of Sodoms Ende to a Biblical
setting. John the Baptist is developed as a typical Hebbel
hero, the forerunner of a new order sacrificed by the old,
but in his preoccupation with the corruption of Herodias'
court, Sudermann lost the balance which characterized
Hebbel's richest works in this genre.

Die drei Reiherfedern (1899) was Sudermann's contribution to the poetic fairy play tradition. The dramatist considered this one of his best works, but few shared his
opinion. The public which applauded Die versunkene Glocke
showed little interest in Sudermann's attempt at the same
genre and he, like Hauptmann, returned after 1900 to a drama
based on contemporary themes, where his real ability clearly
lay.

Realism was in any case the favored mode of the outstanding company Brahm assembled at the Deutsches. The
artistic unity of this ensemble was widely praised, and
Brahm's success in achieving such unity was all the more
striking since the troupe came from different backgrounds
and its leaders had already achieved success in quite differ-

ent styles. Probably the actor who came closest to embody-
ing Brahm's own vision was Rudolf Rittner (1869-1943), one
of the first actors hired under the new administration. In
his Kritischen Schriften Brahm describes his first impression
of Rittner in terms that tell much about his own idea of interpretation:

> I had the impression of something which gained
> extraordinary clarity from its very insignificance:
> I saw him simply go out a door, nothing more.
> He had read a letter and as he mulled it over,
> filled with its mournful tidings, he walked off,
> without any ceremony--I think I have never seen
> anything like it. Since our whole former style of
> acting required an appearance of volition, of care-
> ful attention to detail, the "effective exit" was one
> of the weightiest requirements of this school.
> Every step was defended like the retreat from a
> battlefield, the actor holding every eye on himself
> until the last. The significance of Rittner's exit
> consisted in that he simply went out, adding nothing.
> This delighted me and in this little action I saw
> symbolized the whole revolution of our new method
> of presentation. [34]

Rittner played Oswald in Ghosts, but was best remembered for his Hauptmann roles, Moritz Jäger in Die
Weber and the title role in Florian Geyer. Rittner's most
common partner was Else Lehmann, whose Käthe Vockerath
in Einsame Menschen was often cited by Brahm as the paradigm for naturalist actresses. Though she began her career
playing soubrettes at the Wallner, her great success as
Helene in Vor Sonnenaufgang at the Freie Bühne led Brahm
to offer her a leading position at the Deutsches.

It is hardly surprising that Brahm also gained for his
company the old actor Emanuel Reicher, since the concern
he always showed for the psychological validity of his
characters made him an important precursor of the new style.
His interpretation of Pastor Manders in Ghosts was considered by most of the younger generation as an innovation in
German acting almost as significant as the play itself was
for German dramaturgy. Reicher began his career in
Hungary, appeared in Munich in 1873, then at the Residenz
in Berlin in 1887. His particular skill lay in portraying a
character with a constantly varying tone, of making each role
a process. His idea of the task of an actor fitted in strik-

ingly with the assumptions of the naturalist dramatists and
directors, as Brahm correctly sensed:

> We no longer wish to play effective scenes, but
> whole characters, with the complete aggregation
> of characteristics, internal, external, and sur-
> rounding, which are associated with them. Our
> only desire is to become men who are able to
> demonstrate the feelings of the characters pre-
> sented through the simple natural sound of heart-
> felt human speech; quite unconcerned with whether
> any particular thing is appropriate in a particular
> case, but only whether it harmonizes with nature's
> own unity and whether it gives the spectator the
> impression of a whole man. 35

Despite the effectiveness of his ensemble, not all of
Brahm's major actors fitted so well into the naturalist camp.
Josef Kainz and Agnes Sorma (1856-1927) played with honesty
and truth and opposed the classic formality of the traditional
style, but they preferred elevated and poetic creations and
resisted the underplaying and the scorn for beauty which they
found in the naturalist approach.   Not surprisingly, these
were Brahm's usual choice for leading roles in classic plays,
and such works were a much more important part of the
repertoire before 1899, when Kainz and Sorma departed.
Sorma played tragedy, comedy, and salon drama with equal
success, but her most noted roles at the Deutsches were the
young heroines of Ibsen.   Her Nora was said to be the first
to capture both the lightness and strength of the character.
Kainz, a Viennese, had worked with the Meininger and in the
early 1880s under Possart in Munich.   He was one of the
founding members of L'Arronge's Deutsches Theater, for
which he created such roles as Don Carlos with a new psychological depth.   L'Arronge felt his rich voice was best
suited to the classics, but Brahm's Freie Bühne allowed him
to create modern parts as well, beginning with Wilhelm in
Hauptmann's Friedensfest.   The emotionality of his work
gave him a certain affinity with the romantic actors, and his
greatest success under Brahm at the Deutsches was as Heinrich, the Faustian bellfounder in Hauptmann's Die versunkene
Glocke.

Two members added after Brahm's administration began filled out the roster of leading actors--Oscar Sauer (1856-
1918) and Louise Dumont (1862-1932).   Sauer was a radical
champion of naturalism who joined the company in 1896.   He

began as a comic character actor, but developed the ability
deftly to mix comedy and tragedy, producing striking haunted
characterizations. He excelled in Hauptmann roles--it was
said that all his creations were "einsame Menschen"--and in
such Ibsen roles as Gregers Werle in The Wild Duck and
Brendel in Rosmersholm. Dumont played Schiller roles in
the classic style in Vienna and Stuttgart before coming to
Berlin, and kept always a rather monumental quality. She
adapted her rich delivery to Brahm's requirements, however,
and opposite the deft genre studies of Agnes Sorma created
a series of powerful Ibsen heroines--Hedda Gabler in 1898,
Rebekka West in 1899, Mrs. Alving in 1900.

In this 1900 production of Ghosts Brahm's usual major
talents were employed: Rittner as Oswald, Reicher as Manders, Lehmann as Regina. The carpenter Engstrand was
played by a young member of the company whose fame was
to surpass that of any of his noted colleagues, and whose
productions in the new century would make Germany the theatre center of Europe: Max Reinhardt (1873-1943). He was
discovered by Brahm at the Salzburg theatre in 1894 playing
elderly character parts. Brought by Brahm to Berlin, Reinhardt put his time here to good account studying the great
actors of Brahm's company. He was somewhat more impressed by the imagination and poetic style of Kainz than by
the rough realism of Reicher or the impulsive emotionalism
of Rittner, but he learned from all. At the same time he
entertained his friends by founding a cabaret theatre Schall
und Rauch, which allowed him to experiment with the effects
of a tiny, intimate theatre situation. This led directly in
1901 to the Kleines Theater, the first under his own direction.

In 1905 he became in his turn director of the Deutsches and began to establish a European reputation. The
Deutsches had been conceived in 1883 as a German rival to
the Comédie Française and the Burgtheater, a status it
eventually achieved. L'Arronge and Brahm prepared the way
by assembling a major company and placing them at the fore-
front of the modern tradition. Reinhardt added an experimental theatre, the Kammerspiele, and on these two stages
fulfilled the vision of the Deutsches' founders, providing a
production model, not only for all of Germany, but for all
of Europe.

Notes to Part III

1. M. Grube, The Story of the Meininger (trans. A. M. Koller, Coral Gables, 1963), 40-41.

2. Ibid., 54.

3. H. Herrig, Die Meininger und ihre Gastspiele (Dresden, 1879), 27.

4. M. Martersteig, Das deutsche Theater im neunzehnten Jahrhundert (Leipzig, 1904), 643.

5. M. Grube, Die Meininger (Berlin, 1904), 20.

6. L. Barnay, Erinnerungen (Berlin, 1903), I, 247.

7. M. Grube, Story of the Meininger, 65.

8. Ibid., 71.

9. H. Hopfen, Streitfragen und Erinnerungen (Stuttgart, 1896), 241.

10. A. Antoine, Memories of the Théâtre-Libre (trans. M. Carlson, Coral Gables, 1964), 84.

11. Ibid.

12. G. Fuchs, Die Revolution des Theaters (Munich, 1909), 62.

13. K. Gläser, Das Gastspiel des Meininger Hoftheaters in Berlin (Berlin, 1876), 5.

14. R. Prölss, Das Herzoglich Meiningen'sche Hoftheater und die Bühnenreform (Erfurt, 1880), 51.

15. Letter to Wagner, Nov. 26, 1865, quoted in R. W. Gutman, Richard Wagner: The Man, His Mind, and His Music (New York, 1968), 340.

16. A. Kleinberg, Ludwig Anzengruber (Berlin, 1921), 148.

17. Ibid., 236.

18. R. Holzer, Die Wiener Vorstadtbühnen (Vienna, 1951), 178.

19. H. Bahr, Theater der Jahrhundertwende (Vienna, 1963),
     354.

20. R. Genée, Die Entwickelung des Scenischen Theaters
     und die Bühnenreform in München (Stuttgart, 1889), 78.

21. K. Frenzel, Berliner Dramaturgie (Berlin, 1877), I, 317.

22. Deutsche Rundschau, LI, 464.

23. See W. H. Eller, Ibsen in Germany (Boston, 1918), 72-77.

24. A. von Hanstein, Das jüngste Deutschland (Leipzig,
     1901), 78-79.

25. Quoted in A. I. Miller, The Independent Theater in
     Europe (New York, 1931), 111.

26. Vor Sonnenaufgang, I, 305.

27. F. A. Voigt, Hauptmann-Studien (Breslau, 1936), I, 78.

28. J. Bab, Das Theater der Gegenwart (Leipzig, 1928), 74.

29. E. Steiger, Das Werden des neuen Dramas (Berlin,
     1898), 2.

30. H. Motekat, Arno Holz: Persönlichkeit und Werk
     (Kitaingen/Main, 1953), 15.

31. Letter to Max Burckhardt, Sept. 18, 1893. K. Glossy,
     Wiener Studien und Dokumente (Vienna, 1933), 172.

32. B. Litzmann, Das deutsche Drama in der Litterarischen
     Bewegung der Gegenwart (Berlin, 1897), 203.

33. S. Nestriepke, Geschichte der Volksbühne (Berlin, 1930),
     I, 10-11.

34. O. Brahm, Kritischen Schriften (Berlin, 1913), I,
     472-73.

35. H. Henze, Otto Brahm und das Deutsche Theater in
     Berlin (Berlin, 1929), 12.

CONCLUSION

The theatrical renaissance at the end of the nineteenth century was of course an international phenomenon, but Germany's share in it was so great that it is hardly exaggerating to say that she had taken the lead from France in the theatre as she had done politically in 1870. Much of the theatrical innovation of this period had German roots. Most striking perhaps was the new emphasis on the director and the subordination of parts to the whole while maintaining the integrity of every detail--a clear development of the German tradition reaching from Wagner and Duke Georg of Meiningen back through Laube, Dingelstedt, and Immermann to Goethe. Simplified staging, which came to European attention with various Shakespearian experiments around 1900 and with the beginnings of the new stagecraft at about the same time was clearly prefigured in the Munich Shakespeare stage and the experimental productions earlier of Immermann and Tieck.

In playwriting, Hebbel prepared the way for the revolutionary plays of Ibsen, whose realism was significantly considered "German" by his own countrymen. On the other hand, Germany produced during this century an impressive series of dramatists totally outside the development toward realism, such as Tieck, Kleist, Büchner, and Grabbe, whose importance has only been recognized in our own century as the theatre has followed their example in renouncing conventional approaches. The last author in this independent tradition, Wedekind, launched the expressionist theatre which in its pure form and in such offshoots as the French Dadaist theatre and the epic theatre of Brecht has proven one of the most influential dramatic movements of our century.

The various tensions of the nineteenth century German stage--between stark and ornate production, between visual and oral emphasis, between devotion to native and devotion to foreign drama, between emphasis on emotion and emphasis on elegance--were never definitively resolved. Each of the great theatre leaders of the century worked out a distinctive combination, and the most imaginative and varied theatre was the result. This eclecticism mixed with innovative genius reached its fullest expression in Max Reinhardt, who made Berlin the theatre capital of Europe and Salzburg the festival center of the world. Though his major contributions belong to the twentieth century, they stand as the summation of developments in the nineteenth, and Reinhardt himself can be best understood as the end of a line of powerful German theatre leaders from Goethe through Georg II.

BIBLIOGRAPHY

General

Arnold, R. F.   Das deutsche Drama, Munich, 1925.

Bab, J.   Die Frau als Schauspielerin, Berlin, 1915.
_____ and W. Handl.   Deutsche Schauspieler, Berlin, 1918.
Bahr, H.   Burgtheater, Vienna, 1920.
Bartels, A.   Chronik des Weimarischen Hoftheaters 1817-
    1907, Weimar, 1910.
Bauer, A.   Das Theater in der Josefstadt, Vienna, 1957.
_____.   150 Jahre Theater an der Wien, Vienna, 1952.
_____.   Hundert Jahre Wiener Bühnenbild, Vienna, 1950.
_____.   Opern und Operetten in Wien, Graz-Köln, 1955.
Biberhofer, R.   125 Jahre Theater an der Wien, Vienna,
    1926.
Brachvogel, A. E.   Geschichte des Königlichen Theaters in
    Berlin, Berlin, 1961.
Bulthaupt, H.   Dramaturgie des Schauspiels, Oldenburg,
    1893-1902.

Campbell, T. M.   (ed.) German Plays of the Nineteenth
    Century, New York, 1930.
Coar, J. F.   Studies in German Literature in the Nineteenth
    Century, New York, 1903.

Daffis, H.   Hamlet auf der deutschen Bühne bis zur Gegen-
    wart, Berlin, 1912.
Devrient, E.   Geschichte der deutschen Schauspielkunst,
    Berlin, 1905.
Dietrich, M.   Europäische Dramaturgie im 19. Jahrhundert,
    Vienna, 1961.
Doerry, H.   Das Rollenfach im deutschen Theaterbetrieb
    des 19. Jahrhunderts, Berlin, 1926.
Drews, W.   König Lear auf der deutschen Bühne, Berlin,
    1932.
Droescher, G.   Der Schinkelbau. 100 Jahre Schauspielhaus,
    Berlin, 1921.
Duboc, J.   Hundert Jahre Zeitgeist in Deutschland. Leipzig
    1889, 1893.

231

Eisenberg, L. Grosses biographisches Lexikon der deutschen
 Bühne im 19. Jahrhundert, Leipzig, 1903.
Eloesser, A. Das bürgerliche Drama, Berlin, 1898.

Fechter, P. Das europäische Drama, Mannheim, 1956-1958.
Friedmann, S. Das deutsche Drama des 19. Jahrhunderts
 in seinen Haupt-vertretern, Berlin, 1904.
Fürstenberg, W. Das historische Kostüm auf der deutschen
 Bühne, Kiel, 1924.

Genée, R. Geschichte der Shakespeare-Dramen in Deutsch-
 land, Leipzig, 1870.
————. Hundert Jahre des Königlichen Schauspiels in
 Berlin, Berlin, 1886.
Grandaur, F. Chronik des Kgl. Hof- und Nationaltheaters
 in München, Munich, 1878.
Gregor, J. Geschichte des österreichischen Theaters,
 Vienna, 1948.
————. Kulturgeschichte des Balletts, Zurich, n. d.
————. Das Theater in der Wiener Josefstadt, Vienna,
 1924.
————. Weltgeschichte des Theaters, Vienna, 1933.
————. Wiener scenische Kunst, Zurich, 1924.
Grout, D. J. A Short History of Opera, New York, 1947.

Hadomowsky, F. Das Theater in der Leopoldstadt, Vienna,
 1934.
Hagemann, C. Schauspielkunst und Schauspielkünstler,
 Berlin, 1903.
Herterich, F. Das Burgtheater und seine Sendung, Vienna,
 1948.
Heyden, O. Das Kölner Theaterwesen im 19. Jahrhundert,
 Emsdetten, 1939.
Heym, H. Frankfurt und sein Theater, Frankfurt/Main,
 1963.
Holl, K. Geschichte des deutschen Lustspiels, Leipzig, 1923.
Holzer, R. Die Wiener Vorstadtbühnen, Vienna, 1951.
Hormann, H. W. From Weimar to Meiningen (unpub. thesis,
 Cornell, 1942).

Jacobs, M. Deutsche Schauspielkunst, Berlin, 1954.

Kapp, J. 185 Jahre Staatsoper, Berlin, 1928.
Kaufmann, F. W. German Dramatists of the Nineteenth
 Century, Los Angeles, 1940.
Khevenhüller-Metsch, J. F. Zur Geschichte des Theaters
 am Wiener Hofe, Vienna, 1896.
Kindermann, H. and M. Dietrich. Dreihundert Jahre öster-

232

reichisches Bühnenbild, Vienna, 1959.

Kindermann, H. Theatergeschichte Europas, vols. V-VIII, Salzburg, 1962-1968.

Kirchbach, W. Deutsche Schauspieler und Schauspielkunst, Berlin, 1892.

Kirchner, J. Eine Geschichte der Münchner Volkstheater, Munich, 1910.

Klaar, A. Geschichte des modernen Dramas in Umrissen, Leipzig, 1883.

Klenze, C. von. From Goethe to Hauptmann, New York, 1926.

Klingenbeck, F. Das Theater an der Wien, Vienna, 1963.

Kneschke, E. Zur Geschichte des Theaters und der Musik in Leipzig, Leipzig, 1864.

Knispel, H. Das grossherzogliche Hoftheater zu Darmstadt, 1810-1890. Darmstadt, 1910.

Knudsen, H. Deutsche Theatergeschichte, Stuttgart, 1959.

————. Theater im 19. Jahrhundert, Berlin, 1930.

Kober, M. Das deutsche Märchendrama, Frankfurt a. M., 1925.

Kosch, W. Das deutsche Theater und Drama im 19. Jahrhundert, Leipzig, 1913.

————. Deutsches Theaterlexikon, Vienna, 1951-.

Krauss, R. Das Stuttgarter Hoftheater von den ältesten Zeiten bis zur Gegenwart, Stuttgart, 1908.

Kummer, F. Dresden und seine Theaterwelt, Dresden, 1938.

Laube, H. Das Burgtheater, Leipzig, 1868.

————. Das Norddeutsche Theater, Leipzig, 1872.

Levy, E. Die Gestalt des Künstlers in deutschen Drama, Berlin, 1929.

Licterfeld, L. Entwickelung der deutschen Schauspielkunst, Erfurt, 1882.

Liebscher, O. Münchner Theatergeschichte, Munich, 1913.

Loewy, S. Deutsche Theaterkunst von Goethe bis Reinhardt, Vienna, 1923.

Lohmeyer, W. Die Dramaturgie der Massen, Berlin, 1913.

Lothar, R. Das Wiener Burgtheater, Vienna, 1899.

Mann, O. Geschichte des deutschen Dramas, Stuttgart, 1960.

Martersteig, M. Das deutsche Theater im neunzehnten Jahrhundert, Leipzig, 1904.

Martini, F. Deutsche Literatur im bürgerlichen Realismus, Stuttgart, 1962.

Mason, G. R. From Gottsched to Hebbel, London, 1961.

Mentzel, E. Die Geschichte der Schauspielkunst in Frankfurt am Main, Frankfurt, 1882.

Müller, H. Chronik des Kgl. Hoftheaters zu Hannover,

Hannover, 1876.

_____. Das Stadttheater zu Leipzig, Leipzig, 1887.

Nienholdt, E.   Kostüme des 18. und 19. Jahrhunderts,
   Braunschweig, 1963.

Petsch, R.   Deutsche Dramaturgie von Lessing bis Hebbel,
   Hamburg, 1921.
Prölss, R.   Geschichte des Hoftheaters zu Dresden,
   Dresden, 1878.
Prutz, H.   Zur Geschichte der politischen Komödie in
   Deutschland, Munich, 1919.

Räder, A.   50 Jahre deutscher Bühnengeschichte, Berlin, 1886.
Rapp, F.   Süddeutsche Theaterdekorationen aus drei Jahr-
   hunderten, Munich, 1926.
Ratislav, J.   175 Jahre Burgtheater, Vienna, 1955.
Rieder, H.   Wiener Vormärz: Das Theater ... die Zensur,
   Vienna, 1959.
Riemann, R.   Von Goethe zum Expressionismus, Leipzig,
   1922.
Rommel, O.   Die Alt-Wiener Volkskomödie, Vienna, 1952.
_____. Ein Jahrhundert Alt-Wiener Parodien, Vienna,
   1930.
_____. Die grossen Figuren der Alt-Wiener Volkskomödie,
   Vienna, 1946.
Rosenthal, F.   Schauspieler aus deutscher Vergangenheit,
   Vienna, 1919.
_____. Theater in Osterreich, Leipzig, 1926.
Rub, O.   Das Burgtheater, Vienna, 1913.

Salten, F.   Das Burgtheater, Vienna, 1922.
Schetterer, H. M.   Das deutsche Singspiel, Augsburg, 1863.
Schiedermair, L.   Die deutsche Oper, Bonn, 1940.
Schink, F.   Gallerie von deutschen Schauspielern und
   Schauspielerinnen, Vienna, 1873.
Schlesinger, M.   Geschichte des Breslauer Theaters,
   Breslau, 1898.
Schlögl, F.   Vom Wiener Volkstheater, Vienna, 1883.
Schmidt, L.   Das deutsche Volksschauspiel, Berlin, 1934.
Schneider, L.   Geschichte der Oper und des Königlichen
   Opernhauses Berlin, Berlin, 1852.
Schrickel, L.   Geschichte des Weimarer Theaters, Weimar,
   1928.
Sengle, F.   Das deutsche Geschichtsdrama, Stuttgart, 1952.
Seyfried, F. von.   Rückschau in das Theaterleben Wiens seit
   den letzten 50 Jahren, Vienna, 1864.
Sievers, H.   250 Jahre Braunschweigisches Staatstheater,

234

Braunschweig, 1941.

Smekal, R. Das alte Burgtheater, Vienna, 1916.

Stahl, E. L. Shakespeare und das deutsche Theater, Stuttgart, 1947.

Stigler-Fuchs, M. von. Wiener Theater vor und hinter den Kulissen, Vienna, 1943.

Trojan, F. Das Theater an der Wien, Vienna, 1923.

Troizkij, S. Die Anfänge der realistischen Schauspielkunst, Berlin, 1949.

Uhde, H. Das Stadttheater in Hamburg 1827-1877, Stuttgart, 1879.

Ulmann, H. Das deutsche Bürgertum in deutschen Tragödien des 18. und 19. Jahrhunderts, Elberfeld, 1923.

Wagner, H. 200 Jahre Münchner Theaterchronik, Munich, 1950.

Weddingen, O. Geschichte der Theater Deutschlands, Berlin, 1904-1906.

Weilen, A. von. Hamlet auf der deutschen Bühne, Berlin, 1908.

Weigl, E. Die Münchner Volkstheater im 19. Jahrhundert, Munich, 1961.

Werner, R. M. Gallerie von deutschen Schauspielern und Schauspielerinnen, Berlin, 1940.

Wertheimer, P. Alt-Wiener Theater, Vienna, 1920.

Wiese, B. von. Die deutsche Tragödie von Lessing bis Hebbel, Hamburg, 1955.

Wiesner, A. Denkwürdigkeiten der österreichischen Zensur von der Reformation bis zur Gegenwart, Stuttgart, 1847.

Winds, A. Geschichte der Regie, Stuttgart, 1925.

Witkowski, G. The German Drama of the Nineteenth Century (trans. L. E. Horning), New York, 1909.

Wlassack, E. Afführungen deutscher Schauspiele in den Wiener Hoftheatern von 1748-1880. Vienna, 1881.

Wolkan, R. Das Burgtheater in Wien, Vienna, 1926.

Ziegler, T. Die geistigen und sozialen Strömungen Deutschlands im 19. Jahrhundert, Berlin, 1911.

1800-1830

Altman, C. Ludwig Devrient, Berlin, 1926.

Amend, W. E. T. A. Hoffmann und Bamberg, Bamberg, 1951.

Angollez, J. F. Goethe (trans. R. H. Blackley), New York, 1958.

Anschütz, H.   Erinnerungen aus dessen Leben und Wirken,
      Vienna, 1866.
Appell, J. W.   Die Ritter-, Räuber-, und Schauerromantik,
      Leipzig, 1859.

Bab, J.   Die Devrients, Berlin, 1932.
Bäuerle, A.   Gallerie interessanter und drolliger Szenen der
      Wiener Bühnen, Vienna, 1826-1834.
_____. Memoiren, Vienna, 1858.
Bamberg, E. von.   Drei Schauspieler der Goethezeit,
      Leipzig, 1927.
_____. Die Erinnerungen der Karoline Jagemann, Leipzig,
      1926.
Bauer, K.   Memoirs (trans. anon.), London, 1885.
Bauer, R.   La Réalité Royaume de Dieu, Munich, 1965.
Baumann, G.   Franz Grillparzer, Freiburg, 1954.
_____. Georg Büchner, Göttingen, 1961.
Baumgartner, A.   Goethe und Schiller, Weimars Glanz-
      periode, Freiburg, 1886.
Becker, G. W.   Briefe über Ifflands Spiel in Leipzig zu
      Ende des Junius 1804, Leipzig, 1804.
_____. Die deutsche Oper in Dresden unter der Leitung
      von Carl Maria von Weber 1817-1826, Berlin, 1962.
Bellermann, L.   Schillers Dramen, Berlin, 1905.
Benedix, R.   Bilder aus dem Schauspielerleben, Leipzig,
      1847.
Bielschowsky, A.   Goethe, Sein Leben und seine Werke,
      Munich, 1928.
Bischoff, H.   Ludwig Tieck als Dramaturg, Brussels, 1897.
Bittner, N.   Theaterdekorationen nach Originalskizzen des
      k. k. Hoftheatermalers Anton de Pian, Vienna, 1818.
Blankenagel, J.   The Dramas of Heinrich von Kleist,
      Chapel Hill, 1931.
Blödler, G.   Heinrich von Kleist, Berlin, 1960.
Bobbert, G.   Charlotte von Hagn, Berlin, 1936.
Borcherdt, H. M.   Schiller und die Romantiker, Stuttgart,
      1948.
Brahm, O.   Das Leben Heinrich von Kleists, Berlin, 1911.
Brandes, G.   Die romantische Schule in Deutschland, Berlin,
      1909.
Braun, J. B.   Schiller und Goethe im Urteile ihrer Zeitge-
      nossen, Berlin, 1883-1884.
Brühl, C. von.   Neue Kostüme auf den beiden Königlichen
      Theatern in Berlin ... von Brühl, Berlin, 1819.
Bruford, W. H.   Theatre, Drama, and Audience in Goethe's
      Germany, London, 1950.
Brukner, F.   Ferdinand Raimund in der Dichtung seiner
      Zeitgenossen, Vienna, 1905.

Burath, H. August Klingemann und die deutsche Romantik, Braunschweig, 1948.
Burkhardt, C. A. Das Repertoire des Weimarischen Hoftheaters unter Goethes Leitung, Hamburg, 1891.

Carow, M. Zacharias Werner und das Theater seiner Zeit, Berlin, 1933.
Castle, E. Josef Schreyvogel, Vienna, 1908.
Coenen, F. E. Franz Grillparzer's Portraiture of Men, Chapel Hill, 1951.
Cornet, J. Die Oper in Deutschland und das Theater der Neuzeit, Hamburg, 1849.
Costenoble, C. L. Aus dem Burgtheater 1818-1837, Vienna, 1889.
_____. Tagebücher, Berlin, 1912.
Creizenach, W. Die Bühnengeschichte des Goetheschen Faust, Frankfurt/Main, 1881.

Deetjen, W. Pius Alexander Wolff, Berlin, 1918.
Doebber, A. Lauchstadt und Weimar, Berlin, 1908.
Döring, H. August von Kotzebues Leben, Weimar, 1830.
Dunker, K. Iffland in Berlin, Berlin, 1859.

Eberwein and Lobe, Goethes Schauspieler und Musiker, Erinnerungen, Berlin, 1912.
Eckermann, J. P. Gespräche mit Goethe, Leipzig, 1909.
Ehrenhaus, M. Die Operndichtung der deutschen Romantik, Breslau, 1912.
Eichendorff, J. Werke, Stuttgart, 1957.
Enslin, A. Die ersten Theateraufführungen des Goetheschen Faust, Berlin, 1880.
Enzinger, M. Das deutsche Schicksalsdrama, Innsbruck, 1922.
_____. Grillparzer und das Wiener Volkstheater, Vienna, 1920.
Erdmann, W. Ferdinand Raimunds dichterische Entwickelung, Würzburg, 1943.
Euphrosyne. Leben und Denkmal, Weimar, 1836.

Fambach, O. Schiller und sein Kreis, Berlin, 1957.
Farinelli, A. Grillparzer und Raimund, Leipzig, 1897.
Folgar, A. Grillparzers Ansichten über Literatur, Bühne und Leben, Vienna, 1872.
Friesen, H. von. Ludwig Tieck, Vienna, 1871.
Fürst, N. Grillparzer auf der Bühne, Vienna, 1958.
Fuhrmann, K. Raimunds Kunst und Charakter, Berlin, 1913.
Funk, Z. Aus dem Leben zweier Schauspieler: A. W. Iffland und Ludwig Devrient, Leipzig, 1838.

237

Gearey, J. Heinrich von Kleist, Philadelphia, 1968.

Genast, E. Aus dem Tagebuch eines alten Schauspielers, Leipzig, 1865.

_____. Aus Weimars klassischer und nachklassischer Zeit, Stuttgart, 1904.

Genée, R. Ifflands Berliner Theaterleitung 1796-1814, Berlin, 1896.

Glossy, K. Aus Grillparzers Tagebüchern, Vienna, 1893.

_____. Josef Schreyvogel, Vienna, 1903.

_____. Schreyvogels Tagebücher, Berlin, 1903.

_____. Zur Geschichte der Theater Wiens I, Vienna, n.d.

Gmür, H. Dramatische und theatralische Stilelemente in Grillparzers Dramen, Wintherthur, 1956.

Goethe, J. W. von. Briefwechsel zwischen Goethe und Zelter in den Jahren 1799-1832, Leipzig, n. d.

_____. Goethe on the Theatre (trans. J. Osenford), New York, 1919.

_____. Goethes Briefwechsel mit den Gebrüdern von Humboldt, Leipzig, 1876.

_____. Theaterbriefe, Berlin, 1838.

_____. Werke, Weimar, 1891.

Gotthardi, W. G. Weimarische Theaterbilder aus Goethes Zeit, Jena, 1865.

Grabbe, C. D. Das Theater zu Düsseldorf mit Rückblicken auf die übige deutsche Schaubühne, Düsseldorf, 1835.

Gräf, H. G. Goethes Anteil an der ersten Faust-Aufführung in Weimar, Weimar, 1904.

Grillparzer, F. Sämtliche Werke, Vienna, 1909.

Gropius, C. Dekorationen auf den beiden königlichen Theatern, Berlin, 1827

Gross, E. Die ältere Romantik und das Theater, Hamburg, 1910.

Günther, H. Romantische Kritik und Satire bei Ludwig Tieck, Leipzig, 1907.

Gugitz, G. Der Alt-Wiener Thespiskarren, Vienna, 1925.

_____. Der Weiland Kaperl: Johann La Roche, Vienna, 1920.

Gundolf, F. Heinrich von Kleist, Berlin, 1922.

Härle, H. Ifflands Schauspielkunst, Berlin, 1925.

Hagen, E. A. Geschichte des Theaters in Preussen, Königsberg, 1854.

Hankamer, P. Zacharias Werner, Bonn, 1920.

Harnack, O. Der deutsche Klassizismus im Zeitalter Goethes, Berlin, 1906.

Haym, R. Die romantische Schule, Berlin, 1870.

Helmensdorfer, U. Grillparzers Bühnenkunst, Berlin, 1960.

Heusermann, E. Schillers Dramen, Berlin, 1915.

238

Heusler, A. Klassik und Klassizismus in der deutschen
    Literatur, Bern, 1952.
Hille, G. Die Tieck-Sempersche Rekonstruktion des Fortuna-
    Theaters, Berlin, 1929.
Höcker, G. Die Vorbilder der deutschen Schauspielkunst,
    Glogau, 1899.
Höffner, J. Goethe und das Weimarer Hoftheater, Weimar,
    1913.
Hohoff, K. Heinrich von Kleist, Hamburg, 1958.
Holtei, K. von. Briefe an Tieck, Breslau, 1864.
_____. Der Salon für Literatur, Kunst, und Gesellschaft,
    Berlin, 1870.
_____. Vierzig Jahre, Berlin, 1843.
Houben, H. H. Damals in Weimar, Leipzig, 1924.
_____. Emil Devrient, Frankfurt, 1903.
_____. Hier Zensur, wer dort, Leipzig, 1918.

Iffland, A. W. Briefe an seine Schwester Louise, Berlin,
    1904.
_____. Briefwechsel mit Schiller, Goethe, Kleist, und
    Tieck, Leipzig, n. d.
_____. Theorie der Schauspielkunst, Heidelberg, 1836.
_____. Über meine theatralische Laufbahn, Leipzig, 1915.

Jagemann, K. Erinnerungen, Dresden, 1926.
Jenisch, E. Das Theater der deutschen Klassik, Würzburg,
    1947.
Jenkner, H. A. Klingemanns Anschauung über die Funk-
    tionen des Theaters, Leipzig, 1929.

Kahl, K. Raimund, Velber, 1967.
Kaiser, J. Grillparzers dramatischer Stil, Munich, 1961.
Kapp, J. C. M. von Weber, Berlin, 1944.
Kayka, E. Kleist und die Romantik, Berlin, 1906.
Kilian, E. Goethes Faust auf der Bühne, Munich, 1907.
Kindermann, H. Ferdinand Raimund, Vienna, 1940.
_____. Theatergeschichte der Goethezeit, Vienna, 1948.
Kipfmüller, R. Das Ifflandsche Lustspiel, Heidelberg, 1899.
Klaar, A. Grillparzer als Dramatiker, Vienna, 1891.
Kliewer, E. August Wilhelm Iffland, Berlin, 1937.
Klingemann, A. Kunst und Natur, Braunschweig, 1828.
Klingenberg, K. H. Iffland und Kotzebue als Dramatiker,
    Leipzig, 1959.
Kluckhon, P. Die deutsche Romantik, Bielefeld, 1924.
Knudson, H. Goethes Welt des Theaters, Berlin, 1949.
_____. Ludwig Devrient, Berlin, 1952.
Koch, F. Heinrich von Kleist, Stuttgart, 1958.
Köpke, R. Ludwig Tieck, Leipzig, 1855.

239

Körner, J. Romantiker und Klassiker, Berlin, 1924.
Köster, A. Schiller als Dramaturg, Berlin, 1891.
Koller, Aphorismen für Schauspieler, Regensburg, 1804.
Komorzynski, E. von. Emanuel Schikaneder, Vienna, 1951.
Kopp, H. Die Bühnenleitung A. Klingemanns, Hamburg, 1901.
Korff, H. A. Geist der Goethezeit, Leipzig, n. d.
Kreuzer, O. E. T. A. Hoffmann in Bamberg, Bamberg, 1922.
Kropp, H. Die Bühnenleiting A. Klingemanns in Braun-
      schweig, Hamburg, 1901.
Krosig, H. von. Karl Graf von Brühl, Berlin, 1910.
Kühn, S. W. Kleist und das deutsche Theater, Berlin, 1920.
Küstner, K. T. Rückblick auf des Leipziger Stadttheater,
      Leipzig, 1830.

Lindenberger, H. Georg Büchner, Carbondale, 1964.
Lüdeke, H. Ludwig Tieck und die Brüder Schlegel, Frank-
      furt/Main, 1930.

Mahlberg, P. Schinkels Theaterdekorationen, Düsseldorf,
      1916.
Mantzius, K. A History of Theatrical Art (trans. C.
      Archer), vol. VI, London, 1921.
March, R. Heinrich von Kleist, New Haven, 1954.
Martens, W. Georg Büchner, Darmstadt, 1965.
Martersteig, M. Pius Alexander Wolff, Leipzig, 1879.
Mayer, H. Heinrich von Kleist, Pfullingen, 1962.
Minder, R. Ludwig Tieck, Paris, 1936.
Michalski, J. Ferdinand Raimund, New York, 1968.
Minor, J. Die Schicksalstragödie, Vienna, 1833.
Möller, A. Ferdinand Raimund, Graz, 1923.
Moser, H. J. C. M. von Weber, Leipzig, 1941.

Nadler, J. Die Berliner Romantik 1800-1814, Berlin, 1921.
_____. Franz Grillparzer, Linz, 1948.
Naumann, W. Grillparzer, Stuttgart, 1956.
Nicholls, R. A. The Dramas of Christian Dietrich Grabbe,
      The Hague, 1969.
Niederführ, H. Alt-Wiener Theater, Vienna, 1942.
Noch, C. Grillparzers "Die Ahnfrau" und die Wiener Volks-
      dramatik, Leipzig, 1911.

Parthey, G. Jugenderinnerungen, Berlin, 1907.
Pasqué, R. Goethes Theaterleitung in Weimar, Leipzig, 1863.
Peterson, J. Goethes Faust auf der deutschen Bühne,
      Leipzig, 1929.
_____. Ludwig Tiecks Sommernachtstraum-Inszenierung.
      Berlin, 1929.
_____. Schiller und die Bühne, Berlin, 1904.

_____. Schillers "Piccolomini" auf dem kgl. National-
theater in Berlin, Berlin, 1941.
Pfeiffer-Belli, W. Die Dramen Goethes auf dem Theater
seiner Vaterstadt, Frankfurt/Main, 1930.
Pian, A. de. Theater-Dekorationen, Vienna, 1818.
Pollack, G. Franz Grillparzer and the Austrian Drama,
New York, 1907.
Prothke, J. E. Das Leopoldstädter Theater, Vienna, 1847.

Rabany, C. Kotzebue, Paris, 1893.
Rave, P. O. K. F. Schinkel, Lebenswerk, Berlin, 1955.
Regener, E. A. Iffland, Berlin, n. d.
Rosenheim, R. Die Geschichte der deutschen Bühnen in
Prag, Prague, 1938.

Satori-Neumann, B. T. Die Frühzeit des Weimarischen
Hoftheaters unter Goethes Leitung, Berlin, 1922.
Schauer, G. Album des Königlichen Schauspiels und der
Königlichen Oper, Berlin, 1858.
Schaukel, R. von. E. T. A. Hoffmann, Vienna, 1922.
Schiller, J. C. F. von. Briefwechsel zwischen Schiller und
Goethe, Stuttgart, 1828.
Schinkel, K. F. Briefe, Tagebücher, Gedanken, Berlin, 1822.
_____. Dekorationen auf den beiden Kgl. Theatern,
Berlin, 1819.
_____. Sammlung von Theater-Dekorationen, Berlin, 1862.
Schlegel, A. W. Vorlesungen über dramatische Kunst und
Literatur, Vienna, 1825.
Schlesinger, M. Geschichte des Breslauer Theaters, Berlin,
1898.
Schmidt, H. Erinnerungen eines weimarischen Veteranen,
Leipzig, 1856.
Schneider, H. Von Wallenstein zum Demetrius, Stuttgart,
1933.
Scholz, W. von. Kleists, Grillparzers, Immermanns und
Grabbes Dramaturgie, Leipzig, 1912.
Schreyvogel, J. Tagebücher, Berlin, 1903.
Seyfried, F. von. Rückschau in das Theaterleben Wiens,
Vienna, 1864.
Silz, W. Early German Romanticism, Cambridge, 1929.
_____. Heinrich von Kleist, Philadelphia, 1962.
_____. Heinrich von Kleist's Conception of the Tragic,
Baltimore, 1923.
Smekal, R. Grillparzer und Raimund, Vienna, 1920.
Solger, K. W. F. Nachgelassene Schriften, Leipzig, 1826.
Springer, R. Devrient und Hoffmann, Berlin, 1873.
Stabenow, H. Geschichte des Breslauer Theaters während
seiner Blütezeit, Breslau, 1821.

Stahl, E.   Heinrich von Kleist's Dramas, Oxford, 1961.
Stein, P.   Goethe als Theaterleiter, Berlin, n. d.
Strich, F.   Deutsche Klassik und Romantik, Munich, 1922.
_____ . Franz Grillparzers Aesthetik, Berlin, 1905.
Stubenrauch, P. von. Theaterkostüme, Vienna, 1830.

Tenschert, R.   C. W. Gluck, der grosse Reformator der
    Oper, Olten, 1951.
Thompson, L. F.   Kotzebue, Paris, 1928.
Thürnagel, E.   Theorie der Schauspielkunst, Heidelberg, 1836.
Tieck, L.   Dramaturgische Blätter, Vienna, 1826.
_____ . Kritische Schriften, Leipzig, 1850.
Tornius, V.   Goethe als Dramaturg, Leipzig, 1909.
Trainer, J.   Ludwig Tieck, The Hague, 1964.
Troizkij, S.   Ekhof, Schröder, Iffland, Fleck, Devrient,
    Seydelmann, Berlin, 1949.

Ullmayer, F.   Memorien des patriotischen Volks- und Theater-
    Dichters Carl Meisl, Vienna, 1868.

Vancsa, K.   Ferdinand Raimund, ein Dichter des Biedermeier,
    Vienna, 1936.
Volkelt, J.   Grillparzer als Dichter des Tragischen, Munich,
    1909.

Wahle, J.   Das Weimarer Theater unter Goethes Leitung,
    Weimar, 1892.
Weichenberger, A.   Goethe und das Komödienhaus in Weimar,
    Leipzig, 1928.
Weidmann, F. K.   Maximilian Korn, Vienna, 1857.
Weil, R.   Das Berliner Theaterpublikum unter A. W. Ifflands
    Direktion, Berlin, 1932.
Weithase, J.   Goethe als Sprecher und Sprecherzieher,
    Weimar, 1949.
Wells, G. A.   The Plays of Grillparzer, New York, 1969.
Wendriner, K. J.   Das romantische Drama, Berlin, 1909.
Westra, P.   Georg Büchner, Paris, 1946.
Wiegand, O.   Das königliche Hoftheater zu Dresden, Leipzig,
    1838.
Wienbarg, L.   Die Dramatiker der Jetztzeit, Altona, 1839.
_____ . Raupach und die deutsche Bühne, Hamburg, 1838.
Wiese, B.   Deutsche Dramaturgie vom Barok bis zur Klassik,
    Tübingen, 1956.
Williamson, E. J.   Grillparzer's Attitude toward Romanticism,
    Chicago, 1910.
Wilpert, G. von.   Schiller-Chronik, Stuttgart, 1958.
Witkowski, G.   Goethe als Dramatiker, Leipzig, 1912.
Wittsack, W.   Studien zur Sprechkultur der Goethezeit,
    Berlin, 1932.

242

Wolff, E. Raupachs Hohenstaufenzyklus, Berlin, 1912.
Wolff, G. Das Goethetheater in Lauchstädt, Halle a. d. Salle, 1908.
Wolff, H. M. Heinrich von Kleist, Berlin, 1954.
Wolzogen, A. von. Aus Schinkels Nachlass, Berlin, 1862.

Yates, D. Franz Grillparzer, Oxford, 1946.

Zeydel, E. H. Ludwig Tieck, the German Romanticist, Princeton, 1935.
Ziegler, F. W. Systematische Schauspielkunst in ihrem ganzen Umfange, Vienna, 1820.
Ziegler, G. Theaterintendant Goethe, Leipzig, 1954.
Zimmermann, F. G. Dramaturgie, 1817-1820, Hamburg, 1840.
Zucker, P. Theaterdekoration des Klassizismus, Berlin, 1925.

1830-1870

Adler, G. Richard Wagner, Munich, 1923.
Adorno, T. W. Versuch über Wagner, Berlin, 1952.
Anschütz, H. Erinnerungen aus dessen Leben und Wirken, Vienna, 1866.
Artaker, A. Eduard von Bauernfeld in der politischen Bewegung seiner Zeit, Vienna, 1942.

Baer, H. Deutsche Lustspieldichter unter dem Einfluss von Eugène Scribe, Leipzig, 1923.
Bauernfeld, E. von. Das Theater, das Publikum und Ich, Vienna, 1849.
_____. Dramatischer Nachlass, Stuttgart, 1893.
Baumgart, O. Gutzkows dramaturgische Tätigkeit am Dresdner Hoftheater, Munich, 1918.
Bekker, P. Jacques Offenbach, Berlin, 1909.
Bettelheim-Gabillon, H. Ludwig Gabillon, Vienna, 1900.
Biermann, F. B. Die Pläne für Reform des Theaterbaus bei Schinkel und Semper, Berlin, 1928.
Bietak, W. Das Lebensgefühl des Biedermeier in der österreichischen Dichtung, Vienna, 1931.
Birch, C. Darstellung der Bühnenkunst, Stuttgart, 1856.
Böckh, A., et al. Über die Antigone... im neuen Palais bei Sanssouci, Berlin, 1842.
Börne, L. Sämtliche Schriften, Düsseldorf, 1964.
Bohtz, A. W. Über das Komische und die Komödie, Göttingen, 1844.
Bornstein, P. Hebbels Persönlichkeit, Berlin, 1924.

243

Büchner, G. Gesammelte Werke, Munich, 1948.

Campbell, T. M. The Life and Works of Friedrich Hebbel,
Boston, 1919.
Chamberlain, H. S. Richard Wagner, Munich, 1911.
Corder, F. Franz Liszt, London, 1933.
Craemer, J. L. König Ludwig II. und Richard Wagner,
Munich, 1901.
Crans, H. Fünfzehn Jahr in Weimar, Leipzig, 1889.
Czartoryski, K. Unseres Burgtheaters Glück und Ende,
Vienna, 1876.

Dempwolff, C. Vor und hinter den Kulissen, Skizzen und
Erinnerungen, Vienna, 1869.
Devrient, E. Aus seinem Tagebüchern, Weimar, 1964.
_____. Dramatische und dramaturgische Schriften,
Leipzig, 1846-1874.
Dingelstedt, F. von. Blätter aus seinem Nachlass, Berlin,
1891.
_____. Eine Fausttrilogie, Berlin, 1876.
_____. Literarisches Bilderbuch, Berlin, 1878.
_____. Gesammelte Werke, Berlin, 1877.
_____. Münchener Bilderbogen, Berlin, 1879.
Dobert, E. W. Karl Gutzkow und seine Zeit, Berne, 1968.
Dohrn, W. Das Jahr 1848 im deutschen Drama und Epos,
Stuttgart, 1902.

Fellner, R. Geschichte einer deutschen Musterbühne,
Stuttgart, 1888.
_____. Immermann als Dramaturg, Hamburg, 1896.
Fiedler, C. Die Gesamtgastspiele in München, Munich,
1880.
Flygt, S. G. Friedrich Hebbel, New York, 1968.
Forst de Battaglia, O. Johann Nestroy, Munich, 1962.
Frisch, H. Symbolik und Tragik in Hebbels Dramen, Bonn,
1961.

Gleich, F. Aus der Bühnenwelt, Leipzig, 1866.
Glossy, K. Aus der Briefmappe eines Burgtheaterdirektors,
Vienna, 1925.
Göhler, R. Gutzkow und das Dresdner Hoftheater, Berlin,
1904.
Goldschmidt, R. K. Eduard Devrients Bühnenreform am
Karlsruher Hoftheater, Leipzig, 1921.
Greiner, W. Otto Ludwig, Gotha, 1941.
Gross, E. Hebbel, Lübeck, 1933.
Gutman, R. S. Richard Wagner: The Man, His Mind, and
His Music, New York, 1968.

Gutzkow, K.   Aus der Zeit und dem Leben, Berlin, 1844.
————.   Rückblicke auf mein Leben, Berlin, 1875.

Haase, F.   Was ich erlebte, Berlin, 1897.
Haffner, K.   Scholz und Nestroy, Vienna, 1864.
Hagen, E. A.   Geschichte des Theaters in Preussen,
    Königsberg, 1854.
Hartmann, G.   Küstner und das Münchner Hofschauspiel,
    Dresden, 1914.
Hebbel, F.   Asthetische und dramaturgische Schriften,
    Detmold, 1874.
————.   Briefe, Berlin, 1904.
————.   Sämmtliche Werke, Hamburg, 1867.
————.   Tagebücher, Berlin, 1885.
Holbein, F. von.   Deutsches Bühnenwesen, Vienna, 1853.
Horch, F.   Das Burgtheater unter Heinrich Laube und Adolf
    Wilbrandt, Vienna, 1925.
Horner, E.   Eduard von Bauernfeld, Leipzig, 1900.
Houben, H. H.   Jungdeutscher Sturm und Drang, Leipzig,
    1911.
————.   Laubes Leben und Schaffen, Leipzig, n. d.
————.   Studien über die Dramen Gutzkows, Jena, 1899.

Immermann, K. L.   Düsseldorfer Anfänge, Berlin, 1889.
————.   Theaterbriefe, Berlin, 1851.

Kaiser, F.   Theater-Direktor Carl, Vienna, 1854.
————.   Unter fünfzehn Theaterdirektoren, Vienna, 1870.
Keller, O.   Franz von Suppé, Leipzig, 1905.
Kilian, E.   Beiträge zur Geschichte des Karlsruher Hof-
    theaters unter Eduard Devrient, Karlsruhe, 1893.
Kindermann, H.   Hebbel und das Wiener Theater seiner
    Zeit, Vienna, 1943.
Klaar, A.   Das moderne Drama, Leipzig, 1883.
Kleinmayer, H.   Welt- und Kunstanschauung des "Jungen
    Deutschland, " Vienna, 1930.
Kneschke, E.   Emil Devrient, Dresden, 1888.
Knispel, G.   Erinnerungen an Carl Seydelmann, Darmstadt,
    1845.
Knudson, H.   Küstner und Laube oder Theaterleitung und
    Theaterkritik, Berlin, 1933.
Koch, F.   Idee und Wirklichkeit, Düsseldorf, 1956.
Koch, M.   Richard Wagner, Berlin, 1907-1918.
Köberle, G.   Die Theaterkrisis im neuen deutschen Reich,
    Stuttgart, 1872.
Koffka, W.   Die Karlsruhe Bühne, Karlsruhe, 1855.
Kolb, A.   König Ludwig II von Bayern und Richard Wagner,
    Amsterdam, 1947.

245

Krake, A. Ludwigs Weg zur historischen Tragödie, Leipzig, 1933.

Kraus, K. Nestroy und die Nachwelt, Vienna, 1912.

Kristeller, H. Der Aufsteig des Kölners Jacques Offenbach, Paris, 1931.

Kühne, G. Porträts und Silhouetten, Hannover, 1843.

Kühnlein, H. Otto Ludwigs Kampf gegen Schiller, Leipzig, 1900.

Küstner, T. von. Vierunddreisig Jahre meine Theaterleitung, Leipzig, 1853.

Kuh, E. Biographie Friedrich Hebbels, Vienna, 1877.

Kurnick, M. Theater Erinnerungen, Berlin, 1882.

Landsberg, H. Auguste Crelinger, Berlin, 1911.

Lange, W. Heinrich Laubes Aufstieg, Leipzig, 1923.

Laube, H. Das Burgtheater, Leipzig, 1868.

_____. Erinnerungen 1841-1881, Vienna, 1882.

_____. Meisterdramen, Leipzig, 1908.

_____. Theaterkritiken und dramaturgische Aufsätze, Berlin, 1906.

Lewald, A. Seydelmann und das deutsche Schauspiel, Stuttgart, 1835.

Liebscher, O. Franz Dingelstedt, Munich, 1909.

Lindau, H. Gustav Freytag, Leipzig, 1907.

Ludwig, O. Gesammelte Schriften, Leipzig, 1891.

Malta-Wagner, A. Das Drama Friedrich Hebbels, Hamburg, 1911.

Mann, T. Leiden und Grösse Richard Wagners, Berlin, 1933.

Martini, F. Deutsche Literatur im bürgerlichen Realismus, Stuttgart, 1962.

Mautner, F. H. Nestroy und seine Kunst, Vienna, 1937.

Maync, H. Immermann, Der Mann und sein Werk, Munich, 1921.

Moormann, M. Die Bühnentechnik Heinrich Laubes, Leipzig, 1917.

Moschner, A. Holtei als Dramatiker, Breslau, 1911.

Müller, P. Gutzkow als Lustspieldichter, Marburg, 1910.

Mundt, T. Geschichte der Literatur der Gegenwart, Leipzig, 1853.

Nestroy, J. Sämtliche Werke, Vienna, 1924.

Newman, E. The Life of Richard Wagner, New York, 1933-1946.

Niederle, B. Charlotte Wolter, Vienna, 1948.

Niessen, C. Deutsches Theater und Immermanns Vermächtnis, Emsdetten, 1940.

246

Pabst, K. R. Die Verbindung der Künste auf der dramatischen Bühne, Berne, 1870.
Paoli, B. Julie Rettich, Vienna, 1866.
Poppe, T. Friedrich Hebbel und das Drama, Berlin, 1900.
Prutz, R. Zehn Jahre, Leipzig, 1850.
Purdie, E. Friedrich Hebbel, London, 1932.
Putlitz, G. von. Karl Immermann, sein Leben und seine Werke, Berlin, 1870.
_____. Theatererinnerungen, Berlin, 1874.

Rathje, A. Otto Devrients Stellung in der Theatergeschichte, Kiel, 1923.
Reich, A. Berliner Dramaturgie, Berlin, 1862.
Reich, W. Richard Wagner, Olten, 1948.
Rieger, E. Offenbach und seine Wiener Schule, Vienna, 1920.
Rodenberg, J. Franz Dingelstedt, Berlin, 1891.
Rötscher, H. T. Abhandlungen zur Philosophie der Kunst, Berlin, 1847.
_____. Dramaturgische und ästhetischen Abhandlungen, Leipzig, 1867.
_____. Dramaturgische Skizzen und Kritiken, Leipzig, 1847-1867.
_____. Kunst der dramatischen Darstellung, Leipzig, 1841.
_____. Seydelmanns Leben und Wirken, Berlin, 1845.

Schenkel, W. Roderich Benedix als Lustspieldichter, Frankfurt, 1916.
Schlenther, P. Botho von Hülsen und seine Leute, Berlin, 1883.
Schmidt, E. Otto Ludwig, Frankfurt/Main, 1922.
Schmitt, S. Hebbels Dramatechnik, Dortmund, 1909.
Seiler, F. Gustav Freytag, Leipzig, 1898.
Sitwell, S. Liszt, London, 1955.
Stern, A. Otto Ludwig, Leipzig, 1906.
Strobel, O. König Ludwig II. und Richard Wagner, Briefwechsel, Karlsruhe, 1936-1939.
Stümke, H. Henriette Sontag, Berlin, 1913.

Tappert, W. Richard Wagner im Spiegel der Kritik, Leipzig, 1915.
Teichmann, J. V. Literarischer Nachlass, Stuttgart, 1863.
Troizkij, S. Karl Seydelmann, Berlin, 1949.

Uechtritz, F. von. Das Düsseldorfer Theater unter Immermanns Leitung, Düsseldorf, 1839.

Wagner, R. Uber Schauspieler und Sänger, Leipzig, 1872.
Wahle, W. Richard Wagners szenische Visionen, Zeulenrode, 1937.
Waldstein, M. Erinnerungen an Josefine Gallmeyer, Berlin, 1885.
Wallheim de Fonseca, A. E. Bühnenzustände und Vorschläge zur Verbesserung derselben, Hamburg, 1850.
Wallner, F. Rückblick auf meine theatralische Laufbahn, Vienna, 1864.
Walzel, O. Friedrich Hebbel und seine Dramen, Leipzig, 1927.
Weber, J. Heinrich Laube im Spielplan des Burgtheaters, Vienna, 1935.
Wehl, F. Fünfzehn Jahre Stuttgarter Hoftheaterleitung, Stuttgart, 1866.
Weiglin, P. Gutzkows und Laubes Literaturdramen, Berlin, 1910.
Weilen, A. von. Julie Rettich, Vienna, 1909.
Westernhagen, C. von. Richard Wagner, sein Werk, sein Wesen, seine Welt, Zurich, 1956.
Wiedmann, F. C. Moritz graf von Dietrichstein, Vienna, 1867.
Wienbarg, L. Aesthetische Feldzüge, Berlin, 1964.
Wittsack, W. Karl Leberecht Immermann der Dramaturg, Berlin, 1914.
Wollrabe, L. Chronologie sämtlicher Hamburger Bühnen, Hamburg, 1847.
Wolzogen, A. von. Uber Theater und Musik, Breslau, 1860.
_____. Wilhelmine Schröder-Devrient, Leipzig, 1863.

Ziegler, K. Mensch und Welt in der Tragödie Hebbels, Berlin, 1938.
Zuchold, Z. Gustav Freytag, Breslau, 1926.

1870-1900

[NOTE: general studies on Wagner are found in the previous section. This section contains only studies dealing specifically with Bayreuth.]

Alberti, C. Der moderne Realismus in der deutschen Literatur, Hamburg, 1889.
_____. Herr L'Arronge und das "deutsche Theater, " Leipzig, 1884.
_____. Natur und Kunst, Leipzig, 1890.
Allers, C. W. Die Meininger, Hamburg, 1890.
Amundsen, G. Die neue Shakespeare-Bühne des Münchner

Hoftheaters, Munich, 1911.

Antoine, A. Memories of the Théâtre-Libre (trans. M. Carlson), Coral Gables, 1964.

Arnold, R. F. Das moderne Drama, Strassburg, 1908.

Asphaleia. Projekt einer Theaterreform der Gesellschaft zur Herstellung zeitgemässer Theater, Vienna, 1882.

Bab, J. Agnes Sorma, Heidelberg, 1927.

_____. Das Theater der Gegenwart, Leipzig, 1928.

_____. Deutsche Schauspieler, Berlin, 1908.

_____. Die Volksbühne in Berlin, Berlin, 1922.

_____. Kainz und Matkowsky, Berlin, 1912.

_____. Kritik der Bühne, Berlin, 1908.

_____. Schauspieler und Schauspielkunst, Berlin, 1926.

_____. Was ist uns Kainz?, Berlin, 1905.

_____. Wege zum Drama, Berlin, 1906.

Bahr, H. Der neue Stil, Frankfurt/Main, 1893.

_____. Die Uberwindung des Naturalismus, Dresden, 1891.

_____. Fin de Siècle, Berlin, 1890.

_____. Josef Kainz, Vienna, 1906.

_____. Kulturprofil der Jahrhundertwende, Vienna, 1962.

_____. Neue Studien zur Kritik der Moderne, Berlin, 1897.

_____. Studien zur Kritik der Moderne, Frankfurt/Main, 1894.

_____. Theater der Jahrhundertwende, Vienna, 1963.

_____. Wiener Theater, Berlin, 1899.

Bang, H. Josef Kainz, Berlin, 1910.

Barnay, L. Erinnerungen, Berlin, 1903.

Barnstorff, H. Die soziale, politische und wirtschaftliche Zeitkritik im Werk Gerhart Hauptmanns, Jena, 1938.

Bartels, A. Die deutsche Dichtung der Gegenwart, Leipzig, 1907.

Bauer, L. An Paul Schlenther, Vienna, 1898.

Behl, K. F. W. and F. A. Voigt. Gerhart Hauptmanns Leben, Berlin, 1942.

Behrens, P. Feste des Lebens und der Kunst, Leipzig, 1900.

Benoist-Hanappier, L. Le Drame naturaliste en Allemagne, Paris, 1905.

Berg, L. Der Naturalismus, Munich, 1892.

_____. Geschichte des deutschen Naturalismus, Berlin, 1889.

_____. Zwischen zwei Jahrhunderten, Frankfurt/Main, 1896.

Berger, A. von. Dramaturgische Vorträge, Vienna, 1890-1891.

_____. Einiges über mich selbst, Leipzig, 1900.

_____. Studien und Kritiken, Leipzig, 1896.
_____. Über Drama und Theater, Leipzig, 1900.
Bertaux, F.   A Panorama of German Literature from 1871
   to 1931 (trans. J. J. Trounstine), New York, 1935.
Bettelheim, A.   Anzengruber, Berlin, 1890.
_____. Die Zukunft unseres Volkstheaters, Berlin, 1892.
_____. Reichsbühnen für das Volk, Munich, 1892.
Bierbaum, O. J.   25 Jahre Münchner Hoftheater-Geschichte,
   Munich, 1892.
Bithell, J.   Modern German Literature, London, 1939.
Bleibtreu, K.   Die Verrohung der Literatur zur Hauptmann-
   und Sudermännerei, Berlin, 1892.
_____. Revolution der Litteratur, Leipzig, 1887.
Blumenthal, O.   Theatralische Eindrücke, Berlin, 1885.
Bohla, K.   Paul Schlenther als Theaterkritiker, Dresden,
   1935.
Brahm, O.   Briefe und Erinnerungen, Berlin, 1925.
_____. Josef Kainz, Berlin, 1910.
_____. Kritiken und Essays, Stuttgart, 1964.
_____. Kritische Schriften über Drama und Theater,
   Berlin, 1913-1915.
_____. Theater, Dramatiker, Schauspieler, Berlin, 1961.
Brandes, G.   Moderne Geister, Frankfurt/Main, 1897.
Bromberg, S.   Zur Kritik der Anwendung des Naturalismus
   im Drama, Lemberg, 1905.
Brückner, M.   Bayreuther Bühnenbildner, Graz, 1890.
Büchner, A.   Anzengrubers Dramentechnik, Darmstadt, 1911.
Bulthaupt, H.   Dramaturgie des Schauspiels, Oldenburg,
   1901.
Burckhard, M.   Friedrich Mitterwurzer, Vienna, 1906.
Busse, K.   Hermann Sudermann, sein Werk und Wesen,
   Stuttgart, 1922.
Bytkowski, S.   Gerhart Hauptmanns Naturalismus und das
   deutsche Drama, Hamburg, 1908.

Claar, E.   Fünfzig Jahre Theater, Frankfurt/Main, 1926.
Coellen, L.   Modernes Drama und Weltanschauung, Leipzig,
   1903.
Conrad, M. G.   Von Emile Zola bis Gerhart Hauptmann,
   Leipzig, 1902.

Dehnow, F.   Frank Wedekind, Leipzig, 1922.
Deri, M.   Naturalismus, Idealismus, Expressionismus,
   Leipzig, 1919.
Deutsch, B.   Josef-Kainz-Gedenkbuch, Vienna, 1924.
_____. Wiener Porträts, Vienna, 1903.
Dierlam, R. J.   The Volksbühne Movement (unpub. thesis,
   Cornell, 1948).

Doell, O. Die Entwickelung der naturalistischen Form in jüngstdeutschen Drama, Halle, 1910.
Doublier, G. and W. Zeleny. Hedwig Bleibtreu, Vienna, 1948.
Droescher, G. Die vormals Kgl. jetzt Preussischen Staatstheater zu Berlin, Berlin, 1936.
Dzulko, R. Ibsen und die deutsche Bühne, Jena, 1952.

Ehrenfeld, M. Charlotte Wolter, Vienna, 1887.
Eisenberg, L. Adolf Sonnenthal, Dresden, 1896.
Eller, W. H. Ibsen in Germany, Boston, 1918.
Eloesser, A. Aus der grossen Zeit des deutschen Theaters, Munich, 1911.
Enders, F. Gerhart Hauptmann, Lübeck, 1932.
Engel, E. E. Charlotte Wolter in ihren Glanzrollen, Vienna, 1897.

Fechter, P. Frank Wedekind, Jena, 1920.
_____. Gerhart Hauptmann, Dresden, 1922.
Feigl, L. Arthur Schnitzler und Wien, Vienna, 1911.
Fiedler, C. Das deutsche Theater, Munich, 1877.
Fontane, T. Causerien über Theater, Berlin, 1905.
_____. Plaudereien über Theater, Berlin, 1926.
Frenzel, K. Berliner Dramaturgie, Hannover, 1877.
Freyhan, M. Gerhart Hauptmann, Berlin, 1922.
Fried, A. Der Naturalismus, Vienna, 1890.
Friedmann, S. Ludwig Anzengruber, Berlin, 1902.
Fuchs, G. Die Revolution des Theaters, Munich, 1909.
_____. Sturm und Drang in München um die Jahrhundertwende, Munich, 1936.

Garten, H. F. Gerhart Hauptmann, Cambridge, 1954.
Genée, R. Die Entwickelung des szenischen Theaters und die Bühnenreform in München, Stuttgart, 1889.
Geucke, K. Kunst und Naturalismus, Dresden, 1892.
Gittleman, S. Frank Wedekind, New York, 1969.
Gläser, K. Das Gastspiel des Meininger Hoftheaters in Berlin, Berlin, 1876.
Glossy, K. Wiener Studien und Dokumente, Vienna, 1933.
Goldmann, K. Das Wiener Burckhardtheater, Vienna, 1891.
Gottschall, R. von. Zur Kritik des modernen Dramas, Berlin, 1900.
Graus, H. Die Wunder der Bühne, Leipzig, 1890.
Gregori, F. Bernhard Baumeister, Vienna, 1902.
Grube, M. Die Meininger, Leipzig, 1904.
_____. The Story of the Meininger (trans. A. M. Koller), Coral Gables, 1963.
Guglia, E. Friedrich Mitterwurzer, Vienna, 1896.

251

Guthke, K. S. Gerhart Hauptmann, Göttingen, 1961.
Gysi, F. Richard Strauss, Potsdam, 1934.

Haase, F. Ungeschminkte Briefe, Berlin, 1883.
_____. Was ich erlebte, Berlin, 1896.
Hadamowsky, F. Die Wiener Operette, Vienna, 1947.
Haenisch, K. Gerhart Hauptmann und das deutsche Volk, Berlin, 1922.
Hagemann, C. Schauspielkunst und Schauspielkünstler, Berlin, 1903.
Hale, E. E. Dramatists of Today, New York, 1905.
Hanstein, A. von. Das jüngste Deutschland, Leipzig, 1900.
Harden, M. Berlin als Theaterhauptstadt, Berlin, 1888.
_____. Literatur und Theater, Berlin, 1896.
Hart, H. and J. Kritische Waffengänge, Leipzig, 1882-1884.
Henze, H. Otto Brahm und das Deutsche Theater in Berlin, Berlin, 1929.
Hermann, K. Der Naturalismus und die Gesellschaft von heute, Hamburg, 1886.
Herrig, H. Die Meininger, Dresden, 1879.
Holz, A. Die Kunst, ihr Wesen und ihre Gesetze, Berlin, 1891.
Hopfen, H. Streitfragen und Erinnerungen, Stuttgart, 1876.
Hülsen, H. von. Gerhart Hauptmann, Berlin, 1932.
_____. Tage mit Gerhart Hauptmann, Dresden, 1925.

Ibach, A. Die Wessely, Vienna, 1943.
Ihering, H. Von Josef Kainz bis Paula Wessely, Heidelberg, 1942.
Isolani, E. Josef Kainz, Berlin, 1910.

Jacob, H. E. Johann Strauss, Gütersloh, 1962.
Jacobsohn, S. Oscar Sauer, Berlin, 1916.
Jaspert, W. Johann Strauss, Vienna, 1948.
Jauner, T. Fünf Jahre Wiener Operntheater, Vienna, 1962.
Johannsen, M. Jacques Offenbach, Inszenierungsgeschichte in deutschen Sprachraum, Vienna, 1960.

Kainz, Josef, Briefe, Vienna, 1921.
Kalbeck, M. Das Bühnenfestspiel zu Bayreuth, Breslau, 1877.
Kapp, J. Frank Wedekind, Berlin, 1909.
Kempner, H. Frank Wedekind als Mensch und Künstler, Berlin, 1911.
Kerr, A. Stilisierende Schauspielkunst, Berlin, 1903.
Klang, H. Alexander Girardis Leben und Bühnentätigkeit, Vienna, 1937.
Kleinberg, A. Ludwig Anzengruber, Berlin, 1921.

Klemperer, V. Adolf Wilbrandt, Stuttgart, 1907.
Kloss, J. E. Zwanzig Jahre Bayreuth, Berlin, 1896.
Kober, E. Josef Kainz, Vienna, 1948.
Köberle, J. G. Brennende Theaterfragen, Vienna, 1897.
Kohut, A. Das Dresdener Hoftheater in der Gegenwart, Dresden, 1888.
Kraft, Z. von. Das Festspielhaus in Bayreuth, Bayreuth, 1958.
Kralik, H. Richard Strauss, Vienna, 1963.
Kruchen, A. Das Regie-Prinzip bei den Meiningen, Danzig, 1933.
Kurnatowski, O. von. Georg II., Herzog von Sachsen-Meiningen, Hildburghausen, 1914.
Kutscher, A. Frank Wedekind, Munich, 1922-1931.

Landsberg, H. Arthur Schnitzler, Berlin, 1904.
_____. Los von Hauptmann!, Leipzig, 1900.
L'Arronge, A. Deutsches Theater und deutsche Schauspiel-kunst, Berlin, 1896.
Laube, H. Das Wiener Stadttheater, Vienna, 1875.
Lautenschläger, C. Die Münchner Drehbühne im Kgl. Residenztheater, Munich, 1896.
Legband, P. Das Deutsche Theater in Berlin, Munich, 1909.
Leon, V. Regie, Munich, 1897.
Lewinsky, J. Kleine Schriften, Berlin, 1910.
Lindau, P. Beiträge zur Kenntnis des modernen Theaters in Deutschland und Frankreich, Stuttgart, 1874.
Linden, W. Naturalismus, Leipzig, 1936.
Linsemann, P. Die Theaterstadt Berlin, Berlin, 1897.
Litzmann, B. Das deutsche Drama in der literarischen Bewegung der Gegenwart, Hamburg, 1894.
_____. Wildenbruch, Berlin, 1913.
Litzmann, G. Das naturalistische Drama, Bonn, 1907.
Löw, J. Das neue Burgtheater, Vienna, 1888.
Lothar, R. Das deutsche Drama der Gegenwart, Munich, 1905.
_____. Sonnenthal, Berlin, n. d.
Lublinski, S. Die Bilanz der Moderne, Berlin, 1904.

Machatztke, M. Gerhart Hauptmann, Frankfurt/Main, 1963.
Mahn, P. Gerhart Hauptmann und der moderne Realismus, Berlin, 1921.
Manning, T. Idealismus und Realismus in der deutschen Schauspielkunst, Basel, 1892.
Mar, N. Richard Strauss, London, 1962.
Marcuse, L. Gerhart Hauptmann und sein Werk, Berlin, 1922.
Mayer, F. A. Publikum und Kritik in Wien, Vienna, 1902.

Milch, W. Arno Holz, Berlin, 1933.
Miller, A. I. The Independent Theatre in Europe, New York, 1931.
Minor, J. Joseph Lewinsky, Vienna, 1898.
Motekat, H. Arno Holz: Persönlichkeit und Werk, Kitaingen, 1953.
Müller, A. Der deutsche Naturalismus auf der Bühne, Emsdetten, 1962.
Müller-Guttenbrunn, A. Das Wiener Theaterleben, Vienna, 1890.
_____. Dramaturgische Gänge, Dresden, 1892.

Nestriepke, S. Geschichte der Volksbühne Berlin, Berlin, 1930.
Newmark, M. Otto Brahm: The Man and the Critic, New York, 1938.
Nick, E. Vom Wiener Walzer zur Operette, Vienna, 1954.
Niederle, B. Charlotte Wolter, Vienna, 1948.
Nowack, K. F. Girardi: Leben und Wirken, Berlin, 1908.

Panofsky, W. Richard Strauss, Munich, 1965.
Pinkus, M. and V. Ludwig, Gerhart Hauptmann, Neustadt, 1932.
Pirchan, E. Marie Geistinger, Vienna, 1947.
Porges, H. Die Bühnenproben zu den Bayreuther Festspielen des Jahres 1876, Chemnitz, 1881.
Possart, E. von. Erstrebtes und Erlebtes, Berlin, 1916.
_____. Der Lehrgang des Schauspielers, Stuttgart, 1901.
Presber, R. Vom Theater um die Jahrhundertwende, Stuttgart, 1901.
Prölss, R. Das Herzoglich Meiningen'sche Hoftheater und die Bühnenreform, Erfurt, 1880.
Prüfer, A. Das Werk von Bayreuth, Leipzig, 1910.
_____. Die Bühnenfestspiele in Bayreuth, Leipzig, 1899.

Raeck, K. Das Deutsche Theater zu Berlin unter der Direktion von Adolphe L'Arronge, Berlin, 1928.
Ratislav, K. Arthur Schnitzler, Hamburg, 1911.
Reich, E. Die bürgerliche Kunst und die besitzlosen Volksklassen, Leipzig, 1892.
Richard, P. Chronik sämtlicher Gastspiele des Meiningischen Hoftheaters, Leipzig, 1891.
Richter, H. Josef Lewinsky, Vienna, 1926.
_____. Kainz, Vienna, 1931.
Rieger, R. Offenbach und seine Wiener Schule, Vienna, 1920.
Riegl, A. Stilfragen, Berlin, 1893.
Röhr, H. Gerhart Hauptmanns dramatisches Schaffen, Dresden, 1912.

254

Roseau, R. Arthur Schnitzler, Berlin, 1913.
Rothe, F. Frank Wedekinds Dramen, Stuttgart, 1968.
Rudolph, L. Sonnenthal, Berlin, 1904.
Rüpfer, F. Geschichte des Leipziger Stadttheaters unter
     der Direktion Dr. Förster, Leipzig, 1880.
Ruprecht, E. Literarische Manifeste des Naturalismus
     1880-1892, Stuttgart, 1962.

Salkind, A. Arthur Schnitzler, Berlin, 1907.
Sandrock, A. Mein Leben, Berlin, 1940.
Scharrer-Santen, E. Adolf Wilbrandt als Dramatiker,
     Munich, 1912.
Schlaf, J. Die Freie Bühne, Stuttgart, 1914.
Schlenther, P. Adolf von Sonnenthal, Vienna, 1906.
_____. Bernhard Baumeister, Vienna, 1902.
_____. Das Theater, Berlin, 1906.
_____. Gerhart Hauptmann, Berlin, 1897.
_____. Wozu der Lärm? Genesis der Freien Bühne,
     Berlin, 1889.
Schoen, H. Hermann Sudermann, Paris, 1904.
Seehaus, G. Frank Wedekind und das Theater, Munich, 1964.
Shaw, L. R. Witness of Deceit, Berkeley, 1958.
Simon, O. Friedrich Haase, Berlin, 1898.
Simon, W. Otto Brahm, Kundgebungen zu seinem Gedenken,
     Berlin, 1913.
Sinden, M. Gerhart Hauptmann, Toronto, 1957.
Sonnenthal, A. von. Briefwechsel, Berlin, 1912.
_____. Fünfzig Jahre im Wiener Burgtheater, Vienna,
     1906.
Specht, R. Arthur Schnitzler, Berlin, 1922.
_____. Das Wiener Operntheater von Dingelstedt bis
     Schalk und Strauss, Vienna, 1919.
Steiger, E. Das Werden des neuen Dramas, Berlin, 1898.
_____. Henrik Ibsen und die dramatische Gesellschafts-
     kritik, Berlin, 1898.
_____. Kampf um die neue Dichtung, Berlin, 1889.
_____. Von Hauptmann bis Maeterlinck, Berlin, 1898.
Stein, C. F. von. Die Kunst in Meiningen unter Herzog
     Georg II, Meiningen, 1909.
Stein, P. Henrik Ibsen, Zur Bühnengeschichte seiner Dich-
     tungen, Berlin, 1901.
Steinhauser, R. Das Deutsche Volkstheater 1889-1899,
     Vienna, 1899.
Stern, A. Studien zur Literatur des Gegenwart, Dresden,
     1895.
Stümcke, Friedrich Haase, Berlin, 1911.

Thal, W. Berliner Theater und die "Freien Bühnen," The
     Hague, 1890.

Thomas, W.   Richard Strauss und seine Zeitgenossen,
      Munich, 1964.
Tyrot, R.   Aus dem Tagebuch eines Wiener Schauspielers,
      Vienna, 1904.
_____.   Chronik des Wiener Stadttheaters, Vienna, 1889.
_____.   Vom Lebenswege eines alten Schauspielers,
      Vienna, 1914.
Vallentin, V.   Der Natualismus und seine Stellung in der
      Kunstentwickelung, Halle, 1891.
Völker, K.   Frank Wedekind, Velber, 1965.
Voigt, F. A.   Hauptmann-Studien, Breslau, 1936.
Vollmer, E.   Berliner Theaterkritiker, Berlin, 1884.
Vollmöller, G.   Die Sturm- und Drangperiode und der
      moderne deutsche Realismus, Berlin, 1897.

Weilen, A. von.   Der Spielplan des neuen Burgtheaters,
      Vienna, 1916.
Weingartner, F.   Bayreuth, Berlin, 1897.
Wiegler, P.   Josef Kainz, Berlin, 1941.
Wilbrandt, A. von.   Erinnerungen, Stuttgart, 1905-1907.
Wilbrandt, R.   Mein Vater Aldolf Wilbrandt, Vienna, 1937.
Wolff, E.   Geschichte der deutschen Literatur in der
      Gegenwart, Leipzig, 1896.

Zeiss, A.   Die Katastrophe im Ringtheater, Vienna, 1882.
Zillmann, F.   Max Halbe, Würzburg, 1961.

INDEX

275

Wycherly, W., 63

Young Germany, 5, 7, 37, 92,
93, 94, 101-106, 108, 109,
111, 112, 115, 127, 134,
138, 142, 144, 194, 199, 208

Zacconi (actor), 192
Zar und Zimmermann
(Lortzing), 156
Zauberflöte, Die (Mozart), 51,
52, 53
Zauberin am Stein, Die
(Nissel), 192
Zauberschleier, Die (Told),
133
Zauberzither, Die (Müller), 85
Zeitgenossen (Gutzkow), 102
Zeitung für die elegante Welt,
38
Zelter, Karl, 41, 77
Zenobia (Calderon), 22
Zerbino (Tieck), 26
Zerbrochene Krug, Der (Kleist),
21, 29, 34, 47, 117, 141,
216, 220
Zhukovski, Paul, 184
Zicky, Count, 57
Zigeunerbaron (Strauss), 190,
191
Zirny (Körner), 58
Zöllner, Heinrich, 185
Zola, Emile, 7, 187, 204, 207,
208, 209, 211, 214, 218,
220
Zopf und Schwert (Gutzkow), 109
Zu ebener Erde und im ersten
Stock (Nestroy), 131, 135
Zu Hause (Hirshfeld), 202
Zurich, 158, 197, 213
Zwei Schwestern von Prague
(Müller), 48, 85